CHINESE REFLECTIONS

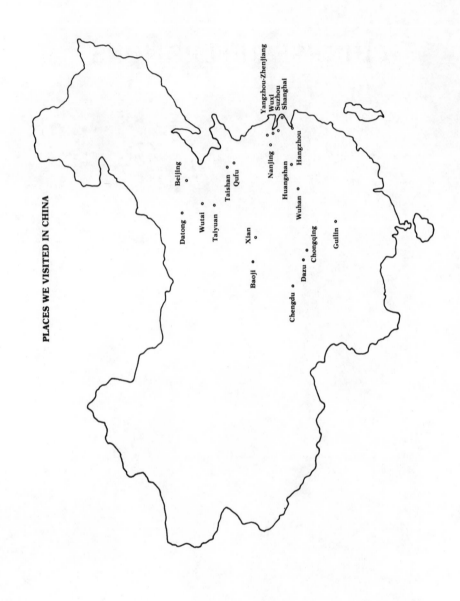

PLACES WE VISITED IN CHINA

Datong
Beijing
Wutai
Taiyuan
Taishan
Qufu
Yangzhou-Zhenjiang
Wuxi
Suzhou
Shanghai
Nanjing
Hangzhou
Huangshan
Wuhan
Xian
Baoji
Chengdu
Dazu
Chongqing
Guilin

CHINESE REFLECTIONS

Americans Teaching in the People's Republic
by
Tani E. Barlow
and
Donald M. Lowe

Library of Congress Cataloging in Publication Data

Barlow, Tani E.
  Chinese reflections.

  Includes index.
  1. China — Description and travel —
1976 —   . 2. Barlow, Tani E.   3. Lowe,
Donald M.   I. Lowe, Donald M.   II. Title.
DS712.B37   1985   951.05′8   85-6467
ISBN 0-03-004792-7 (alk. paper)

Published and Distributed by the
Praeger Publishers Division
(ISBN Prefix 0-275)
of Greenwood Press, Inc.,
Westport, Connecticut

Published in 1985 by Praeger Publishers
CBS Educational and Professional Publishing, a Division of CBS Inc.
521 Fifth Avenue, New York, NY 10175 USA

© 1985 by Praeger Publishers

56789 052 987654321

Printed in the United States of America on acid-free paper

INTERNATIONAL OFFICES

Orders from outside the United States should be sent to the appropriate address listed below. Orders from areas not
listed below should be placed through CBS International Publishing, 383 Madison Ave., New York, NY 10175 USA

Australia, New Zealand
Holt Saunders, Pty, Ltd., 9 Waltham St., Artarmon, N.S.W. 2064, Sydney, Australia

Canada
Holt, Rinehart & Winston of Canada, 55 Horner Ave., Toronto, Ontario, Canada M8Z 4X6

Europe, the Middle East, & Africa
Holt Saunders, Ltd., 1 St. Anne's Road, Eastbourne, East Sussex, England BN21 3UN

Japan
Holt Saunders, Ltd., Ichibancho Central Building, 22-1 Ichibancho, 3rd Floor, Chiyodaku, Tokyo, Japan

Hong Kong, Southeast Asia
Holt Saunders Asia, Ltd., 10 Fl, Intercontinental Plaza, 94 Granville Road, Tsim Sha Tsui East, Kowloon,
Hong Kong

**Manuscript submissions should be sent to the Editorial Director, Praeger Publishers, 521 Fifth Avenue,
New York, NY 10175 USA**

To our friends at Shanghai Teachers College

Acknowledgments

During our stay in China, the Foreign Affairs Office of the Shanghai Teachers College handled all transactions for us. We wish to thank members of that office for their courteous and conscientious work. At the same time, Tani's father, Claude Barlow, supplied us with film from the U.S. and handled the processing. Don's father, C. H. Lowe, efficiently Xeroxed and sent copies of each letter to all those friends and relatives who were its original readers.

When we got home, a number of people encouraged and helped us transform the newsletters into their present form. We are especially indebted to Jerome Ch'en, K. C. Liu, Ruth Earnshaw Lo, Peter Carroll, Gary Hamilton, Howard Goldblatt, M'K Veloz, Ronald Levaco, and Douglas Merwin.

Preface

One pale sunny day in December 1981 we were sitting in our office after a late afternoon lecture, talking to a group of students. At the center of the worn, wood-plank room sat a tiny coal-burning stove, attached to an enormous flue. The students were joking about the Great Proletarian Cultural Revolution (GPCR), and one said, "You know, in those years we felt we were the 'basement' of the world revolution. Our slogan was 'One out of three persons in the world still hasn't been liberated.' " "Yes," somebody else laughed, "we felt it was our responsibility to liberate you." Nobody else sitting on the faded pink sofa-chairs along the east wall of the office paid much attention to her mild joke. But we did. The woman's comments stayed with us. Particularly its mocking implication that in the relation between them and us, one side would eventually "liberate" the other.

We first arrived at the lush, suburban campus of Shanghai Teachers College during the intense heat of the summer, and, quite oblivious to the temperature, stepped into a storybook world any American tourist would have loved. Smiling, innocent Chinese girls and boys sat in well-behaved rows in our classrooms. Delegations of them treated us to welcome songs from the *The Sound of Music*. It took us weeks to see what was in front of us. They weren't teenagers at all, but the adult survivors of the GPCR who ranged in age from their mid-twenties to early forties. Some had been Red Guards. A few might even have put up the military slogans we could still see moldering on the walls near the language lab. And every single one of them could remember a time in their own lives when they had expected to liberate us.

On August 18, 1966, Chairman Mao had urged the million Red Guards parading through Beijing's Tienanmen Square to rebel against entrenched authorities and renew the spirit of revolution. Thus began the Great Proletarian Cultural Revolution. As the inspired Red Guards carried the Chairman's message to the rest of the country, China was convulsed by a decade of mass mobilization, armed struggles, and near civil war. The GPCR did not really come to an end until 1976. In April that year, demonstrators in Tienanmen Square unexpectedly used a commemoration of the recent death of Premier Zhou Enlai to protest the excesses of the GPCR; in September, the 82-year-old Chairman died, followed immediately afterward by the arrest of the "Gang of Four," one of them being Mao's widow, Jiang Qing, on charges of promoting excesses during the GPCR.

The decade of the GPCR saw conflicts and countermovements, countless deaths and personal sufferings, and social groups at cross purposes with each other. Yet certain objectives made the GPCR a significant, politically understandable, though ultimately abortive period, rather than a simple mistake or meaningless tragedy. An understanding of the GPCR rests on knowing the problems and alternatives faced by China since the Liberation in 1949.

Plagued by the internal collapse of the Qing monarchy, the bottlenecks in traditional agriculture, and the exploitation by foreign capitalists and governments, twentieth-century China has been stymied by a series of interrelated structural problems. To enumerate briefly: Excessive population growth pressing on stationary agricultural production; uneven- and under-development of industries due to weak domestic entrepreneurial capitalism and exploitation of Chinese labor and market by foreign capital; emergence of regionalism and warlordism following the collapse of effective central governmental authority; inability of the traditional Confucian elites to confront the new socioeconomic problems; and a general cultural malaise and personal demoralization. These interrelated problems, further exacerbated by droughts, floods, famines, rebellions, civil wars, and foreign invasions meant that piecemeal reform did not work.

With the Liberation of 1949, the Communist Party provided China with a unified central authority and viable ideology for the first time in a hundred years. This in itself was a major accomplishment. But political unification did not resolve the fundamental challenge confronted by contemporary China, namely, how could the government engineer an economic breakthrough that would feed the people and free the country from foreign depredation.

The government's first Five-Year Plan (1953–57) imitated the Soviet Union's approach to socialist economic planning, and initiated the development of heavy industries by extracting necessary investment capital from the agricultural sector. However, China's industrial base in 1953 was smaller than what the Soviet Union had begun with in 1928. Furthermore, actually less investment capital could be squeezed out of China's predominantly subsistence farming. Already, by 1957, there were indications that agricultural production was faltering.

It was then that Mao pressed for the policy of the Great Leap Forward, his vision of mobilizing the human resources of China as a substitute for capital and technology. The Leap failed to live up to its promises, although it did establish a Maoist model of economic breakthrough, and for the next decade Maoists vied with advocates of the more conventional Soviet model. These were the only real alternatives, since its embroilment in the Vietnam War meant China could have no access to the capital and technology of the Western bloc.

On top of crucial economic problems, the Communist Party had by the early 1960s become excessively bureaucratized and was no longer an instrument of revolutionary transformation. With all of China's interrelated problems, to remain stationary was to deteriorate. Finally, in 1966, over the opposition of Liu Xiaoqi and others, Mao once more resolved on a voluntarist approach. This time, however, he would be more thorough.

The GPCR was the most ambitious, sweeping attempt ever made by anyone to transform a society. Falling back on his past successes in organizing a peasant-based revolutionary movement, Mao believed in the power of a *union* between revolutionary leadership and the Chinese masses. This vision underlay the seemingly diverse policies of the GPCR. Economically it meant once again, as during the Great Leap Forward, mobilizing human resources to achieve capital development. But politically Mao promoted a two-pronged attack, against entrenched Party bureaucrats and against all feudal, antiproletarian (that is, anti-Maoist) elements among the people. Herein lay the importance of the Red Guards. They were the first generation of youths born and educated after the Liberation of 1949. Indoctrinated, but innocent of experience, they were the instrument spearheading Mao's drive to purge all antirevolutionary elements in the Party and the masses themselves.

The union of revolutionary leadership and mobilized masses, which had borne fruit during earlier struggles for power, now proved to be illusory in an entirely different social context. Rather than unifying the leaders and the led, every level of the Party and the state, down to the individual workunit, was torn apart by struggle and dissension. Who was a true revolutionary, and who were the class enemies? Was he or she really Red, or just claiming Redness as a strategy for survival? Differences between the old and the new, between the old and young, between city and countryside all came to the fore as occasions for personal in-fighting and vendettas. As a student of ours from that generation explained, in the end no one knew who the enemies were, and who were their friends.

The country in turmoil, the leadership out of control, Mao finally had to call on the People's Liberation Army in 1968 to contain the Red Guards he had originally promoted against the Party. He in effect tacitly acknowledged the failure of his voluntarist vision. Revolutionary mobilization could not overcome socioeconomic realities; instead it strengthened precisely those ties of family, kin, and traditional culture which Mao and his Red Guards had tried to break. Yet he was loathe to give up the struggle entirely. So the politics and rhetoric of the GPCR dragged on until Mao's death in 1976.

Still, international politics were changing the prospect of China's domestic policies, outstripping the Maoist vs. Soviet alternatives. Seeking to wind down U.S. involvement in Vietnam and play the China card against the Soviet Union, Richard Nixon flew to China in late 1972 to end two decades of U.S.-imposed diplomatic isolation of the People's Republic of China. The stage was set for a new and different approach to China's economic development, namely socialist construction assisted by limited capital investment from the Western bloc. However the policy of economic readjustment, or "four modernizations," had to wait for the death of Mao and the downfall of the Gang of Four.

The Red Guards of the mid 1960s, many of them teenagers, thought they were the locomotive of the GPCR. In the end they found themselves riding a roller coaster which left them feeling abused and betrayed. Whether Red or not, most urban youths of that generation had gone through the initial euphoria and eventual disillusionment of the GPCR. Their home life and schooling terminated, many of them volunteered or had been ordered to go down to the countryside. There they experienced unimagined poverty and hardship, loneliness, despair, and estrangement. After the downfall of the "Gang of Four," the lucky ones returned to the cities, leaving the less fortunate stranded and helpless. Finally, at the end of the GPCR, the government announced that all those who had had their schooling disrupted by the GPCR could take the college entrance exam, and if they passed would have another chance at higher education.

We had the incredible good luck to teach the first two classes admitted to the university after the GPCR, during their last semesters at the foreign languages department of Shanghai Teachers College. Fifteen years ago our students had been Chairman Mao's shock troops. Now they call themselves the "lost generation"—childhood, ideals, and political direction all squandered. At first they baffled us with their hunger for everything Western. But, gradually, we learned more. They wanted the information we had to give so they could use it in their own world. In fact, they started pushing us not only to give up our criticisms of the capitalist West, but our fundamentally un-Chinese way of seeing things, too. The people we began meeting all seemed to feel that their way of thinking was universal. Even though they would have denied it, they still wanted to liberate us.

Shanghai Teachers College was not the China we had expected. The two of us arrived with a well-established way of seeing things ourselves. Tani was as much a product of the American sixties as our Chinese students were of the GPCR. Now in her mid thirties, she had grown up in the San Francisco—Bay Area and spent several years traveling and working at blue-collar jobs before she entered college in the early seventies. She chose Chinese history because of her resistance to American involvement in Asia, and her curiosity about the GPCR political style. By the time we left San Francisco in August 1981 she had passed her doctoral exams in modern Chinese history. Don is in his mid fifties. He was born in Shanghai, but left there at the age of nine, and traveled through southwest China, Burma, and India, finally settling in the United States at the age of 16. He has taught history and Marxism for over 20 years, presently at San Francisco State University. Since he is a politically conscious Chinese-American, Don has paid special attention to China and the Third World. Like Tani, he was also affected by Mao Zedong Thought during the 1960s and by the American counterculture. He knew that he didn't belong completely in his American world, no matter how well adjusted to it he appeared to be. But he had no guarantees he'd fit into a Chinese world, either.

So we arrived in Shanghai thinking that at least where America was concerned we were the experts. Eventually, we had to bury our sixties' image of China as a place where human will had triumphed over technology; but we never gave up our critical vision of America. Our "lost generation" students taught us about their need to believe in America the beautiful. We realized slowly that we had encountered them as they rebounded from GPCR propaganda. So the best we could do in the end was to make them measure their new, glossy, advertising image of the West against our experience as people from there. We didn't get the China we expected. And our students didn't get the foreign experts they thought they wanted—at least, initially.

This book is the story of how we came to terms with each other. Each chapter is a letter written home to friends, colleagues, and relatives. We've revised them for publication. Yet we have tried hard to preserve our own ongoing feeling of discovery, even at the expense of naiveté in hindsight. In one sense, the book is a description of life on a small, rather obscure college campus in contemporary Shanghai. But of course it's also the internal dialogue we held with ourselves.

We can't speak for all our students, but we think a lot of them would agree with us in at least one respect. Neither their version nor ours will ever prevail. We did liberate each other. But not in the ways we originally planned. We no longer expect them to accept our vision. Many of them feel the same way about us. The best we can do is to try to look through their eyes sometimes, and learn how best to describe what separates us. The people we know in China will always see experience in moral terms, because their society places ethical matters and human relations at the center of the world. We will never stop seeing our world—and theirs—with post-modern, post-Freudian eyes. And the two cultures will go on defining who we are and how we see each other.

Contents

MAP   ii

ACKNOWLEDGMENTS   vii

PREFACE   ix

LIST OF ILLUSTRATIONS   xvii

LETTERS

1   Arrival *(August 27, 1981)*   1

2   Teaching Assignments *(September 4, 1981)*   10

3   Ways of Seeing *(September 8, 1981)*   18

4   Visit to Suzhou *(September 22, 1981)*   29

5   Lu Xun Day *(September 28, 1981)*   35

6   Students *(September 30, 1981)*   39

7   National Day *(October 12, 1981)*   52

8   Emotions *(October 14, 1981)*   57

9   Teaching *(November 3, 1981)*   69

10   Intellectuals and Power *(November 8, 1981)*   78

11   Modernism *(November 11, 1981)*   89

12   Socialization *(November 18, 1981)*   96

13   Media *(November 30, 1981)*   106

14   Generations *(December 5, 1981)*   112

15   Political Ideology *(December 13, 1981)*   120

16   Maturity *(December 22, 1981)*   126

17   Two Worlds *(December 28, 1981)*   136

18   Children *(January 6, 1982)*   146

19   The Interior *(January 25, 1982)*   158

20   Hometown *(February 6, 1982)*   166

21   Teachers and Disciples *(February 22, 1982)*   173

22   Civic Virtues Month *(March 7, 1982)*   181

23   Feminism *(March 22, 1982)*   189

24   Sexism *(April 4, 1982)*   201

25   Mountain Climbing *(April 27, 1982)*   207

26   Graves and Bound Feet *(May 10, 1982)*   212

27   Aliens *(May 27, 1982)*   221

28   Provincials *(June 20, 1982)*   228

29   Centrality and the Walls *(August 5, 1982)*   235

POSTSCRIPT   245

INDEX   249

ABOUT THE AUTHORS   251

List of Illustrations

Gate entrance to Shanghai Teachers College, with a monument of Mao's calligraphy behind the gate, center rear. (T. E. Barlow) 3

Don with Mingzhang, Peihua, and their children on their veranda. (T. E. Barlow) 6

Calligraphy on the "five stresses and four beautifuls" campaign. (T. E. Barlow) 22

Logo advocating sanitation. (T. E. Barlow) 22

Door slogans on individual responsibility in census campaign. (T. E. Barlow) 23

Blackboard listing the "ten don'ts," a part of efforts to improve sanitation. (T. E. Barlow) 23

Tani with some of her intensive reading seniors, in front of the foreign languages teaching building. (Anon.) 41

Some of Don's intensive reading seniors. (Anon.) 41

This is not a painting, but rather a photograph imitating the "mountain-water" genre of Chinese painting. Taken by Di Feiwan, a student at Shanghai Teachers College. The photo won first prize in a municipal contest. (Di Feiwan) 107

Don with Fourth Uncle in a back alley of Tanhualing, Wuchang. (T. E. Barlow) 168

The divorce portrait of Tan Zhongying and Liu Jungui. (China Daily) 188

Hotel at the top of Huangshan, where we spent the
    night. (China Publishing House)   208

Tani and Don at Huangshan. (Zheng Xuexuan)   209

Bound feet on Taishan pilgrimage. (T. E. Barlow)   217

Don and Tani in front of the Lama Temple, Beijing.
    (Anon.)   237

Aerial photo of Imperial Palace showing the Wumen
    Gate leading to a succession of imperial halls, all
    along the north–south axis. (Beijing Slides Studio) 238

Old Beijing   239

1

Arrival

Shanghai, August 27, 1981

A relaxed man about 40 years old, wearing khaki shorts and smiling a little nervously walked up to us inside the functional, small air terminal and introduced himself as Lao (Old) Zheng, second cadre of the Foreign Affairs Office at Shanghai Teachers College. All work units that deal with foreign experts or foreigners hired for their expertise in something (usually science, language in our case) has an FAO. In fact all dealings with foreigners must take place through a Foreign Affairs Office. Over Lao Zheng's shoulder, behind the heavy glass doors on the other side of Customs we could see Aunt Meixin waving both her arms at us through the heavy, muggy air, and motioning to where she would wait. We had arrived on an unmistakably Chinese jet: Boeing interior with Victorian antimacassars. Directly before the first row of seats in the passenger section the Chinese airline, Minhang, had installed a handrubbed, custom-built, gleaming wooden cabinet, and graced it with a bowl of staid plastic flowers. Out the windows, as the plane descended into Shanghai, we saw the green fields ringing the enormous modern city.

Shanghai has no freeway belt. All traffic into and out of the most in-
dustrially advanced region in the People's Republic of China seems,
at least from the air, to be confined to waterways.

As we stood in line on the ground shepherding our luggage
through customs, Lao Zheng began making slow, deliberate, polite
conversation. At each declaration he appraised the effect, gauging if
it really was true, that "Luo Mingda and wife" could understand
Chinese. Gradually he seemed reassured, almost physically relieved. He spent the long wait listing the ways our speaking the
language would make working together more pleasant, and looking
absent-mindedly through our belongings with the customs officers.
All of them seemed extremely pleased to see our numerous boxes of
books. Then he guided us out through the search tables to the
greeting party.

A tall, slender, elegant man in a gray summer uniform received
us unhurriedly with a slow list of restrained, murmured greetings
and was introduced as Lao Chen, the senior FAO officer. His hands
were remarkably dry in spite of the heat. He completed his protocol
and motioned to Professor Yang Ruiru (Lao Yang) who welcomed us
on behalf on the foreign languages department in beautifully colloquial American English and brusquely shook our hands. Aunt Meixin, Don's father's younger sister, waited until the formalities had
been concluded. Then she hugged and kissed us and told us how
glad she was we'd finally arrived. This took some time. But when it
was over Aunt Meixin dragged over a tall, robust, healthy young
woman, introducing her as Hu Yue, a distant relative of ours, and an
English student in the department. We all got into Shanghai's version of the VW van and slipped out onto the dark, tree-lined road
into the city.

Everything felt so rural. It was about ten o'clock at night, and
we felt keenly alert as the blackened van made its way rapidly down
the unlit road; the driver had turned his headlights off to conserve
energy. After a few miles, shops began appearing along the road.
Then more and more people, walking along the boarded-up shop
fronts. Others sat on stools in the street, chatting, knitting under
lamplights, eating popsicles and playing cards, or lying on small
bamboo cots. The conversation inside the van shifted to tomorrow's
schedule, which they said had already been arranged. The FAO plan
had us lunching at Don's cousin Mingzhang's place, touring
downtown Shanghai the rest of the afternoon, and then a big, formal, welcome banquet dinner for that evening. Not thinking of the
heat, fatigue, or jet lag, we said alright.

Then our journey through the hot night air ended. The van
pulled up to a wrought-iron gate and as it sounded the horn, a man
with white hair yelled something in Shanghai dialect. He opened the

tall gate to let us in, and we drove onto the campus, down a long, dark, tree-lined avenue to a three-storied building. The FAO cadres lugged our bags to the second floor. By the time we got all the luggage upstairs, the heat and humidity started affecting us. Yet exhausted as we were, we still mustered enough energy to sit down in the dining hall for a light snack of sandwiches, excellent Shanghainese European pastries, orangeade, and beer. We negotiated a ten A.M. meeting with the FAO officials to discuss pay arrangements and sightseeing plans for the week before school starts. Then they would take us to Mingzhang's place. That night we slept, wet with perspiration just from the exertion of breathing, on huge beach towels spread over the old-fashioned, twine-strung Chinese bed.

The next morning we walked around the red-brick exterior to look at the turned-up eaves. We live in a 1920s Western-style, two-room apartment which has hardwood floors, lacquered woodwork, high ceilings, and yellow wash plaster wall, not much different from flats in the Sunset district of San Francisco. Walking directly into our quarters from the dormitory hall we step into a large, spacious living room. To the left is a tiny study, to the right a large bedroom, a walk-in closet, and a newly tiled bathroom with a huge Victorian

Gate entrance to Shanghai Teachers College, with a monument of Mao's calligraphy behind the gate, center rear. (T. E. Barlow)

bathtub. The living room even has steam heat radiators and an air-conditioner set into the southern window. Along the hall outside our rooms a half dozen other doors lead into other private rooms. Our rooms abut the small, alcove reading room where a large table sits under the glassed-in newspaper rack. A short hall from the common room leads to the dining hall, the kitchen, and pantry. The third floor and its staff of three cooks and three attendants belong entirely to us, so everyone on campus calls this place the foreign expert building.

At ten o'clock the impeccable Lao Chen rapped on the screen door and stepped inside murmuring courtesies. Lao Zheng accompanied him and so did a heavyset young man who had helped out deferentially at the airport the previous evening but had not been introduced. Xiao (Young) Qian kept his eyes politely fixed on the ground as we all said our good morning. Then he shook hands and explained that he would act as our guide and translator. Then the session began: We get no salary since we are volunteers. But each of us will receive 10 yuan per diem, or about $5.70 per day, plus free room and board, complete medical care, and a ten-day paid vacation at the end of the first semester. None of these details had been settled before, so we were pleased to find ourselves in Shanghai on such good terms. The meeting that morning was the closest we ever got to a formal contract. The staff serves Western breakfast and lunch, Chinese dinner. The FAO will arrange outings such as the one they suggested for the following day, a tour of the Shanghai Industrial Exhibition Hall. The day after that they left free for our course preparation, and then we were scheduled for a boat tour of the Yangtze River. Since we have no idea what courses we will be asked to teach, we accepted the plan which included the free day for preparation. At precisely 10:30 A.M. the gray college sedan rolled up outside, and we left for Mingzhang's place on Urumqi Road South in downtown Shanghai.

Pre-Liberation, European-style buildings still dominate the old French quarters where we're headed, but ringing the older foreign concessions stand rows of new apartment buildings dating from the GPCR. Newer industrial neighborhoods and office complexes give the city its contemporary air. Mingzhang and his family live in an atypical, three-storied private home he inherited from his father and owned once, before turning the lot over to the government. From the outside the house has the genteel Sino-European look of so many former foreign-concession homes. But the interior makes no allowance, with its Chinese-style rooms, staircase, and downstairs common room. Mingzhang's father had a very good reputation as a doctor in the neighborhood, so the Red Guards somehow never attacked the house, and the family has held onto a few antique pieces of furniture. But by American standards the building and the small courtyard it stands in have degenerated badly. The interior feels particularly eerie because once, years ago, someone painted all the rooms a gentle reddish color, which has faded unevenly over time, particularly around the window frames and the doors which lead out onto a small, elegant second-story veranda.

On the dining room wall, so strategically located no one could possibly ignore it, hangs a diplomalike document with a big red seal, stating that on such and such a date in 1952 Luo Mingyi became a member of the People's Liberation Army. Mingyi is Mingzhang's oldest brother. The document hangs on the wall of the Shanghai house rather than in Mingyi's own place in Beijing, because after their father's death Mingyi became the head of their branch of the family, and this house which their father built still remains the center of activity for the four brothers and their families. Chinese terms delineate fine relationships by American standards. There is no such generic term as "cousin" in Chinese. Mingyi is Don's *tangge* and Mingzhang is his *tangdi. Tang* indicates that their fathers were brothers: *ge* means older brother; *di*, younger brother. No one could ever mistake a *tangge* as a cousin on the mother's side, or a cousin through one's father's sister after her marriage, because kinship terms assign other names to these relationships. Since 1949, the government has encouraged people to use the term *airen* (lover) to designate spouses as a way of circumventing the servility of the older terms for wife. *Airen* can be either husband or wife. Of course an *airen* is always a legally married spouse, since no other recognized lovers exist. On top of the old, finely worked kinship system, a new relation of sentiment has been added in an attempt to undercut gender stratification.

Mingzhang met us in the lane in front of the courtyard door. He looks a little bit like Don, but, surprisingly, much bigger and sturdier. The impression is even more pronounced when he stands next to his tiny, delicate wife, Peihua. Somehow we learned immediately that Peihua does not cook and Mingzhang washes no dishes. The lunch was incredible, and we appreciated the enormous energy that had gone into its preparation. But we had really come to meet relatives: Peihua, the two children, Peihua's American-educated father, one of her brothers-in-law (she is the youngest of eleven children), and Aunt Meixin. It wasn't easy at first. But the food began to disappear, and we started talking and toasting. They filled us in on family news, and everyone who could began reminiscing about the past when all the "Mings" were children. Donald is Mingda, part of the generation of cousins whose personal names all begin with the ideograph for "bright" in accordance with the Luo family's naming couplet.

Don with Mingzhang, Peihua, and their children on their veranda. (T. E. Barlow)

At two sharp, Xiao Qian returned for us and we drove in our huge gray coupe down one of the city's main shopping avenues, Huaihai Road, to the Bund, and back up the other, Nanjing Road. We saw what all tourists see—the European architecture, the enormous offering of consumer goods, the crowds. We even spotted a coffee shop jammed with people who were all eating cream puffs. We got out at the Bund and felt that well-known, inquisitive, unsmiling but nonhostile Chinese stare for the first time. It is unnerving.

We have never seen so many people, ever. Our first glimpse came on the ride from the airport. We've since learned that Shanghainese do not go into their houses at night, but bring their beds outside to avoid the heat. Downtown Shanghai is a mob scene. Many of the stores open directly onto the street, which means the shops are as crowded as the street. Right in the center of downtown people sit on stools eating, retired women walk around crocheting or talking to their friends, a team of workers might be patting coal dust into tiny balls for the brazier stoves people drag out into the street at dusk to cook on, half a dozen workers stand outside the gate of their factory taking a cigarette break: all this as masses of pedestrians make their way through the neighborhood. It's a little like New York City at rush hour. Except Shanghai has untidier crowds, since nobody worries about cars. People drift in and out of the street barely avoiding bikes and buses, slowed to a crawl by the incredible heat.

After lunch we felt so uncomfortable in our heavy, northern California clothes we asked Xiao Qian to take us to the Number One Department Store on Shanghai's famous Nanjing Road, so we could buy something lighter. The tall, many-storied, pre-Liberation building almost visibly sags from overuse, age, and the heat. We followed Xiao Qian up the huge round staircases gawking like bumpkins from Gansu Province before it hit us that we were the major display. We aren't used to thinking about ourselves as strange or peculiar. Oppressed by the heat and close bodies and stares, both of us started sweating heavily. People were shouting in dialects we couldn't understand. They come from all over China to shop in this store, and many of them seemed torn between wanting to buy and wanting to stare at us. The crowd made both of us feel terribly shy. We did not want them to laugh at us or find us buying the wrong things, so we let Xiao Qian handle everything in Shanghai dialect. As people pressed into us more and more tightly even he looked uncomfortable. We finished the transaction and ran out into the mob scene on the street, gasping with relief.

Two days in China and we are beginning to see why our cousin Guoxun, who recently migrated to the U.S., told us he felt so lonely when he first arrived. We have read about the importance of family, neighborhood organizations, and work units, but now we can feel it. The Bund was the only place we'd been so far where we saw a group of farmers who looked totally disoriented. Everyone else seems to have a place in this enormous city of 11 million. What reinforces this impression is the different human atmosphere. People generally have more sensitivity to community than what we're accustomed to. That in itself makes comparisons difficult for anyone who knows only China, or only the West. For example, letters to the editor of *China Daily*, an English-language newspaper that is delivered to the foreign experts dorm every morning, come from both Chinese and Western readers. The non-Chinese seem more service-oriented—the waiter in my hotel was rude, why can't people line up at the bus stops. Those letters signed by Chinese almost inevitably comment on the social consequences of certain wrong attitudes or behavior. One letter said the city government should set up a "smiling school" for medical doctors because doctors who have "numb faces" scare their patients. Another argued persuasively that since book publishing is like getting married and brides want to wear lovely gowns on their wedding days, so, too, books should be beautifully designed and well packaged. The readers of such books will enjoy possession even more.

We knew before we arrived that compared to the U.S. China is a more personalized society. We hadn't thought about how sensitive to mood and nuance this would make the people around us. Probably the warmth and tact of people here is what visitors find so attractive about China. Tani has mostly a reading knowledge of Chinese. Though she follows conversations, she really hates to make mistakes so she tends to avoid talking—much to her own chagrin. On the way back from our excursion, Lao Gu the driver suggested in a friendly, gentle way that she try a bit harder. In itself there was nothing at all remarkable about his advice. But Lao Gu offered it in a sensitive, indirect way. First he complimented Don on how well he spoke Chinese. Next he mentioned that returning to China was a wonderful opportunity for people to learn the language. Then he told a story about another foreign woman who had come to Teachers College with no knowledge of Chinese at all, but miraculously, inside a year she could talk like a native!

We know that certain imperatives lie underneath all the charm. We recognized the FAO cadres' relief when they made certain we did not need a Chinese translator, though Xiao Qian will help us out in other ways. Particularly from the affable, smiling, inquisitive Lao Zheng we felt pressure once he could stop worrying about language; his voice has risen a little, his Shanghai accent seems to have broadened, and we feel a certain unmistakable determination in his efforts to show Don, especially, how things should be done. Not one person has made the slightest effort to try and understand how really foreign we are. They do not express any curiosity about the alien, only in the uses to which foreign things—technology, for instance—could be put in a Chinese world.

That evening, dressed comfortably in our light summer clothes, we attended the official welcome dinner. Don found himself watching Lao Chen constantly. All things revolve around Lao Chen, at least everything that touches on us. He appeared in the dining room early that evening to supervise the last touches on the table, supported on one side by Lao Zheng who seemed a little tense, and on the other by the very junior Xiao Qian. Crisply, in a manicured, understated way the senior man moved through the kitchen to look at the hors d'oeuvres and opened the wheezing refrigerator to make sure the beer was chilled; then he adjusted the angle of the tall standing fans set around the banquet tables. But he wasn't exactly a host. All night he ran around making sure food got to the table properly, pouring wine and beer, insisting on toasts, in an almost junior-man fashion. Lao Chen fascinates Don. He sets our exacting schedule and manages our affairs. The younger men make a point of deferring to him. He is also our first ideologue, in the sense that ideology necessarily forms the center of his working world. His job is to handle foreigners and so his attitude must shift abruptly in line with current Party decisions.

Lao Yang managed a relaxed informality even on a formal occasion. She shook hands warmly with Don and then, tucking Tani's hand in the crook of her arm, she escorted us to the corner and introduced us to our department head, Dean Chen. In very slow, measured, unnatural but faultlessly grammatical sentences, the Dean, a fat version of Deng Xiaoping, apologized to us. He explained that he had forgotten how to speak English during his many years in prison. He had just finished learning the language all over again. Then there was a mild commotion and Vice-Chancellor Zhang, a really jovial Party man from Shandong arrived to represent welcome from the highest administrative level. He spoke execrable Chinese, so thick with Shandong patois that no one could understand him.

As things slowed down we rose to thank our hosts formally for inviting us to teach in their college. We stated our eagerness to contribute to the educational modernization campaign at Shanghai Teachers College and requested that they help us and when necessary criticize us in the future. There was a sudden, almost shocked pause. Our faux pas was to bring up memories of the GPCR when harsh practices of "criticism and self-criticism" humiliated many and drove some to suicide. But as we toasted and turned back to eating dessert, conversation livened again. Finally the banquet ended. They walked us politely from the dinner table down the hallway to our apartment door. Somebody told us Xiao Qian was taking care of our police registration, work permits, health and library cards, and would have them all done when he picked us up for the trip to the Shanghai Industrial Exhibition Hall tomorrow. Then everyone said goodnight and left.

2

Teaching Assignments

Shanghai, September 4, 1981

*T*he FAO finally assigned us our teaching schedules and we got started this week. Don has been given one class or section of "intensive reading" with seniors, and four sections of sophomore "Introduction to Contemporary America." Tani also has a senior intensive reading. Both sections of intensive reading seniors are from the entering class of 1978 that will graduate at the end of this academic year. The rest of Tani's time will be taken up with a lecture survey in "History of American Literature," to all 200 of the class of 1977 who get assigned jobs at the end of this semester.

Everyone in the classes of '77 and '78 passed the first national college entrance exams given immediately after the GPCR. Previously, students were selected on the basis of different kinds of merit—political correctness, personal morality, class background, leadership potential, and so on. Our seniors simply outscored everyone else on the entrance exams. The classes of '77 and '78 are also distinctive because for the two years right after the GPCR the authorities raised the cutoff age to 35 for students taking the exams, giving "sent down" youths two chances to compete for university spots. So unlike the freshmen, sophomores, and juniors, these two senior classes range in age from kids in their early twenties to men and women around forty. The older ones are about the right age to have been politically active during the GPCR. Almost all of them spent time, anywhere from a month to five or six years depending on their age, working on state farms, communes, or in factories. These older, more experienced students seem to have very little problem following our lectures, and when they approach us in class or in the halls speak fluently in English. Don's sophomore students, on the other hand, are all teenagers or in their early twenties. Their language level is low and Don found himself struggling in the first lectures to find a vocabulary simple enough for them; otherwise all he gets are blank faces and a lot of rustling noises. But it's more than just language. The sophomores are inexperienced and kind of dull.

We weren't fully aware of all this until we got to the teaching building on the other side of campus and actually met our classes for the first time. Tuesday morning we were both scheduled to meet our intensive reading sections at the same hour. Penciled schedules in hand, we walked out of the foreign expert building, down the long, shaded road, protected by stands of sturdy green plane trees on either side, which joins the two halves of the campus. We crossed over the crowded, concrete bridge which bisects the eastern and western parts of the college, and continued past the performing arts building, skirting the grassy quad, to the foreign languages department on the west edge of the campus. The department has two red brick buildings. The three-storied teaching building houses home classrooms for each section, a language lab that doesn't seem to work, the department's Party branch office, and some larger, lecture halls. The administration building is an exact duplicate of the teaching building and stands 200 feet to the north. All the foreign languages faculty except the foreign experts have offices in the administration building. The department's library and mail room are also located there. Our joint office is on the second floor of the teaching building, down the hall from the department's Party secretary's office.

We arrived at the teaching building, walked up the broad, clammy steps to the second floor and down the hall to find our sections' home rooms. Each of us opened a classroom door; 30 students waited, seated in small wooden chairs behind rows of long desks. At the head of the room was a tall podium and a big, recently washed blackboard on which was painted "Warmly Welcome Ms. Tani Barlow-Lowe" or "Class Warmly Welcomes Prof. Mingda Lowe" in colored chalk. The moment each of us opened the door to our classroom a voice shouted "stand!" and by the time we had stepped inside the entire class had risen to attention. After just a few meetings we both feel tremendously drawn to our intensive reading classes. The students still greet us too formally, leaping to their feet when we enter the room, but otherwise they act as though we were their special property. They hang on our words, laughing riotously even at our silliest jokes. When the recess comes they follow us around the halls to hold impromptu discussions. Their determination to squeeze everything out of us, from how to pronounce a word to what a certain slang expression really means, seems to us entirely unaffected. We have asked them why they feel such determination to know these things. They almost always reply that we are their "great opportunity" to learn about the West.

Students are so unfailingly polite and eager to have us with them that we can't help but be amused and moved. Our American students at home seem so world-weary and knowing in comparison, and have so little faith in what we can offer them: after all it can't get them a job, can it? Here, the students make us the center of everything and don't ever appear to question what we can offer them. That is why we keep coming back to the feeling that they are innocent. They have to be a little innocent to take us so much on faith. But there is more to it than that. Foreign tourists talk about sexual innocence in China and we see it too; even knowing what we do about this society it's still a novelty seeing young men holding hands or draped all over each other, and young women in each others' arms as they intently watch an athletic competition on the big field outside our dorm window. To us the sudden absence of sexual tension between people signifies a kind of childish innocence, since in our world only children behave this way. And of course they are really incredibly innocent about the Western world, which adds to the unreal feeling. We have both tried to tell them that their ideas are really off the mark. They happily resist our efforts, and have their own ideas about what things mean. We just don't know what to make of a 25-year old, unmarried, female student, the absolute picture of rosy-cheeked innocence, who stays after the history lecture in order to tell the foreign teacher she is "entranced" by the brooding sense of guilt in the *The Scarlet Letter*. All this, smiling gently and unperturbedly. By her own admission, she doesn't know anything about original sin, the basis of Hawthorne's darkness. Something really does move her about the novel, but we have no idea what. Another student has insisted that literature's only purpose is to convey the inevitable tragedy in life. We also think our students appear innocent because they are unguarded when they talk to us, and because they are all so unbelievably intense. All we have to do is smile at a passing student or crack a little joke, and in return we get a genuinely emotional response. Of course, they can also withdraw it at will. When we do not give them what they want in lecture the whole class emanates boredom. Far more often, they exhaust us with their single-minded desire to know more. They keep saying they are ignorant, many claiming to have been cheated out of their "golden years" by the GPCR.

Sometimes people are attracted to us for more complex reasons. Last week we saw a Beijing opera based on an episode from the traditional epic, *Water Margins*, which dealt with a problem of military strategy. Song Jiang and his bandit heroes try three times to rescue their comrades, and failing in his first two efforts, Song delivers an aria to express his grief at being unable to find a winning strategy. We see the carry-over into daily affairs, in the sense that *strategy* has a very clear role in social relations. One day, a student came up to Tani to discuss a problem of personal strategy: how could she get her "cousin" through the new, stricter policy at the U.S. consulate, now that visas are being granted only to students who can prove they have reasons to return home. Tani had to explain that she had no "back door" at the consulate. Chinese seem to accept the necessity of strategizing in daily life, much more so than the average Americans. This may explain why students here like Western detective novels so much. Many of them have told us they prefer reading detective stories to any other kind of foreign literature. Partly, they have trouble picking out the themes and motifs in sophisticated fiction because they know so little about Western cultures; but also they just like reading plots, the longer and more intricate the better. And, according to one man, they particularly appreciate clever strategies which result in happy endings.

The special treatment we get from students and faculty has strategic intent. Everyone wants us to reciprocate, to live up to their expectations; and with the two of us they are working on fertile ground. After very little prompting we've already promised an awful lot. If we ignore convention and do not reciprocate for all the special treatment, we would show insensitivity to our hosts. And of course we would be shut out of the campus community we want so very much to join. We want to respond in as Chinese (that is, un-"barbarian") a way as possible, partly so we won't feel so out of place, but also because if we acted here the way we do in San Francisco we would confuse them. It isn't that easy. Everyone has a very definite idea of what Americans are like. Particularly when students talk to Tani they project all sorts of fantasies. Apparently being with a foreigner requires extra politeness, such as making sure the foreigner gets enough to eat by introducing her to the Chinese custom of eating with chopsticks (they don't know that many San Franciscans eat Chinese food with chopsticks now), and a great deal of arguing in Shanghai dialect about what the foreign teacher should be told next. It's linked to student's desire to know about the "America," where everything is clean, rich, powerful, intelligent, superior, modern. . . . They sure don't want to know about that real America where problems arise precisely from the concentration of the wealth and power which they admire so much.

On Monday we attended a departmental welcome tea party. We walked into a small sunlit room down the hall from our office, to greet representative students, including some familiar faces from our intensive reading sections, Professor Yang, Professor Fang Quan whom we met at the banquet party, other faculty we had not met before, and a group of Party officials. After seating Don in the most prominent position, and Tani next to him, Professor Fang gave a formal introduction in British English and began calling on students to speak or sing. One boy (students refer to themselves as boys and girls) finished "Doe a Deer a Female Deer" in a lovely tenor voice, then everyone insisted it was our turn. We reciprocated by promising we would teach them as much as we possibly could, but that was not enough. They demanded a song. Tani wracked her brains and came out with "The Battle Hymn of the Republic." At least it wasn't "Onward Christian Soldiers." Afterwards we regretted we had never learned the "Marseillaise."

We try to figure out what we are seeing. Is it Communist or Chinese? Each of us has been in other Chinese communities outside China, and in other, non-Chinese socialist countries; but we've never seen this combination before. And, at least for now, we tend to see it as the heritage of the Chinese Revolution. Maybe we will have to revise our judgment. We are getting more information about people's politics. Everywhere we go people tell us about the destruction and suffering that went on during the so-called GPCR. The "so-called" has just been inserted before the GPCR in all Chinese periodicals, the reason being that, as one student put it, "It was not a revolution and it had nothing to do with culture." Several people have assured us that Shanghai Teachers College suffered fewer violent confrontations than other local colleges, and we know that is true. But the fading slogans on the building walls—"down with so-and-so, down with this, down with that"—still make us uncomfortable. Nothing seems to have been done to remove them.

We feel an inexplicable depth to the people we meet, particularly middle-aged students and professors. There is no doubting that people here are warm and emotional, not at all like the silly American stereotypes of the formal, stilted, Chinese. But we also realize that in many cases this warmth is a luminous, deceptive facade. On reflection it does not seem particularly strange, since the GPCR disrupted every entrenched system of personal relations on this campus, every academic habit, every one of the special social graces we are now enjoying so much. Each time we speak to a middle-aged person we wonder what crimes he or she was accused of committing then. Every time we run into a Chinese teacher surrounded by students we cannot help but envision Red Guards, because a percentage of these students *are* former guards returned to this campus. The even more puzzling matter is how students like these, the same faculty, the acculturated patterns of behavior could all have ever been anything other than what we see now?

That's why the intensity of the students frightens us a little. Now they are channeling it all into school work. We see dozens of them working steadily in huge, brightly-lit study halls late into the night—and the semester has just begun. Every afternoon, we see the younger students standing in doorways, window bays, corners, any convenient, out of the way, quiet places, backs to the passerby, textbooks held squarely at eye-level chanting the English lesson out loud in clear, confident voices. We feel students snatching at whatever we can offer them.

Complicating everything is our own reticence about asking people directly what happened to them during those years. Maybe it's because the GPCR made such a positive impression on us in the late sixties, we feel almost responsible for the tragedy in a minor way, by our previous misunderstanding of its nature. It was very hard for us to accept the aftermath of Jiang Qing's arrest. It's doubly difficult to be reminded daily of the difference between how we saw the GPCR then and what the experience was like for people here. One day Lao Chen took Don aside evidently rather put off by our idiocy, and suggested politely that we learn more about Shanghai before boring him with our "friendship" platitudes. Another colleague tried to explain the whole period once by saying that during the GPCR men were not men and women were not women. But last night we saw a movie that made us feel a whole lot better.

Every Thursday the whole campus goes to the movies, just as Friday afternoon everyone attends the mandatory political study. Everybody likes movies, so the audience is a mixture of students, faculty, officials, staff and their families, and even peasants from the commune next door. First showing starts at noon in the fine arts department's largest performance hall, followed by a second and a third in the afternoon and evening. This Thursday we saw *Yanwei* (Long Separation). A young woman falls in love with a handsome young male pianist, whose mother is a lovely soprano. The younger woman witnessed the persecution of her own parents during the GPCR. For many years she has lived as a sent-down youth in Inner Mongolia. The audience knows, but the boy does not, that many years previously when she was a Red Guard this young girl struck a famous soprano on the ear in the course of a violent struggle. Naturally the blow deafened the singer. And naturally the singer was none other than the young piano player's mother. The audience finds this out through a series of extraordinarily unsubtle flashbacks, just before the narrative shifts to the mother's perspective. The younger woman has applied for admission to the music conservatory headed by the older woman. After a series of emotional climaxes and a long chase scene through the snow drifts of Inner Mongolia—one woman on a horse, the other in a jeep—the two are reconciled, and the film ends with a triumphant duet on the glowing conservatory stage. After the movie we felt ridiculous. If terrible potboilers like these were being made about the GPCR our shyness was unrealistic.

Yet we could not be completely sure. Last week Tani brought up the subject in class and things got very crazy. Her intensive reading section had been assigned a text explaining the uses of I.Q. tests in Britain. So Tani asked what they thought were differences between social intelligence and measurable intellect, and whether anyone had had his or her concept of "intelligence" changed during the GPCR. Instead of getting the anticipated critique of I.Q. tests as biased, racist, classist, and unscientific, Tani got something really unexpected: a boy student rose out of his chair, no handraising or asking permission, and, ignoring the original question, lit into the teacher for her ridiculous representation of the GPCR. Other students also got up. Six or seven seemed so angry and upset they were ready to shake their fists at her. Tani literally froze, as every student in the room from the most inarticulate boy to the shyest girl student took turns telling the teacher what bad form it was to suggest anyone learned anything in the GPCR. Partly we suspect the class just wanted to tell the foreign teacher a thing or two. But the tension in the air was genuine and unmistakable. Everybody wanted to say that each one of them had been cheated, their years in the countryside wasted. If they had learned anything at all it was to avoid politics and distrust slogans. A student who had only moments before class told Tani very reflectively that working as a peasant had at least taught him how deadening manual labor could be, got up to berate her, too. The emotional intensity made Tani apprehensive. After all, the Gang of Four was not smashed yesterday.

The movie was really terrible, and we didn't know exactly what to think. This morning Xiao Qian made us feel better. When Don tried indirectly to find out if the sound he thought he'd heard last night really had been the audience snickering, Xiao Qian said yes, the audience had hated the movie, too. He told us about a number of films he'd seen that had dealt with GPCR themes a lot more successfully, and that from his perspective *Yanwei* was particularly unconvincing because of the phony love scenes. Everybody in Shanghai falls in love, and movies about romance have been especially popular here; but this film was hackneyed, formulaic, the audience had figured out the plot almost from the outset and even the flash-backs—a relatively new technique in Chinese films—had been badly handled. We asked what he thought about all the characters being privileged musicians with personal luxuries like telephones and cars; would that bother the audience? He said no.

Both of us have had complaints from students that their assigned reading texts are too boring, and requests for new readings. To help us provide them with new texts Xiao Qian walked us through the "publication" process several days ago. Books in foreign languages are expensive and hard to get, so the foreign languages department has an entire staff of workers to type and mimeograph assignments for our classes. Previously we just handed over the assignments to Xiao Qian and he took care of it. Now we have started taking selections up to the spacious, well-ventilated, brightly-lit office in the department's administrative building, where Mr. Wang and a typing crew work on heavy, oversize typewriters; there are seven or eight machines for English, French, Italian, and German, and several for typing in Chinese. The smell of stencil corrector hangs in the air. Tall, bony, bald Mr. Wang is a retired, middle-school English teacher. He has been assigned to us exclusively since he is the fastest typist, and our students need the material most. Everytime we walk into Wang's office he welcomes us in a gallant, almost European way; he politely claims he gets a lot of reading in by typing our assignments. From this office the stencils go across the campus to the campus publications office, where workers run them off on stencil machines. Mr. Wang says that the student leaders in each section pick them up and distribute them. The amount of human labor that goes into this process is staggering.

3

Ways of Seeing

*R*ight after the GPCR, Arthur Miller made a trip to the P.R.C. and wrote a very moving article in *The New York Times Magazine*, about meeting Chinese intellectuals and artists, and hearing of their horrible experiences over the previous decade. This seems to have initiated a love affair. Miller has continued to promote literary and other cultural exchanges with China, and Chinese intellectuals have begun taking quite an interest in his work, particularly in the anti-McCarthy era drama *The Crucible*, which they see as meaningful in their own GPCR context. Anyway, several days ago an extremely shy woman came up to Tani right after a lecture and asked if Professor Lowe would like to learn about the revival of Western-style theater going on in Shanghai student circles lately. If so, he and Ms. Barlow-Lowe might like to see the Chinese adaptation of Miller's *The Crucible* now running downtown. (This has happened several times now, that female students approach Don through Tani.) And it would be nice if Professor Lowe could give the theater students a lecture on the development of Western theater in the twentieth century. We explained that neither Professor Lowe nor Ms. Barlow-Lowe knew anything about the history of Western theater in the twentieth century. The student was disappointed but gave us the tickets anyway.

She met us again as we stepped off the bus on downtown Nanjing Road, steering us around the crowds toward the theater where an intense young man from the Shanghai Academy of Dramatic Arts met us at the door. We walked into a crowded house. No one except the two of us appeared any more formally dressed than the people on the street. Our hosts told us tickets to this play were almost impossible to get now, and we do have a lot of trouble distinguishing Shanghainese by their dress, but it still seems to us that there were a lot of workers in the audience.

Suddenly the lights went out and the curtain rose on a highly-lit Western-style realistic stage set of Salem, Massachusetts. On walked the actors in Puritan costumes, all very convincingly Caucasian in blonde wigs and big putty noses. But in spite of the theatrical realism of costume and setting, once the dialogue began it became clear that the production was heavily stylized in the Chinese fashion. Actors delivered lines as though the entire cast had rehearsed with a metronome. Stage action felt exaggerated, almost to the point of mime at points. The cast seemed to be relying more on the aural effects they could get by manipulating the timbre of their voices, than on the kind of "method" emotionalism we knew from our brief encounters with theater in San Francisco. That is not to say we were unmoved. Quite the contrary. As soon as we got past the staginess of the delivery, we felt ourselves getting carried away by the rising dramatic tension.

Yet the audience did not react as a Western audience would have. Throughout the performance people kept on making comments about the actors—a few times in very loud voices—like the Beijing opera patrons had several days ago when we had attended a very good opera performance. The situation reminded us of going to the kabuki in Japan. There the audience walks around, people cheer or eat, hold long conversations during the boring parts, and generally view the "play" as a spectacle, ignoring the one element that so thoroughly dominates all Western theater—the illusion of the proscenium arch. Similarly, here the audience did not want to mistake the events happening on stage with "real" events. Theatrical illusion requires the cooperation of a silent audience, but that did not happen. The viewers made no effort to join the actors in the conspiracy of the proscenium. And they did not applaud very enthusiastically after the last curtain, either. However we could not tell whether it was out of convention or disappointment at the performance.

We wondered whether *The Crucible*'s run will be affected by the Central Committee's latest policy statement issued early last week urging Party members to resume criticism and self-criticism.

The government promised to restrict rectification to Party members, partly because of widespread fears that any "criticism" might indicate the outbreak of a new Cultural Revolution. But a certain tension has emerged between Deng Xiaoping's "hundred flowers" policy, which encourages innovation and independence in the arts, and the most recent warnings about "bourgeois liberalism." The controversy came to a head this summer over a movie titled *Bitter Love*. In the film an Overseas Chinese returns to China but is horribly persecuted during the GPCR. He dies, after enormous suffering, frozen to death in a snowstorm at the center of a great question mark etched in the snow. The film provoked the inevitable question: Why, if he loves China so much, cannot China love him in return? It was banned soon after production, but many people read the script when one of the Shanghai dailies published it in full so that everyone could know what they were supposed to criticize. A foreign friend of ours said he stood in a line stretching around the block to get a copy. Even now, months later, the authorities are still using *Bitter Love* as a ripe example of bourgeois liberalism. Newspaper editorials refer to it as a "sugar coated bullet of the bourgeoisie."

Yesterday on our way across campus to see if any mail was delivered to our office, we saw some students writing on the blackboard that stands between the two red brick foreign languages department buildings. We stopped to take a look at the message, which turned out to concern this Friday afternoon's political study agenda. These days, the topic is the historical re-periodization of the "so-called Great Proletarian Cultural Revolution," specifically who should be held personally responsible for the disaster. Friday afternoon discussion topics are determined by the authorities, so whatever our students discuss here is also being studied all over the country, published in the newspapers, put on propaganda billboards, editorialized in major newspapers, and even written up in *Beijing Review* and *China Reconstructs* for export. In the case of this week's topic, we can honestly say that people talk constantly about who should be blamed for the GPCR.

Even in the U.S., we would have followed the course of criticism against a major work like *Bitter Love* very carefully, since no one is ever sure when a small criticism will blossom into a major campaign. But here in Shanghai we realize how powerful an influence these propaganda campaigns really have, even the relatively minor ones. Take the current etiquette movement. Remember us mentioning the "smiling school" someone had suggested in a letter to the editor of *China Daily*. The comment turned out to be linked to a larger campaign known as the "five stresses and the four beautifuls" (*wujiang simei*) intended to encourage beautification of everything, beginning with personal habits and ending in the national environment. This does not appear to be a noteworthy effort, but even this one amazes us because the city is completely blanketed with reminder-slogans. The four characters appear everywhere, on large red banners in front of shop entrances, as part of photo layouts on the street displays instructing cyclists and drivers in good manners. Don leaned out the window of a bus one afternoon, and there, etched in tiny characters on one of the poles holding up a bus-stop sign was "five stresses and four beautifuls." Xiao Qian patiently explained what was being referred to in the "five stresses" and "four beautifuls," although even he had a little trouble recalling specifically what the last stress was. Most people we ask just laugh rudely in our faces, and some say that, while everybody thinks the effort is ridiculous, shopkeepers suffer most of all because the red paper and gold lettering come out of their budgets.

Even so, to us the posture of the critics does not feel that much different than the position being taken by the government. Both sides agree that what destroyed the old social values of politeness, cleanliness, civic pride, was the GPCR, and that some larger coercive action should be taken to restore civic virtue. In other words, critics and proponents both believe people will change only if they are subjected to moral pressure. In America we would probably find people arguing that it is against the law to litter or spit, so if a person violates the law he or she deserves to be fined or punished. No one we have discussed the matter with here has ever raised this argument. Usually people begin by saying that the campaign, such as it is, addresses a real moral problem, and then launch into a long explanation about how the acts of a handful of people at the top, usually the Gang of Four, caused bad social effects among the ordinary people. To undo the harm, society must either wait for the bad effects to wear off, or (for those who endorse the campaign) impel people to change their personal morality. There is consensus on the problem—the tie-up between civic virtue and personal morality—and to some degree on the solution, though very little on the specific means.

The other thing we have discovered about this campaign is how thoroughly consistent the propaganda machinery seems with the rest of the social environment. The slogan belongs to the tradition of calligraphic emblems. Brushwork hangs in all public buildings and in almost any empty interior space. At the entrance to Shanghai Teachers College stands a huge iron obelisk inscribed with Comrade Mao's handwriting—not just a message, but also a work of art. Written characters can also be inscribed on rocks and cliffs, steles, tombs, gravestones, even mountains; they can be lifted off one surface onto paper by a simple rubbing or printing process. Their design elements can be exaggerated, or collapsed, made huge or reduced.

Calligraphy on the "five stresses and four beautifuls" campaign. (T. E. Barlow)

Logo advocating sanitation. (T. E. Barlow)

Door slogans on individual responsibility in census campaign.
(T. E. Barlow)

Blackboard listing the "ten don'ts," a part of efforts to improve sanitation.
(T. E. Barlow)

But under all circumstances the calligraphic emblem has two qualities, extreme plasticity and irreducible signification, which cannot be destroyed. Therefore, not just ideograph, but calligraphy get drawn into political discourse. In the West, we usually express our political ideas in the print media, and even more commonly and powerfully now with images in the electronic media. But we no longer have a viable calligraphic art.

Chinese cultural aesthetics endow the handwritten characters with extra virtues. Calligraphic representation is a high art, and even now exerts powerful influences in the social world in a number of ways—by communicating beautiful images, by transmitting meaning, and by implying that "good" calligraphy exudes personal and moral virtue. This is what political discourse avails itself of when it blankets the public world with calligraphic slogans. We think the calligraphed character is the visual counterpart in China to the photo image in the West, connoting levels of signification. People here still look at a sample of handwriting and claim to be able to "see" the moral character of the person who wrote it. In any case, the secret of the proliferation of well-written slogans—well written in the sense of good calligraphy—is that while you might try to resist the message you can't escape the medium.

Obviously both of us are exhilarated to be actually here. But we are finding that the new environment affects each of us somewhat differently. Don has a whole set of Chinese clothes now and a new Chinese haircut. The only thing he hasn't given up yet are his sturdy, leather, American walking shoes with the crepe soles. But when we go on a walk he can easily disappear into the crowd if he wants to. He enjoys that, even though he doesn't really feel like the people around him. Don left China forty years ago. He went to high school, college, and graduate school in the U.S., and he has taught American students for over twenty years. Until we came here he almost always thought and dreamt in English. But he had a Chinese childhood, and his parents raised him to be a Chinese person. Just in the last few days he has started seeing things in the people around him that feel very familiar—responses and automatic habits, movements, ways of laughing or talking. He can't claim to feel a strong connection to this community yet, and maybe he never will; but to be finally part of the racial majority has made him unexpectedly euphoric, and the extraordinary rush of relief at having been emancipated forces him to reconsider his roots.

Don's father and two of his uncles were educated in the U.S., where they learned to value certain elements of American culture like technology, efficiency, symphonic music, nineteenth-century paintings, and even (no kidding) apple pie. But for all their Americanization they never lost sight of the other side of apple pie and the

YMCA—the obvious fact of Western imperialism. Don can still remember the "days of shame" in Chinese grammar school, when he and his classmates ritually commemorated modern China's political tragedy. His uncles still tell the story about Don's father striking a white man on a Shanghai bus back in the 1930s, for making insulting remarks about Chinese. This branch of the Lowes are upper-middle class, and Don has benefited from his "Americanization." But here, suddenly, he feels relieved of the nagging sense of being different, of having to explain, of having to sit politely through endlessly meaningless ethnic jokes and American stereotypes of the Chinese. He can just forget about his ethnicity here. Further, he feels a rapport or ease with certain men around him here, like his cousin Mingzhang and Lao Chen, who always treats Don like a Chinese rather than as an American—a Chinese who has been away from home for many years, to be sure, but someone who has valuable things to tell them about where he has been. To them Don is first of all a Chinese.

In San Francisco, Tani is in the majority and Don the minority. Reversal of the racial role liberates Donald but adjusting to minority status is not always easy on Tani. After all, Don has been a Chinese-American for decades, whereas Tani is just starting the experience of being a foreigner in China. The very pressures on her shows us a lot about general attitudes toward strangers and Western things in general. Several days ago she took a walk down Hengshan Road to buy cigarettes at the foreigners' hotel; the FAO hasn't issued her any tobacco coupons yet, so she can't buy them at the campus canteen. As she turned onto Hengshan from Guilin Road she became gradually aware that the traffic was slowing down. Everyone was leaning out of the cars, trucks, tricycles, or bikes to take long, long looks at her. Even the well-mannered cop in the elevated tower leaned out for a look. Never in her life had she ever felt more like an object than at that moment. Yet she did not feel anything sexual in the gaze. We have noticed that Chinese men and women don't seem to notice each other's bodies the way we do in the West. Don saw a woman on the bus one day wearing a tight sweater that outlined her breasts, but noticed that no one turned around to look at her. Another time we spotted two extraordinary skinny people walking around in tight U.S.-style blue jeans, apparently interested in appearing fashionable, but under no definition could they have been seen as sexual. No one on Hengshan Road stared at Tani's breasts, buttocks, or even her legs; their attention seemed mostly fixed on her ordinary summer shoes and her bright yellow hair.

After 45 minutes of walking, the staring had worn her out, so she ducked into a little shop to buy some chocolates. A dozen people stared rudely as she asked for the candy. Then Tani reached into her pocket for her work-unit identity card showing she has permission to use Chinese currency rather than the special "foreign certificates" issued to tourists. All of a sudden the atmosphere changed. The shopkeeper took the card and began smiling very hospitably questioning Tani in heavily Shanghianese-accented Common Language (*putong hua*). Then everyone began telling stories about the other foreigners that they had seen on the street over the last five years or so, in particular a chubby man with a beard who came riding by on a bicycle almost every day and whose Chinese name was something like Ge. Somebody said they thought he had a married a Chinese woman, and everybody started making cracks about Shanghainese mothers-in-law, so Tani told them she was married to an Overseas Chinese, but from Hubei, and that the two of them were teaching English at the college. We are still not sure what impressed the people in the shop so much about Tani's work card. Maybe it just gave them a good enough reason to talk, or maybe they know enough about the college to feel even foreign workers from the college *danwei* or work unit have a definite location, a legitimate place, in their neighborhood.

The point is that unless Tani can demonstrate she belongs somewhere, her coloring and her race signify that, quite the contrary, she obviously cannot possibly belong to wherever she is. This experience of never being in the right place wears Tani out. It means partly that she can never be at ease without literally ignoring everyone around her, or that she does not go places alone. She also finds herself responding to the warmth of colleagues and students even more needily, because their initiatives are based on an unspoken pact—she belongs to them—even though underneath she can sense them classifying her as Mrs. Lowe, their teacher, the foreign expert, and so on. Tani feels the alienness more because she presents a bigger challenge to those around her, unlike Don who with his Chinese appearance and clothes can be absorbed with little fuss and indecision.

Living as a foreigner here feels doubly peculiar because everyone else is so firmly connected. A couple of days ago we came across two beggars sitting on the pavement across from the Xu-jiahui bus exchange, heads on their knees in front of a huge poster explaining who they were and why they had come to Shanghai to beg. In Shanghai any street event, no matter how trivial, draws a crowd immediately, and usually when we come around Tani is the event, but this time the beggars' story was too absorbing and the crowd never even glanced up at Tani. In fact they actually elbowed us out of their way in their efforts to get closer to the front. The point is not just that the story was interesting but that beggars and foreigners do not belong and the crowd was as interested in the beggars' justification for camping out on the sidewalk as the candy-store clerk had been in Tani's work-unit I.D. card.

Every legal resident of Shanghai (and everyone here is supposed to be legally registered) belongs to a variety of social, political, residential, and recreational organizations, beginning with the residence small group, residence committee, street committee, the district committee, and the city government, to enumerate just those directly political organizations mandated by the state. Furthermore, everyone with a job belongs to a work unit or *danwei*, contemporary urban China's most crucial social organization. A good *danwei* tries to provide its workers with housing and health care at a minimum, and certain kinds of social welfare, for example, education, vacation, and even now, as the first generation under socialism ages, jobs for the children of mature workers. As it is a corporate body which controls birth, regulates individual's economic welfare and, in many cases, even arranges marriages, the *danwei* obviously competes in importance with the old family system. Many people belong to the same work unit their entire lives.

But all sorts of other groups intervene in community life, such as more or less ad hoc committees to aid old people. Just now neighborhoods are organizing committees to develop employment schemes for young people slipping back into Shanghai from the countryside, or who are being legally returned to their urban families.

Chinese culture stresses immediate, reciprocal personal relations, so these organizations tend to strain in the effort to be social and political at the same time. This is true at the college too, where each class has been divided into sections, each section presided over by a class monitor who organizes the section's activities with the help of a study head or "boss," an athletic head, a recreation head, and an art head (the last being responsible for blackboard slogans and illustrations). These activities are social and political simultaneously, being inextricably intertwined. Party organizations such as the Communist Youth League are at the top of this pyramid, with a great deal of overlapping so that a monitor is almost always either a Youth League member or a Party cadre.

In any case, you can imagine what the entry of a foreign person from a capitalist country might mean to people in this nexus. In the neighborhood people feel uncomfortable unless they can place foreigners in a *danwei*. On campus people express their anxiety in many ways. Some students seem to worry that we will make fun of them or get angry if we find out too much about the political apparatus that structures college life. Tani's students wobble between trying to represent the best their country has to offer and making sure she is aware of the very worst. Don's students don't seem either so solicitous or so worried about what he might think or feel since, we suspect, they reason that because he is Chinese, anticipating his needs should be relatively simple. What we are describing is in no way hostility. How can they relate unless they know where you belong? In fact, Tani already feels a great deal of affection coming from many quarters. But it is still uncomfortable to be objectified, no matter what the circumstances.

You won't believe our daily schedule. The campus amplifier starts blaring the bugle call at 5:45. Fifteen minutes of music followed by another 15 minutes of calisthenics, then the national news from Beijing. We eat at 7. Most days, our classes begin at 7:45 and are over by 9:25, except for the two afternoons when we have classes. On our free afternoons we prepare lectures, do chores, go shopping, or visit relatives. The cooks at our foreign expert dorm serve lunch at 11:45 and dinner at 5:30. We have absolutely no night life, but then we never did. At 9:40 we are already in bed, except when the students throw a rock-and-roll dance party or play basketball under our windows.

4

Visit to Suzhou

Shanghai, September 22, 1981

We have been in Shanghai exactly one month.

Our social life astounds us. Last week the college president invited us to a moon festival buffet, where we expected to view the moon, but instead, spent a staid few hours eating and politely conversing. The following day Peihua and Mingzhang threw another holiday dinner and Mingren, his older sister, came all the way from Nanjing with her husband (and a justly famous Nanjing duck, which tastes better than the Beijing duck) to welcome Don whom she hadn't seen in over 40 years. On Sunday, distant relatives came to get us at the foreign expert dorm in a van they had "borrowed" from their *danwei*—through a "back door," they bragged—and took us to the old Xubei slum district in north Shanghai for one of the most awkward meals we have ever had. Their little girl wore imported jeans and their son a shirt with US NAVY stamped all over it. They kept up a level of defensiveness about their apartment which seemed quite unrealistic under the circumstances since they had enough room to keep several members of the family living illegally in Shanghai on everyone else's ration tickets. Anyway the place seemed

29

to us unusually spacious. When conversation shifted to how "dirty" Shanghai is and how talented their children are at learning foreign languages, we got the message.

Beyond the formal, scheduled events we find ourselves spending blocks of time in office hours consulting with students, getting briefed by colleagues, and dropping over to Peihua and Mingzhang's place whenever we can just to eat and relax. Both of us are usually very quiet, retiring people. So while we get exhilarated by all this it also makes us very, very tired. Then on top of accelerated social lives we eat communally with two other foreign experts, both British, one a younger woman and the other seemingly in her dotage. Probably the older one would not irritate us so much if we didn't see her so regularly. After a month we just got to the point where we really wanted to get away together, alone, for a weekend.

It took a week to arrange. We knew where we wanted to go. We'd read about Suzhou, the "Venice of the P.R.C." in *The New York Times* travel section, and the area was also of enormous historical interest because it had been a center of gentry culture since the Song dynasty. Getting there involved a short hour and a half train ride. But before we could leave our FAO had to do a series of things. Lao Chen sent Xiao Qian down to the Shanghai Public Security Bureau to apply for our Alien Travel Permit, and then to the train station where he stood in line for an hour to get a soft seat reserved on the crowded four o'clock train. The Shanghai Teachers College's FAO then placed a call through to the Suzhou municipal FAO to arrange for a guide to meet us at the train station with a car and driver, and escort us to the luxury hotel. They finally completed all the necessary connections and reservations.

Friday afternoon Lao Gu picked us up in his gray sedan. We have learned recently that drivers don't just drive, they clean, maintain, and repair their cars, and are responsible for stretching their unit's gas rations. So whenever he can get up the speed, Lao Gu turns the ignition off and lets the car glide until it's nearly stopped, before turning the engine back on. He also knows every shortcut and alley in Shanghai. Lao Gu pulled into the enormous parking lot in front of the Shanghai North Train Station, carefully weaving the car through a crowd of hundreds of travelers, many of whom were standing with cartons or seated on rope-bound suitcases; he discharged us in front of the first-class waiting room. The uniformed woman did not question our prerogative and let us into the cavernous, marble-floored station decorated with the most beautiful "miniature landscapes" (limestone rocks shaped into tiny mountain ranges and covered with years' growth of moss) we'd ever seen and banks of flowering plants and trees. Xiao Qian strode over to meet us. We had not been able to dissuade him from this courtesy of seeing us off, even though it's just for a weekend. He escorted us through the gate onto the first-class, reserved "soft seats," handed over our return tickets, Alien Travel Permits, letter of introduction from the Shanghai Teachers College's FAO to the Suzhou municipal FAO, and then left us to enjoy our vacation.

We couldn't help enjoying ourselves. The passenger car was built of wood and had been lacquered and polished to a gleaming yellow color. All the soft seats had pale pink slipcovers and white cotton antimacassars; on the tables in front of us stood potted palms. We bought packets of thick tea and a young female usher came by every few minutes to pour hot water. We felt we had entered a 1930s movie set, and kept waiting for Humphrey Bogart and Mary Astor to step on at the next stop. Ninety minutes later in Suzhou an efficient FAO officer picked us up and took us in another gray coupe to a secluded hotel in a residential part of Suzhou. Out the curtained window of the car we could see the team of workers building a new false mountain in front of the hotel entrance.

Suzhou really changed the way we experienced Shanghai, and put some of our early impressions into a new context. Several days after our arrival in Shanghai we had gone for a walk around Xujiahui, the large bus exchange and shopping area for much of southeast Shanghai. The Xujiahui bus terminal is a large, roundish open area at the foot of Huaihai Road, one of the city's main east–west thoroughfares. On the corner across from the terminal is the neighborhood's major shopping mart, Number Six Department Store, and behind it we discovered alleys crowded with pre-Liberation houses, tea shops, a yarn and thread market, even a place where men were repairing plastic basins that had worn out, wielding enormous tools that looked like outsized welding irons. Furniture and baskets were displayed out in the street. Peddlerstyle fruit stands, set up for business on carts, had bananas for sale. With our San Franciso eyes we felt as though we'd been put back in time. The low, one-storied, wood buildings seemed to shimmer in the heat—no skyscrapers, no modern hotels, no cars, no British banks or French mansions obscured our illusion of a China almost beyond Western influence.

Since that walk we have learned that what in the U.S. might take one worker seems to take a whole group of workers in Shanghai. We feel ambivalent about this. We can't dismiss it as "inefficiency" exactly, since everyone must eat and premature mechanization would create a horrendous unemployment problem. We also know that overpopulation lies at the root of most of this. Labor intensiveness is part of the cycle. A subsequent visit to the Shanghai Industrial Exhibition Hall taught us to reverse our usual notion of the relation between machine and human labor. At each of the heavy industrial machines stood a smiling woman who recited a description and then politely motioned the guests on to the next machine and the next woman. There are huge numbers of clerks in department stores, but no cash registers. In Number Six Department Store at Xujiahui, for example, if you want to buy something, you give the money to a clerk, who fills out a bill in triplicate by hand, clips the receipt and your cash to a small box in an overhead dolly and shoots it to a cashier sitting in a elevated chair above the cash box who checks every receipt on an abacus.

However, in Suzhou the tallest building in the downtown area is the renovated Daoist temple, where the temple fair has recently been allowed to open once again. The low-storied whitewashed plaster and wattle houses have back doors that open onto the picturesque sluggish canals for which the city is famous. The government constructed a north–south boulevard to ease traffic, but in many areas you can still easily imagine what life must have been like generations ago. People walk more slowly in Suzhou, their food tastes sweeter, and they are fantastically polite as we found out when we walked down the street and no one ogled Tani. We had originally thought of Shanghai as slow compared to San Francisco. But in Suzhou even the local dialect sounds more musical and genteel than frenzied Shanghainese. We don't mean to sound disloyal, since we still have a big crush on Shanghai, but Suzhou is an easy place to love.

Tourists come to Suzhou to see the private gardens built over the generations by wealthy, retired dynastic officials. Our favorite was the Garden of the Net Master in the southern part of town. Like all Chinese gardens it lies enclosed behind walls, cut off from the world. Strolling down an ordinary narrow alley, we stopped at a window set into the mud wall to buy a ticket and then stepped through the gate into a small courtyard. The open area just beyond led to farther spaces each laid out to form a meandering pattern. Walls gave way to more, inner walls. Moon gates prepared us to accept the spaces lying beyond them as enclosed, prefabricated views. Yet when we stepped through the doors, and got farther inside, everything felt like it was collapsing into a completely different shape. As we walked along, these deftly spaced views gave way one after the other until we were sure the small acre and a half garden was actually very large. We lost a sense of exact dimensions. What intrigued us most were the tiny cultivated areas we viewed from the second story of one of the teahouses, where we got a bird's-eye view of one part of the garden. The designer had placed several rugged rocks, a tuft of long grass, and a cluster of drooping bamboos into one small plot. Mosaics of stone formed geometric patterns, or images or animals, insects, and birds. At the center of all these enclosed spaces lay an artificial lake surrounded by artificial mountain ranges.

Enclosure—whether of the world behind the wall, nature in the rock, the courtyard in the household, the person in the family—is a fundamental organizational principle in the Chinese world, quite different from Western concepts of "transcendence," or "objectivity." Instead of the Western ideal of an individual standing apart, the Chinese person is surrounded and defined by the world.

We sat and stared at a microcosmic version of nature molded to the human eye. You need to enjoy the Chinese garden in person because photographs cannot duplicate the shifting perspectives without necessarily flattening the whole into one dimension. The Net Master's Garden gives exactly the reverse impression from a formal European garden. To appreciate Versailles' landscape you have to imagine that you are the Sun King standing on the veranda looking beyond, with the wings of the palace stretching out behind you. Versailles was built from the perspective of the king, for other eyes to reflect on his grandeur. The Chinese garden, on the other hand, resists the single-eye perspective. Each of its parts softly, methodically focuses your senses inside, to the perfectly regulated, miniature enclosed world. Wherever we stood, the garden formed a microcosm of the natural world outside the walls, and every step forced us to revise the way we looked at the whole. The world reflected in its part; the stone a synecdoche of nature; in the elegant tufts of grass what we saw was not a replica but a reduced image.

For a few cents anyone can visit the gardens. Crowds are in fact beginning to overwhelm them, so except in the early morning you have to use a lot of imagination to depopulate. In the larger, less highly compressed gardens, like West Garden, old workers and retirees sit all day drinking tea and reading the newspaper. We met a man who was just killing time waiting for a train. People take their lunch hours or afternoon breaks and students come to sketch or study peacefully. Kids swarm all over the artificial mountains. West Garden is actually a Buddhist temple with 20-foot images in the main hall, and side halls containing 500 larger-than-life-size arhats or spiritual guardians, each with its own distinctive face and persona. We were not surprised to find old peasants worshiping the Buddhas and the arhats. But we even caught a few of the young people very self-consciously imitating the kowtows of the older worshipers. At the entrance of most gardens you can rent Brownie cameras already loaded with black-and-white film. We saw honeymooners and groups of young people posing formally in front of rocks or flower beds to have their portraits taken. As you leave, the shop develops your film on the spot; so, often you see people walking happily out the gates trailing long rolls of negatives behind them like the tails on kites.

Sunday we rested quietly in the small Joyous Garden near the center of town, sipping tea, taking naps, and periodically talking to curious young workers. A few men wanted to know about wages and working conditions in the U.S. A young student came over to talk, asking in Chinese if we knew any German and told us about his plan to learn German and translate scientific articles. A middle-aged man came over, who turned out to be an intellectual, and we talked about recent popular literature. Then it was over. At the Suzhou railway station the conductor ushered us into the first-class waiting lounge.

Shanghai's North Station discharged us back into the human maelstrom. We decided to try the North Station Restaurant across the street and stood with our ration tickets in a long line with 50 or 60 other hungry people to purchase meal chits. Inevitably, a worker saw Tani and pulled us out of line. She seated us and brought our food out and then shooed away the people who, chits in hand, had already gathered behind us waiting for us to give up our chairs. We just could not tell what they were thinking. Did they accept the justification we had come to accept, that this is the way China does things, and, since Chinese and foreigners are two different categories of human beings, the foreigner inevitably gets special treatment and should not protest too much?

5

Lu Xun Day

Shanghai, September 28, 1981

Friday, September 25, was the great writer Lu Xun's birthday, and we foreign experts joined the rest of China in celebrating the centennial of his birth.

Wednesday night, September 23: Shanghai Teachers College sponsored a showing of the newly released, black-and-white film version of Lu Xun's famous short story, "Medicine." The film stuck meticulously to Lu Xun's vision of decadent late-Qing dynastic Chinese society. Lu Xun originally set the story in his own hometown of Xiaoxing, and it follows a bizarre connection between two local families. In the first family an only son attempts but fails to assassinate a corrupt official and is executed by the government, leaving behind his completely destitute, widowed mother who will certainly starve to death. The other family hovers over its dangerously ill son. A quack doctor convinces them that only human blood will save him, so they feed the invalid a roll soaked in the murdered revolutionary's gore. The sick boy dies, anyway. Don felt very moved by the film and particularly appreciated the good effect of the black-and-white film in recapturing the atmosphere of a bygone society. It did nevertheless strike him that this story's utter despair might not sit well with audiences fed a steady diet of optimistic, social realism and he wondered what the general reaction was going to be.

Thursday night, September 24: Tonight the FAO sent us off to the Shanghai Municipal Theater to view three one-act ballet adaptations of Lu Xun sketches. This time the audience was composed primarily of the foreigners and foreign experts in Shanghai. Before each act, a man dressed in a Western suit and tie appeared on the stage and told the audience what story the dancers would perform; obviously the choreographer and producer considered the plot to be extremely important. "Soul," an adaptation of Lu Xun's "Autumn Sacrifices" concentrated on the fantastic part of a plot about a widow forced to remarry, by choreographing her dream that her two husbands' ghosts pursued her through hell. The second ballet was so trite, sentimental, and romantic that we could not connect it to anything Lu Xun had ever written. "The True Story of Ah Q" dramatized the author's great fable about a twentieth-century Chinese anti-hero, using a combination of Western and Chinese dance techniques, and leaning heavily on narrative mime. Of the three, we both preferred "Ah Q."

We knew a little about how China had acquired ballet from the Soviet Union, so we looked at the performances as a way of understanding more about how Chinese adapt alien art forms. The first two pieces were nothing more than derivative, but the third, "The True Story of Ah Q," combined elements of Russian art, yet insistently emphasized Chinese narrativity. This meant that the dance movements had frequently to give way to obviously mime sequences to insure that the audience would concentrate on the story, rather than become absorbed in the spectacle. Probably a sophisticated Western audience would find "Ah Q," and many other Chinese performances too literal for their taste, but we enjoyed it thoroughly; although we have to confess we haven't seen anything here so far as good as *The White Haired Girl* which we saw on American television years ago. We did learn to keep our opinions on ballet and opera mostly to ourselves. Once we happened to mention our preference to Lao Yang who winced and said in her blunt, friendly way that we had better not say so widely, since most people had very strong negative feelings about *The White Haired Girl.* Jiang Qing banned all but eight plays during the GPCR, yet kept insisting that tickets be issued. So the *danweis* began forcing people to sit through the same eight operas over and over again. No one ever wants to hear their names mentioned again.

Friday, September 25: The official Shanghai municipal celebration of the Lu Xun centennial took place in the same theater where the evening before we had witnessed the ballet. The government "invited" the foreign experts and diplomatic corps to attend. Guests walked into the large empty auditorium. The stage held two long rows of empty chairs and tables which soon filled up with Party, government, and civic officials. The ceremony began with the national anthem (Don recalls it from the thirties as "The Guerilla's Marching Song"), followed by the Shanghai Party branch secretary's welcoming remarks. Next the propaganda chief of the Shanghai Party branch read out aloud a 36-page speech on the significance of Lu Xun's literature, Lu Xun's relations to the Chinese Communist Party, Lu Xun's importance as a cultural hero before the downfall of the Gang of Four, and Lu Xun as a model to emulate during the present period of the four modernizations. The speech sounded a little bit like the one delivered by Chairman Hu Yaobang in Beijing at the same time to commemorate the day:

> Lu Xun forcefully debunked such theories as that which considered literature and art as outbursts of individual "inspiration." He stressed that revolutionary literature and art belonged to the masses and was created for them. It was a tool to reform society, a reflex action, a means of attack and defense. . . . To promote the healthy development of literature and art, it is absolutely necessary to practice criticism and self-criticism.

Following the speech by the Shanghai Party branch secretary, the ballet troupe gave another performance of "The True Story of Ah Q." Mercifully, Lao Zheng excused Don early. A slight stomach upset brought on by eating too much prevented Tani from attending.

Saturday afternoon, September 26: The FAO arranged for us to visit the Lu Xun tomb and the Lu Xun Memorial Museum in Hongkou Park in northern Shanghai. A guide gave us a detailed lecture tour through the chronologically arranged display of Lu Xun memorabilia, published and translated works, important books he had read, and so on. We then went on to the tomb to pay our respects. Baskets of flowers from all sorts of organizations and delegations covered the lovely monument, including some from Japan where Lu Xun had spent several years. Later in the afternoon we visited Lu Xun's Shanghai apartment nearby. We really were lucky to have had this chance, since the residence is not open to the public. It has been fully restored to its original, 1930s' decor, so it felt quite eerie to walk around the place where one of the twentieth-century's greatest writers had lived and worked.

After that we decided to search for the compound on nearby Shanyin Road where Don lived as a little boy in the early thirties. It was so long ago, Don could barely remember anything. But he had a vague notion of what the exterior had looked like and how the second-floor windows of the house jutted out at a certain angle. We think we found it. But now rows and rows of workers' apartment buildings stand where the spacious green lawn used to be.

6

Students

S tudent life here is factionalized, hierarchical, and full of conflict. Individuals compete not only for grades, but also for books, facts, correct pronunciations, new terminologies, the latest trend in Western literary criticism, and all other scarce academic resources because here knowledge really is power. We finally realized that if we assign something to a section, we must personally force students to circulate the material. Otherwise the person with the book refuses to let anyone else read it. When we criticize, the students shift the blame to the teachers and say the faculty sets a bad example. The students claim only the faculty can check certain books out of the library but they hoard all the good books at home, so no student will ever learn more about a subject than the teachers. (We have never seen that. But we have met librarians who seemed to think that the library books belonged to them personally.) Everyone claims the problem is too few foreign books. We strongly suspect that actually the hoarding pattern indicates a prevalent attitude toward accumulating and using knowledge.

Outside of their own familiar sections, students have little contact with each other. Some of them live at home with their parents or spouses and commute to school every day. But most have been formed into groups of six or eight and live together in the dormitories adjacent to the teaching building. Students who live on campus know seven other persons very well, since the group lives, eats, and studies together in a room the size of a large walk-in pantry. They know another fifteen classmates fairly well, because of the four years they spend together in their home-room section. And they know everyone else in their class of 200 not at all. Both of us have found that if we ask two or three sections to meet with us at the same time, everyone, even the most voluble male students clam up, because they all feel too bashful to speak English in front of people they "don't know."

Our senior students are experienced adults. A substantial fraction of them have been teaching middle-school English for years. But most came to school directly from their GPCR jobs—barefoot doctor, shoemaker, ditchdigger, farmer, factory worker, and so on—occupations that were physically grueling and yet allowed them enough spare time to study English on the side, in preparation for the national entrance exam. One of Tani's special students is old enough to be her father, and is taking intensive reading as part of a re-education project his school has just started offering its older faculty. The median age of the classes of 1977 and 1978 is about 32 or 33. The college faculty considers these seniors hard to teach, by which they mean that these two "special" classes do not conform to the acceptable juvenile pattern Don sees in his young sophomore students, and that these older students have had extraordinary experiences outside the classroom. By and large, our older students are politically disillusioned young adults who managed to come out on top after the turmoil of the GPCR and can speak extremely knowledgeably about their generation's peculiar experience.

We did not see this at first because all students have to abide by the national student dress and behavior codes. So our middle-aged students sit behind the kind of rickety little wooden desks we associate with gradeschool in the U.S., wearing dowdy, almost uniformstyle clothing—students are forbidden to wear any fashion or piece of clothing that might signify an interest other than service and scholarship. They trade their extremely high social position against a code of dress and action that indicates they are willing to identify with the workers and peasants, at least on a symbolic level. (Workers and peasants now, of course, want perms and bright coats made out of plaid material with belted waists that we see in the department stores downtown.) Our students almost never express their opinions openly and always defer superficially to authority.

Tani with some of her intensive reading seniors, in front of the foreign languages teaching building. (Anon.)

Some of Don's intensive reading seniors. (Anon.)

These seniors really shock us. They don't seem to believe in anything, and even more frustrating they have no interests beyond their own personal lives. Most of them (and this is true of the sophomore students, too) do not trust anything that seems even vaguely political; they refuse to think in political terms and they reject everything we say about American social structure and political economy. Anything seeming at first glance "Marxist" in vocabulary or analysis, even something as bland as the sort of pop sociology you can find in any liberal, American magazine, students tend to reject with courteous but absolutely profound boredom.

Students in their early thirties would much rather talk about love and marriage, particularly about the political aspects of arranging a good match. During one intense discussion a group of men said the state's new policy of returning confiscated money to the big capitalists had been a mistake. Now, with rich, older men around again, some ambitious women concentrate all their energies on trying to marry into Shanghai's remaining bourgeois families—the point being apparently that this competition in the marriage market dims the prospects of intellectuals like themselves.

People also keep telling us about Mr. Gross.* We have gathered from the students' description that their Mr. Gross must be the fat, foreign man with the big beard the shopkeepers told Tani they saw on Huaihai Road so often riding around on a bicycle; the one they claimed had married a Chinese woman and gotten a Shanghainese mother-in-law. Many of our seniors studied with Gross during the two years he taught here, just before we arrived. At the end of his stay he shocked all of them by announcing his engagement to a student. Usually the point of the story is that Ms. Wang made a politically poor marriage choice. She might possibly have been correct in her decision to use Mr. Gross as a passport (no one seems to grudge her that), but she made a big mistake leaving China before she got her degree and, some say, in marrying an American instead of some other kind of foreigner, because Gross will probably divorce her in a year and get another wife—the United States being the land of slipshod marriages. A few people have told us they worry over the possibility that Gross might humiliate Wang because of her race; others, that her American in-laws might mistreat her. No one we have met so far has directly criticized Ms. Wang's supposed motive. They always point out that the entire Wang family suffered a lot during the GPCR and that Ms. Wang deserves to leave China. Her strategy concerns her friends (and she appears to have had many, many friends) because they do not trust Mr. Gross.

---

*Out of a sense of fairness to him, Gross is a pseudonym. All other names in this book are real.

A request to choose essay topics they thought would help Tani understand China turned up a more serious concern about the "marriage crisis." Women have also mentioned the crisis in discussion, but the men used the assignment to voice vociferous concern about threats to their ability to marry well coming from "high-priced" women who demand dowries of furniture, electric lamp, fan, recorder, television. Women and men complained about parental interference in the planning, problems meeting good partners, and the expense of the wedding banquet. One essay claimed to be a true story. A man lied to a woman about his financial worth. He took extra jobs to be able to buy all the things she demanded. On their wedding night the bride's family found him dead of a "myocardial infarction," a corpse stiffening on the marriage bed. This was the most lurid of all the treatments of the "high-priced" woman problem. But students generally expressed great anxiety about how marriage brokering might be conducted, particularly those unmarried people whose prospects had been damaged by the "wasted years" of the GPCR.

Our students just assume they will become China's new elite. Also, as educated Chinese have since Confucius's time, our students see high social status as somehow connected to special moral standing. Students have the attitude that because they are now intellectuals they have more rectitude than the masses they used to consort with when they were workers or peasants or laborers. This predisposition on top of the years they spent as teenagers studying the ethical writings of Lin Biao and Mao Zedong means they read moralistic overtones into all of their assignments. When we give them a genuinely didactic piece, this is what we get in response:

> I like Emerson, particularly his essay, "Self-Reliance," especially these sentences—"the secret of fortune is joy in our hands" and "insist on yourself, never imitate." It is really true in our practical life. Everything depends on yourself. No one could help you in your fortune. So relying on others is silly. Because the world itself is ever-changing, let alone those people who are being relied upon. One day he might turn back on you, and you will find yourself at the bottom of the world. And the second sentence is also true. You should always insist on yourself, because if you insist on imitating someone else you can never be a great man. Every great man is unique. You should create something new, let the others follow you. That is the way to become a great man.

Looking at our students from the Chinese faculty's point of view is quite instructive as well. Professor Luo, a vigorous, white-haired, chain-smoking man in his seventies with a no-nonsense attitude toward almost everything, except nineteenth-century British novels, gave us a glimpse of the generational conflicts we suspect rage around us. Luo had a typical GPCR experience for an intellectual of his generation: 18 months in prison, 10 years at hard labor. He told us he believed the student fad for American things would pass quickly. He was far more concerned about what he calls the immediate ideological crisis facing the entire GPCR generation—people contemporary with the American baby-boomers. As he sees it young people will become political and moral nihilists if they accept "learning" itself as their only justification for years of grueling intellectual work. Right now, he agrees, the generation does not believe in anything. That social tragedy far outstrips the individual hardships, because nihilists will never be able to govern China.

Professor Luo's analysis of political nihilism differs a little from our own view partly because we presume we are hearing different things from our students, and in part, because students expect different things from their Chinese teachers than they do from us. Also, our point of view is basically different from his. We don't share the professor's assumption, quite common here, that the foundation of government ought to be the personal morality of the government officials. What we see in our students is a sort of escapism. Students displace their aspirations and longing onto us, because we don't belong to their society and we come from a place where, as they see it, every need has been satisfied. In this regard we act like powerful magnets for their fantasies. Beyond fantasies about migrating to the West, the other current addiction among students is Western literature.

Tani asked her survey classes to submit answers to the questions: What do you get from literature? Why do you like it? Does literature have a purpose? One student responded:

> Literature is the language which connects people who are unknown to each other. No matter how far people are from each other, no matter how long ages have gone from now, literature of the times always faithfully recorded the stream of thought of the minds of the elite of the times concerned. Through literature one can not only have an opportunity to add more colors to his life, but also can feel the pulse of the human vein. You will always have a sense that you're in tune with the pace. There is also a realistic function to literature. Through literature we may absorb others' experiences, generally the experiences of great people, so that we may know how to deal with problems you will encounter in life.

Another wrote even more pointedly:

> Literature gives me nourishment in life. Literature sometimes flows like music through me; I like music, and literature

resembles it in rhythm and taste. I often think that music and literature are the twins appreciated only by the highbrows. The more you read, the more you enjoy. In short, it roots in men and always rings within my recess. Different people have different ideas about the purpose of literature. Those who never think will consider literature has no purpose. In fact, literature is one of the main factors to promote moral spirit and human culture.

Foreign literature obviously gives our students a counter-weight to Marxist ideology. One man bragged that he had purposely tried to flunk his political education exam as a protest, to show up his teacher's incompetence, and the fact that the highest marks always went to the stupidest students. In Don's lecture courses the students have such a poor grasp of even rudimentary Marxist concepts—they don't understand what political economy means or why he is using it to describe contemporary America. But just ask any student about Hemingway, or to name a novel written by William Faulkner, and you always get a correct answer, even when the student has never read the original novels. Part of their interest in fiction can be explained as the natural dispositions of foreign language majors to read books in the language they are learning. Our students, on the other hand, have discovered in foreign literature a moral system outside the political one established by the state.

Everyone in the class of 1977 must write a senior thesis. Students may choose to write either a long essay (difficult, because of the shortage of research material) or to do a translation provided it has a short introduction. One man came by during office hours several days ago to go over the introduction he'd written to his translation of a Hemingway short story, and we got a real education in students' literary taste. The fellow is a tall, heavyset, middle-aged man who is also the class monitor for one of the average track sections. His ten-page essay explored Hemingway's brilliance, Hemingway's life as a moral leader of the Western world, Hemingway's maturity (particularly his breakthrough from sterile individualism to social concern in his old age, as shown in *The Old Man and The Sea*), and most interesting to us, how Hemingway's universal message spoke to the concerns and experience of Chinese.

As we sat and talked to this man a number of things came into focus. Students do not like us to criticize "their" writers or to criticize the hagiographic essays they write about them. (We have students who even resisted reading critical essays written by American scholars.) You cannot, we found, ever suggest to a Hemingway fan that the notion of grace under pressure is corny. The student who had brought in his essay had absolutely no interest in the story's historical context, or really in the period that had formed

Hemingway's thought, beyond his belief that the experience of armed struggle made Hemingway's generation similar in certain respects to his own generation of Chinese men who went through the GPCR. Hemingway's description of dying—like a silk handkerchief pulled by one corner out of a pocket—moved him, and he was only moderately infatuated with "his" writer.

One tiny, bombastic student spent weeks arguing and finally had to accept the bad news that O. Henry is no longer considered one of America's most popular and respected geniuses of all time. Our student got over his disappointment and he still loves O. Henry's greatness, but it took some struggle. Another, more sensitive student defensively rejected the suggestion we have started using to pry students away from hero worship, that Chinese readers select foreign authors because of occurrences in China, not because of any intrinsic importance those writers may have in contemporary North America. We can only explain her defensiveness as part of the general longing students feel about literature outside China, outside history, which they believe can give them true moral guidance.

This is what the Party calls "bourgeois liberalism." And actually quite a good-sized fraction of our students seem to have come from rehabilitated "bourgeois" families. They talk about their aunts and uncles working in embassies abroad, factories their parents used to own, and their older sisters and brothers who received medical training before the GPCR or who have jobs as middle-level managers in "companies" in the city. Precisely because of their privileged class backgrounds many of these people grew up seeing parents suffer at the hands of vigilante committees, or enduring neighborhood struggle sessions during the GPCR. Many talk about going to the West for advanced training. They always explain that they want modern skills to serve China, yet in the very next breath will tell us the Chinese are not as "civilized" as Western people, not as cultivated, or even as clean. Conflicting attitudes mark this generation in a very special way. Still they are not that different from the disaffected Chinese revolutionaries of the early twentieth century, in that they too live inside a tightly knit social network of personal relations which they neither care to nor could leave, even if they wanted to. Some of the most cynical and disillusioned students pose as Western "individualists." Yet even they find it impossible to maintain that persona very long outside the classroom or study group. The seniors' remarkable experiences make us sympathetic but their escapist and limited interests make us feel extremely odd since they expect us to feed their fantasies.

We don't mean to imply that all students identify with foreign literature and recoil from Chinese politics. Particularly our genuinely middle-aged students, who grew up during the golden age of socialism in the 1950s, talk about their feelings with terrible ambivalence. One man ended an office discussion almost in tears by confessing he still, even after all these years and all these disappointments, wanted to be like Lei Feng, the utterly selfless martyr to the Revolution who plays an intermittent, important part in political propaganda.

Similar feelings appeared in another, moving essay by a woman student. The narrator explained how the police had recovered the body of a neighborhood girl from the river near the narrator's house sometime after the GPCR. The girl had stolen some money from the narrator, had been caught, and the narrator had graciously exonerated her. Much later this girl leaped in the river. Her parents were too ashamed of their daughter's bad reputation even to claim the body. At the end of the story the narrator delivered a homily.

> Some months later I moved to my new house. I never saw her again. I was satisfied with myself that I never had given the child a contemptuous look. And I was secretly proud of my generosity to people. But now she had killed herself! I can't be satisfied with myself anymore. If I had made friends with her and given her some comfort, if I had had some talks with her to encourage her. . . . Poor creature! Why is there so much hypocrisy, so much ugly selfishness? Isn't it a kind of mental pollution? Now I sometimes come across her mother in the street. We nod to each other. She's beginning to get wrinkles around her eyes. Her hair turned grey, gone was the light from her fine eyes.

The suicide had forced the narrator to see her own moral weakness. She had been proud of her socialist ethics until then, and had believed she had a talent for being good to people. But the GPCR with its epidemic of suicides had taken hope out of her, and without realizing it she had neglected to help a girl in need. That suicide signified for her the breakdown not just of personal, but general social morality. This essay provoked beliefs she had held before the disappointment of the GPCR, and the saddest part of it all was, as she put it, "since the Cultural Revolution I have heard too many horrible incidents that would make your hair stand on end" to really think that one case mattered.

Our slightly awkward, yet genuinely warm relationship with Xiao Hu, our distant relative and student, has given us a little insight into students who are younger, less alienated, more closely identified with political authority and not nearly so critical of the status quo. Xiao Hu has been visiting us regularly, which in itself is a rather remarkable achievement since her connection to us is very tenuous and students do not ever come visit us at our private quarters. We sometimes get the feeling that she comes partly out of the same concern that motivates the Welcome Wagon; here are some people who live in Shanghai now and have only a handful of relatives, so anyone with a kinship tie is really obliged to step into the gap. One day she showed up with mooncakes from her parents. Another time she brought a bowl of egg dumplings. Her attitude toward Don is familial and quite appropriately deferential given that he is almost her professor (she is only auditing his lecture), a generation older than she, and since Don's aunt's husband is in some way related to Xiao Hu's parents. Tani she treats like a cripple. Walking down the street she holds Tani firmly under the elbow to prevent the foreigner from falling down. We always get the funny feeling that she checks the contents of the refrigerator before she leaves just to make sure we are getting enough to eat.

Xiao Hu is a "three good" student, meaning she excels in politics, scholarship, and physical education. She lives with four other women in the student dorm, although every weekend she returns to her elderly parents' home in central Shanghai to do the shopping and housework for them. On top of that she has many extracurricular duties because of her job as class monitor. (Whenever we tease her about applying for Party membership she just blushes and won't say anything.) Xiao Hu was too young to get involved in the GPCR and never was sent down to the countryside because she is an only child, and so, although we suspect she is substantially older than she looks, she represents the experience of the younger students to a great extent. She reinforces the impression of girlish youthfulness by wearing her short hair in two fat little pigtails which poke right out from under her ears, as regulation requires, and always dressing so that a bit of a frill sticks out of her regulation jacket. On the other hand, Xiao Hu wishes she had been born a man. She and all of her roommates hate to think about graduation because then they will have to be married. That will destroy their strong friendship. In fact sometimes they wish they could stay single so they could live together forever. None of them knows anything about the heroines who meant so much to their grandmothers' generations, Qiu Jin or Madame Roland, or, not surprisingly, the demimondaines idealized by their parents' generation during the May Fourth years. Xiao Hu and her friends instead idealize Madame Curie (a biography of her has just been published in Chinese), and Prime Minister Margaret Thatcher. That last one made us wince, so we asked why. Xiao Hu and her group said a female hero should be a good wife as well as a brilliant, modernizing scientist or the leader of a great country. That is why they do not admire Indira Gandhi, because her "relationships are not good."

Xiao Hu's job as class monitor is to keep in touch with student opinion and she was very open about various tensions, particularly the rift between the senior students and the younger faculty trained during the pre-examination period, when only workers, peasants, and soldiers were admitted to colleges. Monitors find it difficult to maintain discipline in the classes taught by young faculty, because the present students who passed the examination process have only contempt for the political graduates. Xiao Hu has to make sure students do not openly ridicule such teachers or behave badly in their classes. As far as her ideological work goes, things move fairly smoothly because the students in her section are all adults and know they must have a superficial grasp of current politics so they can plan their careers. Everyone pays attention in Friday afternoon political study. They all want to know the current line, particularly what it will mean in terms of concrete government policy, although most skip over theoretical issues, having no interest in Marxism. Xiao Hu said she found her responsibility to remind people to do their homework the easiest part of the job. Older students have no trouble studying on schedule.

Most of Xiao Hu's energy goes into what we would call public relations work, a kind of ideologically motivated affirmation of community social relations. She gave an example. If the parent or grandparent of one of the class members gets sick, or if a serious family problem comes up, monitors visit representing the whole section. She almost refused to believe us when we told her American colleges don't have sections, not to say monitors; and that even if they had, chances were that student representatives would not make calls on sick parents or grandparents. Xiao Hu just thought we were joking. She could not imagine a world where immediate personal relations took a back seat to almost everything else. And she is not the only one.

The belief that personal relations form a meaningful part of everyone's work cuts across the political spectrum. Even the most disaffected students expect monitors, faculty, Party officials, and classmates to give them personal attention. One day we spent an hour with a bitterly critical student who cursed the government, the Party, Chairman Mao, the old men running the country, corruption in high places, the interference in orderly government by the sons and daughters of high officials, and so on. At the end of the hour Tani happened to mention she would probably be unemployed when she got home since overproduction of Ph.D.s was a problem in the U.S. now. He couldn't believe his ears. He felt sure that a democracy like the United States would guarantee jobs for all intellectuals because, he snorted, a truly humane government always takes charge of the lives of its people.

Xiao Hu has quite a reputation. Some of the more demanding students ridicule her for being a prig and a Pollyanna. And there is no denying she is a straight arrow. We value her for what she teaches us about the more politically oriented students. They all strike us as more naive than the others, but they do have a much broader social sense than the limited horizon of the cynical, disillusioned students. Actually, the gap between Xiao Hu and the majority of the students isn't that great. Even the most cynical long to believe in something, be it only Ralph Waldo Emerson or Harriet Beecher Stowe.

Our relationships with the students have been shifting recently. Don finds that increasingly the students approach him the way he himself remembers approaching his Chinese teachers when he was a boy. Although he requested that they not do so, his class continues to rise each time he enters the classroom, because, as the monitor told him, they need to express their respect for him and feel a sense of frustration when they cannot rise. Their possessiveness grows daily, as does their deference, and now that Don's reputation has begun to spread all over campus they seem virtually tongue-tied with admiration for "their professor." Don's intensive readers do not exactly drop in as much as send delegations. A group representing the section, composed of three grave, older students came to the office to meet with Don some time ago and said they did not think intensive reading was the best use of their time with him. Don suggested a condensed version of his Western civilization course, instead. So he began teaching a Western civ survey course with emphasis on the interacting relation between culture and political economy, supplemented by mimeographed readings from Perry Anderson, E. J. Hobsbawm, and lectures from his own book on the history of communication and perception in the West. To put it baldly, a neo-Marxist analysis. Don enjoys teaching them very much. Class 1978 section I is considered the top class in the department. Whereas Tani's section II group seems evenly balanced between men and women, Don's is dominated by very serious, older men. Most of these men are in their mid to late thirties and all the students are tremendously motivated and quite capable of absorbing what he can offer. The Western civ course was such a success that its reputation spread and the history department just sent its own representatives over to the office to ask Don to repeat it during the six-week winter break for those of their majors who understand English. The senior students will leave the campus to do their teacher training then and Don will be free, so he accepted at once.

Don's contemporary U.S.A. lectures for sophomores continue to be a problem. Tani has asked her most active, capable seniors from the literature survey group to audit, and that gives Don a more responsive audience. But most of the sophomores still have problems fully comprehending Don's analysis of contemporary American society. Actually the trauma caused by the entrance of the senior auditors turned out to be the most interesting event so far. The sophomores threw a collective tantrum. They may be younger but the auditors were in their classroom and they refused to give up their own chairs to the usurpers. Those auditors who had sneaked in early and grabbed all the seats refused to budge—a conflict between hierarchy and territoriality. Luckily, Xiao Qian happened to come along. Qian, who is turning out not to be at all diffident, has a remarkable effect on our students. With us he is not only unfailingly polite and generous but also witty, intelligent, able to anticipate our questions, and curious about our perceptions of his country. He is absolutely commanding with students. Politely he ordered the unhappy sophomores to go to the next room and get themselves some chairs and stop sniveling. Then he dressed down the auditors and told them next time they should bring their own chairs. Students carried out his instructions with unusual haste. The department later settled the overpopulation problem by moving Don's afternoon lecture to a larger lecture hall and opening it to auditors campuswide.

Students are having a tougher time figuring out Tani. So many of them are older than she, an important distinction in a society where people automatically order themselves by age. Yet by virtue of her position and academic training she has authority over them. Chinese students, it is quite clear, expect authority to be authoritarian. None of Don's students would ever consider being rude to him, and we suspect that is partly why they cannot bring themselves to stay seated when he enters the room. But in Tani's case the students began with the age problem and then got very confused by Tani's rather relaxed, anti-authoritarian, Californian lecture style. "You ask us questions," one student complained, "but you smile when you do it. It's very confusing." Tani's impatience with exaggerated signs of deference and the students' expectation that all teachers behaved in certain ways affected how her students acted at first. Older, male students particularly eyed her with a great deal of skepticism. Some of this must have gotten to old Professor Luo, because one day he cornered Tani in the hall, cigarette blazing, and ordered her sternly to "crack the whip a lot." Tani's own breaking point came when a student opened his newspaper at the start of a lecture and began studiously to read it. She gave in. The more grossly authoritarian she gets the more pleased her classes are, as though she had somehow proven her value. Now they clean her desk, wipe her blackboard, and close her windows just like they do for their Chinese teachers. A number of students have come by to say they appreciate her "frankness," meaning apparently her informal, underplayed style. But they insist that she link it firmly to discipline.

7

National Day

Shanghai, October 12, 1981

Several days before October 1, red placards and banners went up all over campus. The Party is still in the middle of its major reassessment of the GPCR, meaning that everyone's political attention has been focused again on the past and how to reinterpret it; a similar but more subdued attempt than last year's public trial of the Gang of Four, which several people have described to us lately. There was no major celebration this year. In our *danwei*, the college, people seemed to be more interested in the "reunification with Taiwan" slogan than any other single political issue.

As with the other celebrations that have taken place since we arrived here, we took part in the official proceedings. The FAO invited us to attend the official National Day reception for Shanghai's overseas business, consular, and foreign communities. A large crowd was already milling around inside the Municipal Building when the two of us and our British colleagues, Valerie and Anne, arrived. Since the guests were all foreigners, the individual *danweis* had not sent along many representatives. This affair was organized as a stand-up party, because after the last intracity function foreign guests complained to their FAOs that foreigners do not like Chinese-style sit-down parties, and had explained the Western custom of mixing and circulating. A very aggressive blond man seemed to be bothering everybody when we got there, taking flash photos. We introduced ourselves to get closer to the strange striped tie he was wearing and found that it wasn't stripes at all, but rows and rows of computerstyle letters spelling out the slogan "capitalist tool." Hoping it was a weird joke, we asked, "Are you really a capitalist tool?" He said that's what he really considered himself to be. "China stinks," he told us seriously. "The people are a real drag, but I think I can do business with them." We assumed he must be an overseas business representative, but it turned out that he had come as a foreign expert in order to gather information for his obscure, little, American company. On the other hand, IBM had been a lot more aboveboard and had sent a pleasant, easygoing Chinese-American from San Jose to train technicians and negotiate for the company. We also ran into Robert, our French Sinologist friend who is teaching twentieth-century French poetry at Fudan University this year. We mixed very happily until the officials set up a microphone and the vice-mayor of Shanghai gave a welcome speech, in which he emphasized the new importance the Party had decided to place on negotiations for reunification of Taiwan with the rest of the country. After the short, subdued speech we all ate and drank for another hour, then an official thanked us for coming and dismissed us to our FAO officers who put us in the sedan and brought us home.

We were very curious about this new diplomatic move. The unification drive has accelerated gradually, with relatively little public fanfare. The low-keyed speech at the mixer contrasted remarkably with the Lu Xun day celebrations, for example. The Party had already made plans to celebrate the 70th anniversary of the 1911 Revolution this year with almost as much ceremony as October 1. The Guomindang has always celebrated the 1911 date, October 10, as its national day, or "double ten celebration," so the CCP has arranged a number of festivities honoring this day, including planned academic conferences, publications, and on September 30 released a nine-point outline for resumption of talks between the two sides. Shortly after that Chairman Hu Yaobang personally invited *Mr.* Chiang Ching-kuo and *Madame* Chiang Kai-shek to visit China, adding that in honor of their trip Chiang Kai-shek's home at Fenghua would be renovated, including the grave of his mother.

We have no way of knowing what reception the idea had in Taiwan (although we can sort of guess), but, interestingly, people here in Shanghai were genuinely excited about it. Our relatives were pleased, and faculty have mentioned the new initiative. But knowing enough not to assume our students will endorse just any policy the government proposes, we were a little surprised when Tani's students gave her a friendly dressing down even for asking how they felt about this official reunification decision. They went to the trouble of deputizing class members to give impromptu speeches on the historical logic of uniting Taiwan with the beloved motherland, and others to criticize her for not being more aware of their feelings. Later someone explained privately that patriotism is different from agreeing with the state because to a patriot, China the country consists of the mountains and the plains, rivers and valleys, whereas China the state just means the discredited Chinese Communist Party. However, since both "country" and "state" are the same word in contemporary Chinese, the Party mobilizes people's patriotism on behalf of the state, and ends up getting the credit.

Since we had no further official functions to attend that long National Day weekend we had arranged with the FAO to take a three-day vacation to Hangzhou. We should have been a little suspicious when Xiao Qian had to spend two full days downtown arranging the trip. National Day is the equivalent of Thanksgiving Day weekend in the U.S. Anyway, without giving it too much thought, we got on a very crowded train and pushed over to our compartment. Our fantasy of Hangzhou as a rustic paradise where we could forget our cares and escape the pressures of overpopulation in Shanghai evaporated as soon as the train arrived. Thousands of Chinese tourists had gotten there before us and had already started celebrating the long, holiday weekend. Hangzhou is always paired with Suzhou as the other of China's great garden paradises. Hangzhou, however, reverses the effect the Suzhou gardeners sought, and places the human beings into a very large panorama of hills, lakes, bamboo groves, rustic shrines, lily pad fields and long dikes, all of them just as studied and artificial as the little Suzhou gardens, but on a macrocosmic scale. We were thrilled to be there, but in order to see the famous spots and drink the spring water tea and climb the Six Harmony Pagoda or even take the boat trip out into the lake to see the Three Pools Mirroring the Moon, we had to push our way through huge, exhilarated, boisterous crowds. We almost didn't get to see the most popular place of all; an enormous mob of people had gathered in front of the grave and temple of the twelfth-century patriot and national hero, Yue Fei, who fought against the barbarian invaders and then was betrayed by a "gang of three"—an evil minister, a vicious, scheming empress, and the incompetent emperor. People particularly like to stand in front of the old metal statues of the three and just stare down at them reflectively. A good-sized element of the crowd didn't seem that interested in really looking at the monuments at all, although we suspect they never missed a one: newlyweds. These people were the most uninhibited cooing lovers we've ever seen in China. There seemed to be a pair of them on every bench along the long courseway dikes stretching across the artificial lake. Once we even stumbled on a pair seriously necking in the bushes. Newlyweds give themselves away; they have flaming red faces, bright new clothes and shoes, and they hold hands and giggle a lot. Xiao Qian confirmed our suspicions later, blushing a little bit himself, that October 1 is a very popular time to get married and go on honeymoon. Maybe the couple in the bushes had very poor hostel accommodations.

About a week after our holiday Lao Zheng knocked on our door at the foreign expert building and Tani let him in. He asked for Don, and when informed Don was out, got very agitated. Lao Zheng is a very excitable man. He gets provoked easily and when he does he starts talking really fast in a jazzy provincial dialect neither of us can follow. When he realizes he's left us behind, he tries to do Common Language but forgets and puts in lots of dialect. Anyway, something had gotten Lao Zheng really upset and Tani couldn't figure out what. He sat down and fidgeted with an enormous red envelope for a while, and even when she directly asked him if he cared to leave the letter for Professor Lowe, he seemed reluctant to give it to her. Eventually he left the invitation, and later the two of us opened it up. It invited Professor Luo Mingda to a celebration of the 1911 Revolution to be held the next day. Clearly the implication was that Professor Luo would attend himself, without his foreign wife. Don thought the invitation was very rude, and anyway he could not figure out why he had been asked. Tani was offended.

Lao Zheng arrived the next morning and with Don—both dressed in blue, serge, cadrestyle *zhongshan* suits—drove off in Lao Gu's sedan to the Shanghai Municipal Theater once again. Lao Zheng loves to escort Don because they can really talk about things, and he can question Don about the standard of living in the U.S. and complain that a cadre's pay is less than what a peasant in the Shanghai suburbs can make these days. When they reached the theater, ushers guided them to their first-row balcony seats. Don hung over the edge and watched the huge auditorium fill up. He noticed that the area where he was sitting seemed to be reserved exclusively for overseas Chinese, most of them dressed in expensive Western business suits, all of them accompanied by FAO guides. He turned around in his seat to look at them and recognized the man from Vancouver who was seeing relatives in Shanghai, and the Harvard economist he'd met at the October 1st Day celebration. Then he saw the IBM man from San Jose waving at him, and went over to see him. As they talked it dawned on Don what they were all doing here. He and all the others were "representatives of the Overseas-Chinese communities in the West" to the function that was just about ready to commence.

Distinguished officials, Party, and civic leaders filed onto the stage and sat down in hierarchical precision at the three rows of tables. Ushers appeared and handed out a long, mimeographed program containing the four speeches to be delivered, a copy of Chairman Hu's statement of the previous day, and a reprinted article by Lenin on the historical significance of the Chinese Revolution 1911. A military band struck up the national anthem. When it ended the secretary of the Shanghai Party branch rattled some papers into the microphone in front of him and began reading his speech, which, it became clear very quickly, was a major policy statement. The secretary reevaluated the historical significance of the 1911 Revolution by calling it a necessary stage in the development of semi-feudal, semicolonial China, and then connected 1911 with the Communist Revolution of 1949. In his old age, the speech continued, Sun Yatsen, the father of the 1911 Revolution, began to understand the need for alliance between the CCP and GMD (Guomindang), setting a historical precedent which Chairman Hu wished to renew by inviting the Taiwan government to begin negotiations for reunification.*

As he sat in the balcony, listening to the proceedings and rather bemusedly watching a television camera marked with the logo of the Shanghai TV station move leisurely over his group of overseas Chinese, Don thought about his predicament. He couldn't help feeling a bit used. He really wished Lao Zheng had warned him what they were walking into; but then he didn't know how much Lao Zheng would appreciate his feelings. Besides, had the FAO come over and made the proposal flat out, Don would have taken them up on it since he has no objections to acting as a representative of progressive Chinese-Americans, and anyway he would like to see reunification take place. He almost laughed out loud when he thought of how angry Tani had been, and how funny she would think it was now. It was so consistent.

We have noticed a number of times how the etiquette of formal occasions works, even with our own relatives. They never tell you what the event will be like, and, unless you know and can decide on that basis, you accept invitations at your own risk. Maybe the FAO has gotten so used to Don, they just assume he knows how things work. Maybe they figured he wouldn't mind anyway. The rule of thumb, in any case, is as it is with so many other things in China: those who know, know; those who don't, find out later.

---

*This probably was the signal which initiated the negotiations between the British and Chinese over Hong Kong.

8

Emotions

One day in section, an irritated student got up during the free discussion period and said he resented the way everybody carried on about Tani. People act as though she's a queen and give her special privileges just because she has blonde hair and round eyes. Tani made no attempt to defend herself since she agreed absolutely with him. So she just said mildly that she found the exaggerated courtesy exhausting because it turns every encounter into a formal occasion, and she can never be her natural self because she has to smile constantly and respond to all the courtesies. Then she turned the question around and asked the class why they accept what Donald tells them about America as being true, but reject the same information when they hear it from her. After all, she, being the native-born American should be an even more trustworthy informant than Don who was an immigrant to America. People agreed that they did tend to accept things from Don more easily. One thoughtful woman said it was because she and the others just automatically trusted Chinese more than foreigners, no matter what issue was involved.

Both of us, though, are still having trouble explaining the inner lives of Americans to our students. "I know social inequality exists in America," one woman told us, echoing the feelings of many. "But that is true everywhere in the world. I just still believe that most people in America are happy, rich, and satisfied with their lives." We routinely recommend Studs Terkel's *Working* to them and a story by Anne Beattie, both available in mimeographed form. They don't believe the Terkel interviews. They seem half-convinced that we are actually propaganda agents for their own government and complain that Terkel is just reinforcing the inaccurate, boring Party rhetoric. But they worship writers and almost never question the truths expressed by fiction. A number of people who have been reading a lot of recent American fiction have started coming into our office with the inevitable question: Why, if the country is so rich and happy, do our writers produce so much fiction about loneliness, alienation, despair, violence, and sickness? One way we force them to be more realistic about the U.S. is by appealing to their unquestioning assumption that everything has two sides, bright and dark. Students have to grudgingly agree with us that a "dark" side of America must exist and that they should know about it. So some of them have decided that since they have to learn about America's darkness, they at least should have rebuttal time to teach Tani about the dark side of their country.

Lots of people have told us about students' mental problems. The *China Daily* carries a large ad for "Neurozin," a "nutritive tonic for the prevention and treatment of neurasthenia, general debility, poor memory, insomnia, and anorexia." We have been particularly curious about neurasthenia, ever since Tani came across literary descriptions of it in her research on Chinese women writers of the 1930s. American psychiatry no longer recognizes neurasthenia as a diagnostic concept, though it was a fairly common phenomenon in the late-nineteenth century. So we asked Lao Yang what kinds of people get neurasthenia and whether it was a widespread mental disease. She said she wasn't sure but her impression was it was most prevalent among middle-aged female faculty. But it was not a severe problem and at worst led to periodic inability to work. Students have another story. They say boys and old people are most prone to neurasthenia. This does not completely surprise us, since we assume that culture determines the specific patterns emotional stress takes and researchers have found neurasthenia in contemporary Chinese communities all over the world.

Overstudy, tension, lack of physical exercise, family quarrels are all common stresses in students' lives and do not necessarily lead to any specific mental syndrome like neurasthenia. People also list speech disorders and eccentric behavior, like "insensitivity" to roommates and inappropriate actions, along with memory loss as fairly common mental problems for students. Neurotic students consult Chinese and Western-style doctors at the college clinic, where they are usually treated for physical weaknesses and given tonic, exercise regimens, or herbal remedies. Schizophrenic students go to an off-campus psychiatrist. What surprises us a lot is how much schizophrenia the students claim exists on campus. Everyone mentions that it is the very worst form of emotional illness, and one student listed its symptoms as insomnia, disconnected, random questions, losing the ability to read, extreme nervousness, and sometimes maniacal brilliance and ability to perform under pressure. Our guess is that neurasthenia affects older people primarily, and neurosis the younger ones. But personally we have yet to meet anybody who exhibited symptoms of either. Apropos of schizophrenia, Valerie told us a story she had heard from another British teacher in the city.

A British foreign expert gave a take-home exam and received two identical papers. She called the students into her office one by one. The first claimed to have written the exam herself and could not understand how it could have been duplicated, until the teacher happened to mention the name written on the second exam. The student left abruptly, promising to return, then the teacher interviewed the second examinee, who also claimed to have written the exam. Minutes later the first student reappeared with a class monitor who apologized on behalf of the second student, saying he was "mentally disturbed" and often did peculiar things like this. The monitor looked very angrily at the student and asked how he had cheated and the "disturbed" boy explained, in a peculiar, off handed way, that he just took the finished paper from his friend's desk and copied it word for word. He still did not seem to understand that any teacher would immediately recognize duplicate exam papers. The monitor demanded the student apologize, and asked the instructor if this student could retake the exam. In answer to the foreign teacher's questions, the monitor said this was not the first time the student had behaved inappropriately but that his case was not so severe as to require he be removed from school, although they didn't know what sort of job he might be able to hold down after graduating, certainly not a teaching position.

Now that we are beginning to feel comfortable on campus we have started monitoring our own emotions very closely. Mostly we are discovering our own level of tolerance for Chinese-style sociality. Our interest in Chinese life means we go everywhere we can and meet all kinds of people, so our social life is more strenuous than in the U.S. But the two cultures also involve people with each other in very different ways. Here people have many directly personal relationships.

That intrigues and delights us because it means we are suddenly living inside the "community" we want but do not have in our own country. But since we're not Chinese, we also find the burden of other people's presence intolerable at times. Our friend Robert says he feels the same way: social life is so much more demanding in China than the West, it ends by exhausting foreigners, which explains why we are always getting sick even though our diet is so much better than anybody else's. You can never say to a Chinese colleague, "Hi, look I'm in a hurry, so I can't stop to talk." Each encounter involves an elaborate greeting and affirmation of the connection between you, and of course in a work unit where many people actually live on campus—Lao Zheng, for example, lives right down the road from us in the staff dormitory—you see people almost every day.

Only colleagues fully briefed on Western customs seem to understand how exhausting this is for us. And even they don't really believe that Western people like to be left totally and completely alone sometimes. Tani mentioned this to a student once, who said solitude was the one Western habit she found utterly repulsive. Under other circumstances this student would never have used Party language, but in this context she called our need for privacy "bourgeois individualism." The only Chinese person, she said, that she had ever known who spent lots of time alone had turned out later to have serious "moral failings!"

So while the sense of community attracts us very much and we find ourselves being sucked into intense personal relations, we also are having a terrible time finding enough privacy to keep ourselves sane. If either of us stops anywhere on campus to talk to a friend, students we don't know cluster around to listen to the conversation. The popular spot for ambushing us is the campus post office. Right at the intersection of Guilin Road, leading onto the campus, and the cross-campus thoroughfare, stands a large green metal post box, and across from it a small gatehouse where the Cantonese postmaster sells stamps and hands out packages. People in Shanghai don't use the telephone much because it is inconvenient, expensive, and there aren't many public phones. But they write letters, and the mail comes twice a day; so communication by mail is easy, and the post office is almost always crowded, with students standing in line outside to use the pastepots. (Stamps here have no glue on the back.) when they see us coming they always crowd around and gaze at the addresses on our letters. One day a really pushy man got Don quite irritated and he asked the student what he was looking at. "I want to know where your letter is going," the man replied matter-of-factly. The Cantonese postmaster who actually came from Singapore years ago says that's just an excuse for being rude. The postmaster says the GPCR ruined everyone's manners and this generation of students is just running wild. We think he is being overly polite. Nothing here is ever private. Not your letters, not your room, not your diary. During the GPCR it became conventional to write highly rhetorical political diaries and leave them half-opened on your bed for other people to "happen" to read. These chronicled your inner struggles to achieve Redness. But genuine diaries also got read, which led to enormous political problems for those with improper feelings.

So we find ourselves constantly "spending" emotion. October 10 is a good example of this, because the schedule called for a series of activities. That morning Don went off to the Shanghai Municipal Theater with Lao Zheng for the 1911 celebration while Tani stayed at home. After lunch we were scheduled for a visit to the Meilung People's Commune, so we took our nap,* and joined Lao Zheng and Lao Gu downstairs for the half-hour drive out into the vegetable fields.

Visiting a commune has already become a cliché. We recommend it very highly, anyway. Meilung had just opened for tourists and our hosts seemed to feel a little awkward delivering their speeches. But, they were also very obviously proud of their showplace. A very commanding woman met us in front of the blackboard with its color-chalked English inscription, "Welcome to Foreign Guests." She introduced us to a male school teacher, an old peasant grandfather, and a "son-in-law," that is a man from a neighboring village-commune who had married matrilineally, a real rarity and a subtlety we're afraid will probably be lost on most visitors. These people had been carefully selected to "represent" the commune to outsiders. They ushered us into a brightly painted, Chinese-style banquet room, and after some pouring of tea and introductory words, began the briefing.

Meilung People's Commune has 1,440 acres of cultivated land, 147 acres of private plots, for a total population of 25,000 people or 7,368 families, of which 16,665 persons work. There are 13 work brigades, subdivided into 157 production units. The commune produces grain, cotton, garden vegetables, and has, in addition, 26 light-industrial units. It had a total income of Y17,690,000 in 1980, of which Y4,150,000 was profit. It owns 197 tractors, 29 irrigation pumps, plus chemical fertilizers, and insecticides. In 1980 it sold to the state 4,760,000 kilos of grain, 300,000 kilos of vegetables, 13,440 pigs out of a stock of 24,626, 462,144 poultry, and 321,822 kilos of eggs. In addition the commune produces mushrooms and cut flowers. Twelve elementary and middle schools with a staff of 263 people serve the commune's schoolchildren. There is one hospital, 63 medical workers, a cinema, a drama unit, a cable broadcasting

---

*In late 1984, the government announced its intention to abolish the afternoon nap.

station; each production unit collectively owns a television, and a number of families have even purchased TVs. Since the members own their houses and farm private plots, they spend nothing on rent and very little cash on food. They do spend approximately Y2 per year, individually, for medical insurance. Workers retire at 65 and get a pension of Y20 monthly. Wages are based on work points. The average pay is Y50 per month plus an annual bonus of Y100–200. Meilung is an extremely prosperous commune.*

This initial briefing had all the intimacy of a dialed telephone recording. And we noticed a certain uneasiness in our hosts, who asked us where our translator guide was, and why Lao Zheng had come, since he speaks no English. Gradually, after we started asking questions, slowly reassuring them we really did understand Chinese, they warmed up. The cadre in charge said that when we first came in she had been confused, thinking Don was actually the cadre in charge of Tani. Everybody laughed. And as they relaxed, they began probing us, extending that incredibly warm, unhurried, mildly insistent yet polished feeling so characteristic of a group of Chinese who have been able to submerge or forget the tensions between them. We recognize this atmosphere now. It is as genuine and as learned as the distance one American stands from another in order to shake hands in greeting. The briefing lasted somewhat longer and then the cadre reluctantly gave the sign. The two of us looked at each other, realizing they would probably feel more comfortable if each of us played the roles their own internal briefing had prepared them to expect from us. So Tani graciously let her guides open doors for her, show her each display, all the while thinking up good questions to ask each of the women assigned to direct her through each of the rooms we toured. The guides didn't seem to be able to shake off their first impression that Don was a cadre. They let the "Chinese with American citizenship" trail along behind the tour, chatting comfortably with Lao Zheng.

We started in light industry. In the first building, we watched women sorting, cleaning, drilling, and stringing tiny low-grade pearls. The guide who took us through this room told Tani that women workers at Meilung have very high social status because their wages in light industry, stringing pearls or knitting and crocheting for the Japanese market, raise the family income substantially. From women's work we rushed to the clinic, where obliging volunteers pulled up their shirts or dropped their pants so medical workers could demonstrate how to apply needles for re-lieving arthritis. Then we drove across the commune to the

---

*Since then the commune has been modified by the individual responsibility system.

kindergarten where we finally got to see the handsome, healthy tots singing a collective song about pulling up a big turnip. We suspected from the hassled look in their teachers' eyes that they'd kept the kids late to accommodate us. But at each stop we felt the same probing, curious emotional extension from our guides as we had felt in the earlier briefing as soon as we opened our mouths and spoke Chinese.

At dusk we pulled into the first of two peasant homes. A man was sitting on a low-slung chair playing with his daughter as he waited for us to show up. His wife hadn't gotten home yet from her job at a factory in Shanghai. We met him because he represents the current, ideal marriage between one worker and one peasant—they spend one income and bank the other at 5 percent interest in the People's Bank. With the Y2,000 they already have saved they could add a second story to their house, as many prosperous peasants are already doing. Or they could buy furniture, a new TV, curtains, or some nice clothes. At the second stop next door, the woman welcoming us into her brand new, concrete, two-storied house said a little nastily that the first man was just plain lazy. He cultivates his private plot but never sells anything on the free market, considering that too onerous. Instead he gives his extra produce to relatives. This woman was proud of her family's traditional frugality and their successes. She makes a very good salary as a knitter and her husband works in the field. They also have side-line occupations, including raising rabbits, sinking wells, and cooking at commune banquets. The profits from all this enabled them to build the four-unit building where the three brothers, their families, and their old mother all live together—a peasant ideal.

We found our tour of Meilung fatiguing because we ended up feeling more than we thought we would. We did exactly what thousands of tourists have done, except we made our conversation directly, rather than through a translator. But because they could talk to us, we aroused the curiosity of the people performing for us and they seemed to really put their heart into it. Their performance was a peculiar mixture of obligation, since this is their job, and curiosity at getting to talk directly to a foreigner. Particularly the critical peasant woman who seemed to consider Don a sort of out-of-town cadre (since he dressed in his usual *zhongshan* suit), and spoke directly to him about her work, and the pressures on the family because of all the economic possibilities that had opened up lately. The guides were even more emotionally demanding. Talking directly to Tani, finding out she was just a foreign version of a young, friendly woman, they put their arms around her in a gesture of intimacy, held her hands, and told her to ask them anything, even waited for her to think up other questions for them to answer. Tani loves the physical contact, and would not want it to stop. But she also began to feel the drain it had on her feelings. Breaking cultural taboos, even the ones we want to break—like the prohibition against women touching each other in friendship—ends up exacting a cost. At the end of the tour the social contact had become unbearably fatiguing.

We couldn't really afford to be exhausted. We had invited Xiao Qian to bring his fiancée over to dinner because we like Xiao Qian so much and we really were looking forward to meeting Xiao Shen. We assume Xiao Qian was assigned to us because we know a lot more about China than the average foreign expert does. Several times he has mentioned his "discipline" by which we understand him to mean his Party membership. We have no idea if it is standard practice for all FAO guides to be also Party members, but for us he is perfect because he can answer all our political questions. Evidently he comes from a working-class background and spent years during the GPCR in the northeast where he worked in an open pit coal mine, on a state farm, doing road construction, and other kinds of punishing physical labor. Somewhere along the line he was selected as a worker-peasant-soldier student, and was sent to Shanghai Teachers College. The authorities told him to major in English, and in a few years he had mastered the language and now teaches English and politics and works in the FAO.

We rushed upstairs after a ride home in the dusk from Meilung, and found Xiao Qian waiting for us. Sitting next to him in the reading room was a short, sturdy woman with a heart-shaped face, carefully permed hair, and a shy, controlled manner. They rose from their seats, and he introduced us to Xiao Shen. We took just a few moments to refresh ourselves and sat down immediately to the banquet we had arranged for the evening. Probably the most intimate social contact available to Chinese who are not related to each other is banqueting. A good banquet offers a lot more than just good food. It requires a sort of warm, jovial honoring of the special guests, a carefully controlled atmosphere of jokes and wisecracks, teasing, talk about the food, exaggerated fun, and toasts. (We have never attended a dinner where people discussed serious matters.) Every possible satisfaction should be wrung out of the food and drink and company. To create and maintain this feeling is a full-time job. We had to keep the guests' glasses full, of course, Xiao Qian had beer and Xiao Shen had orange juice; but hosts also feed their guests, piling food onto their plates; particularly the young women, since no woman under thirty-five will ever serve herself at a banquet. The guest of honor (usually a man or older woman) must be served the shoulders, best part of the fish, and an entire chicken drumstick which is considered the choice cut. A guest of honor does not select what she or he prefers but waits for the host to distribute what are generally perceived as the choicest tidbits. Don had to invent more and more toasts to get Xiao Qian a little high, and Tani had to insist that Xiao Shen eat, talking uninterruptedly since Xiao Shen's role required that she blush politely and almost never speak out loud. We like Xiao Qian very much and that is why we had him over. But for the kitchen staff having one of their own people come as the guests of honor, it turned out, inspired them to a truly great meal. The banquet was an unquestionable success and later, when we retired into our rooms to have a little tea and conversation, we had no trouble getting the couple to tell us how they had met.

One of Xiao Qian's colleague's wife works in Xiao Shen's *danwei*. This couple thought their mutual friends should meet so they held an introductory meal, and had the two look each other over. After dinner Xiao Qian and Xiao Shen took a stroll on the Bund and realized they lived right across the street from each other. They decided they had enough in common to meet again. Each went directly home to investigate the other. Xiao Shen giggled when she told us just how thorough she had been. The sister-in-law of her father's apprentice had gone to school with Xiao Qian's older brother and through that connection she found out Xiao Qian was generally considered to be an honest, hardworking, all-around good prospect. (Presumably she also heard he was a Party man, a very valuable qualification.) They left the sequence of their early "dates" a little vague, but Xiao Shen said she decided to let herself fall in love with Xiao Qian when he assured her that his *danwei* had an excellent housing policy, and would assign them a decent room fairly quickly. We asked her why she had given up her own place in line at the hospital where she works to let Shanghai Teachers College take care of housing, since that will mean a long commute for her. The two said they had weighed many factors: Xiao Shen's nursing work schedule; length of estimated time before room assignment (since they can't get married until they have gotten a room); the possibility that either one might be transferred in the future; childcare; and distance from the center of the city. In the end, the campus seemed a better location. Also of course it is very beautiful. Xiao Qian and Xiao Shen are practical people who have spent enormous energy considering every angle of their courtship, engagement, marriage, and future life together. They see each other on a schedule in order to avoid gossip, which is difficult because their families live so close. Both families have had a guiding hand in every decision, from the initial one of getting married to the specific details of the marriage plans. According to them—and of course the FAO teases Xiao Qian mercilessly about this, to his delight—they spend their dates discussing life goals, proper deportment, ethics, moral character, how to be a good parent, and their future bank savings account.

Obviously not everybody has the patience or discipline for this sort of upright, moral calculation. The GPCR generation has reached the age when they must marry and people are falling in love, having love affairs, breaking up, or getting married all the time. Many students argue that love ought to be completely different from the experience described to us by Xiao Qian and Xiao Shen. That is, it should be overwhelmingly powerful and spontaneous. The fact that it almost never is, people say, is due to China's poverty and the terrible material conditions, even in Shanghai. Individuals must divert too much energy from the "spiritual" aspects of marriage in order to bargain for a barely decent material existence. Even so, the prevalence of what the Party officials see as "selfish" romantic love has many people concerned, and the government is trying to channel some of the passions into what it considers more socially constructive avenues. Recently a series ran on TV about model romances, and needless to say, approximated the sort of courtship and ideal family life Xiao Qian and Xiao Shen described to us—serious, ideological, morally scrupulous, affectionate, and family centered. Xiao Shen and Xiao Qian both take very seriously their obligation to set an example for the masses.

Whether you marry out of blind passion or a more regulated sort of affection, marriage is still the biggest event in anyone's life. Nowadays it cost several thousand yuan to have a decent wedding in Shanghai. (The official exchange rate is about 1 yuan to U.S. $0.52, and the average monthly wage is about Y50–65.) The groom buys or makes all the furniture. A specified number of items, usually a TV, radio, sewing machine, electric fan, or sofa, is negotiated in advance. The bride usually supplies bedding, dresses, clothing, dishes, and household utensils. The groom's family pays for the wedding banquet, which runs about Y60–75 per table. The problem lately is that many families try to impress friends and colleagues by having lots of guests. But wedding guests must each contribute a gift of Y20.00, which is leading to genuine hardship among our students, and even among young workers who make over Y50 a month, because with the whole sixties generation now getting married, it is not unusual to get a wedding invitation every month. No one can refuse an invitation without seriously damaging social relationships, so the financial burden of the wedding is rapidly overwhelming everyone. The government has tried to regulate the spiraling cost of marriage by raising banquet prices, and limiting the number of guests one can invite. It has just begun offering inexpensive group weddings, also. On October 1, the Shanghai municipal government sponsored one, which attracted only about 300 couples. Lots of people get around the regulation easily by hiring a few cooks and throwing an enormous private banquet in their *danwei*'s hall or at home, thus bypassing the state-owned restaurants.

Xiao Shen and Xiao Qian would very much like to keep the cost of their wedding down, but aren't too hopeful because they represent only one voice in the planning and must convince their parents and even all their grandparents that cheaper is better. The older generations have reasserted their control over marriage, in the wake of the GPCR, finding the return to older social conventions very reassuring. This situation strikes young people as more than a little ironic. Their own parents, who married in the 1950s during the first marriage reforms, were rebelling against their parents. They married for love and didn't have weddings at all, just registered at the state's marriage bureau—no banquet, no furniture, no worries. So, the generation which benefited most from marriage reform is, according to their children, now making it difficult for love to survive, by insisting on elaborate weddings and many times selecting spouses for their children. This of course is the younger generation's perspective. Lao Zheng has his own strong feelings about the marriage crisis. He complains about how the spoiled GPCR kids expect all sorts of electrical appliances while he and his wife married in the late 1950s with nothing, and still don't have anything except two kids to feed and a lot of responsibilities.

By 8 P.M., October 10, we simply could not go on. We really wanted to. Our guests, Xiao Qian and Xiao Shen, still looked fresh and seemed to be genuinely enjoying themselves. But Tani just started to buckle. Even Don, whose capacity for Chinese-style conviviality not only far exceeds hers but also seems to be expanding the longer we stay in Shanghai, also began feeling a terrible need just to be alone and unwind. We love the incredible warmth and sense of belonging Chinese sociality gives. Tani's irritation at always having to be the foreigner is slowing giving way to the realization that there is much security in having a role assigned to you, even that one. But we keep running into internal, socialized psychological limits. We like Chinese communality. But we cannot always join in it.

October 10 was a very full day, and it pushed us to our limits. But we don't want to give the impression that our lives are hectic. Pressures exist, but the organized regularity of our scheduled lives actually reduces the tension from the level we experience at home. It takes us a lot of time to cultivate so many warm social relationships, and we find ourselves slowing down our work pace. Mostly our colleagues have an unhurried way of life. There are constant conversation breaks, shopping trips, newspapers to be read, tea to be drunk. There are lots of meetings, lots of frustrating delays. People aren't anxious about their work. They work fairly steadily at it, but at a greatly reduced level of productivity.

9

Teaching

Shanghai, November 3, 1981

*B*oth Shanghai Teachers College and the larger, richer, and more prestigious East China Normal University train middle-school teachers. Our students say they actually wanted to be assigned to the municipally controlled S.T.C. because it guarantees them a teaching assignment in the Shanghai area. A Normal University diploma is far more glamorous, but it means graduates may find themselves teaching anywhere in east China, from Jiangsu to the impoverished rural interior of Anhui. Since city people despise the countryside, and Shanghainese particularly cannot imagine living anywhere but in Shanghai, our graduating students' anxiety level has been soaring, despite continuing assurances from the authorities. The class of 1977 has just gone into its final phase of training and examinations. By the end of this semester they will be assigned jobs, a process called *fenpei*. They know they won't get sent to the boondocks. But a lot of them are terribly afraid they might end up teaching in one of the new suburban schools an hour away from the center of the city, servicing one of the so-called satellite towns ringing Shanghai. Everyone says the students in those schools are inferior because they're all from workers' families. Also, living an hour from town means it is difficult to stay in touch with friends, since commuting is impossible except on weekends. Not only in our school, but at every campus in Shanghai, the class of 1977 is so keyed up over *fenpei* that the newspapers have started running stories about the government's efforts to crack down on "back door" favoritism in teaching assignments.

Last week Don talked with one of the history majors who has been auditing his Western civ survey. Since the two of us are historians, we were naturally curious about the college's history department. This man took the national college entrance exam and, like all applicants, he selected ten colleges in order of preference. This initial part of the selection process has been honed to a fine art, because everyone has to weigh their chances of getting into a prestigious university against the chance that a more obscure school might be looking for very good students. If you lose out with the prestigious university, the others may already have filled their quotas. Also, job assignment is an important element of calculation. Applicants need to find out the general area of likely assignment, the kinds of advancement possible after assignment, and how individual personal situations may ameliorate assignment. Being a single child, the child of aged or single parents, or a person whose sibling is already in hardship areas all might be invoked as special circumstances. Anyway, this particular student had gotten assigned to S.T.C. He named English as his first major preference, history second. He told us that for nonscience students, English is now almost always the first choice. It is considered the most glamorous major and knowing a foreign language obviously improves the chances of studying abroad. But the foreign languages department's quota was full, so he found himself in the history department. Actually he was not too disappointed because he likes history and the revival of college journals lately has made it possible for history students to publish highly controversial interpretations of recent history and see them debated all over the country. What every liberal arts student dreads is the chance that he or she might end up in the political education department. During the GPCR everyone wanted to do political education, but right now it has sunk to last choice; it's even considered a stigma to have a degree in politics we hear, because only people too old or too stupid to learn new materials end up there. At present, in the student popularity contest, English ranks first, history a close second, Chinese studies third, and politics way at the bottom end of the scale.

This history student said the college accepted 70 history majors in 1977, 120 in 1978, about 100 in 1979, 60 in 1980, and only 40 in the 1981 freshman class. Since all S.T.C. grads are assigned to teach in Shanghai middle schools, the supply is calibrated with expected demand. History majors take a standard four-year program, including three years of Chinese history and world history, plus mandatory political economy and historical materialism, English, and a senior thesis. Without exception, the faculty organize history courses around lectures and emphasize chronological, political narrative. They use economic history as the basis of their periodization, a concession to Marxism. Modern European intellectual history, offered as a senior elective, starts with Francis Bacon (the beginning of modern scientific thought) and finishes with Ludwig Feuerbach (the predecessor to Marx and Engels).

Don's lecture series on contemporary U.S.A. has finally taken off. He is now attracting between 80 and 100 people to his Wednesday afternoon section, ever since the authorities allowed auditors. Some are seniors in the foreign languages department. But news about good courses travels fast in Shanghai's academic community. (Even Mingzhang and Peihua hear about our lectures from a distant relative of theirs who keeps them well informed.) Auditors are coming in from other departments, and other campuses; some are students, others faculty. The auditors naturally are far more interesting than the regular sophomores in his other sections, and it really helps his morale to have them there. Last week, after a rousing Wednesday afternoon lecture, a group of older students came around for some questions:

Student: "The love between one woman and another, aren't there laws against that in America?"

Don was very intrigued by this question, since usually no one ever mentions sex, whether privately or, as in this case, in public. So he asked,

"Where did you ever learn about that sort of thing?"

"In an American magazine. I read that a female athlete had 'love' for another woman."

Don guessed that the student was referring to the Billie Jean King affair. *Time* magazine recently ran a cover story on Billie Jean King's admission that she had had a love affair with a woman. Since students in our department read *Time* whenever they can get their hands on it, we suspect this man isn't the only one with questions about this "open American custom." Students read the magazine for what it tells them about the outside world. But they also translate small articles from *Time* (China does not subscribe to copyright law, so translators are free to use whatever texts they can find) about medical breakthroughs, scientific miracles, and peculiar, or interesting social phenomena. Translators can earn a little extra money selling their work to the new, popular journals like *October, Present Age, Harvest,* and others. Don figured maybe this student had a translation project.

Don: "That is called homosexuality. Sometimes it happens between two women; sometimes two men fall in love."

Student: "Isn't it illegal?"

Don: "Some states have laws against homosexuality, some don't. States which do are generally not enforcing their laws presently."

Student: "Oh, thank you, teacher." He walked away, flabbergasted. How could there be no law against it? How could existing laws not be strictly enforced?

We are aware of student interest in Freud, because we've both been approached about the issue of sexual repression. But this is the first time anyone has mentioned lesbianism. We have to be extremely careful, even with students we know are very interested in sexual matters, that we are not off-color, or even very explicit in our occasional reference to sex. Even necessary literary references have unanticipated effects. One afternoon, Tani told the Oedipus myth in order to illustrate a lecture point; a shocked titter rippled through the room. Actually, their response restored a real sense of horror to the myth, but it also reminded us of how easily our students shock when it comes to these matters.

Anyway, the students were not finished with Don yet.

Junior faculty: "Excuse me, teacher, can you tell me something about existentialism?"

Don: "What do you mean by existentialism?" Just lately students have been coming to the office wanting to know about existentialism, which they tell us is the most popular philosophy in America today. That's certainly not true, and we keep wondering where they got that idea. Nor do we really understand why existentialism is so attractive to them. But Don does not feel like getting dragged off on an intellectual wild-goose chase today.

Junior faculty: "I mean the philosophy of Jean Sartre, and the German philosopher whose name I am not too sure of." He meant Heidegger.

Don: "Existentialism is not particularly important in the U.S."

Junior faculty is not going to be put off that easily: "Do you have any books on American philosophy?"

Don: "I'm sorry, but I did not bring any books on philosophy. We have mostly books on history and literature. Why are you interested in philosophy?"

Junior faculty: "I'm going to be teaching it to our students in the future."

Don: "I'm very interested in intellectual history, too. But I always try to place intellectual ideas in their proper social historical contexts."

Junior faculty just walked off. He did not get what he thought he wanted. And he was certainly not interested in any historical approach, particularly one tinged with historical materialism.

Literature teachers in both the P.R.C. and the U.S. tend to ignore social, historical contexts when they present the texts to students. We both have been trying to force our students here to read all the assignments against a historical background. We don't know how well we are succeeding. Sometimes, things come up that make us very discouraged.

Last week, Tani lectured on the Local Color School of American literature and used *Gone with the Wind* as a popular example of more recent plantation literature. She knew many students were familiar with the novel and she pointed out how Margaret Mitchell had romanticized antebellum plantation culture. During the break, two distraught students came to the office. Teacher, they pointed out, had to be aware that *Gone with the Wind* is a world masterpiece. How could the teacher criticize such a marvel of literary invention, such a compelling vision of American black slave life? (Support for *Gone with the Wind* is so strong, we're beginning to suspect maybe students see it as an antidote to official state patronage of black literature. We find ourselves siding with the Party when it comes to race; we've run into some extraordinary racists here. Party members are the exception, but even they tend to patronize the very fiction they translate.) Students do not like teachers to deviate from the textbook, either. One week Tani was lecturing on Walt Whitman and Emily Dickinson. Immediately after lecture, a student arrived at the office to announce that since his textbook (a Chinese translation of an out-of-date Russian work) did not have a chapter on Emily Dickinson, the teacher had obviously made a big mistake in claiming such great significance for what was obviously a relatively unknown poet. It is not easy to change their minds, either. Han chauvinism, that funny, frustrating habit our students have of assuming that all cultures are basically variations of their own, makes the job doubly difficult.

We interpret our students' reverence for textbooks in part as a throwback to the old scholarly tradition of establishing orthodoxies, even in bodies of fiction. People accept the idea that there are objectively superior literary masterpieces which will confer benefits on readers, and they pay relatively little attention to individual or eccentric personal preferences. Or to put it another way, readers expect their own tastes to be formed through exposure to a selection of correct literary masterpieces—a masterpiece being any book which received an award, the National Book Award, the Pulitzer Prize, the Nobel Prize. This is an intellectual habit. Students don't seem to think it peculiar that each year their government issues a list designating "the ten best short stories of 1981," and they get as partisan about selections for "Golden Cock Awards" for films as we do about the Academy Awards. The assumption that one correct answer exists about literary taste, as about everything else, means students rely very heavily on anthologies—collections of orthodox texts—and that now, as in the past, students learn about literature by memorizing what consist of almost Talmudic literary lineages.

All this reinforces a rather bookish attitude toward language. One day Tani received an essay in intensive reading called, "The Mills of God Were Slowly Grinding." She altered the title to fit the subject more closely, and to give the story a little more colloquial tone. The next day, the author came to the office to complain about the title change. He produced a second essay, which helped explain his obvious distress. It was titled "Three Thousand Five Hundred and Twenty-six English Idioms," which described how he had spent two years compiling an enormous list of idioms with Chinese translation, two indexes, all neatly written out in longhand. Tani spent the next two hours trying to convince him that (1) colloquial, literary, and dictionary English are all different languages; (2) because English is a living language it changes through time, just like Chinese, so that many of the idioms in his list were no longer in use today; but (3) that the list was still very useful for people reading nineteenth-century literature.

An awful lot goes on under the surface that we never learn about. Weeks ago, Professor Fang Quan started appearing at Tani's lectures. She would come in and sit right smack in the middle of the room and listen intently throughout the lecture, then smile her gentle, unutterably polite smile, and disappear. We usually work closely with Lao Yang, who actually suits us beautifully because she is so "Americanized" (that is according to students' perceptions, and we are beginning to see why). Lao Yang always tells us what types of exams we should prepare and helps us learn students' names, or answer questions when we don't understand what students want. All the other foreign experts deal with Fang, who is about Yang's age and is the department's administrator in charge of relations between foreign experts and the Ministry of Education in Beijing. There is something so ultrafeminine, so genteel and controlled about Fang Quan that we jokingly say she must be Japanese (never to her face, of course, since she and Yang were young during the Second World War and have bitter memories of Japanese atrocities). Fang Quan never explained what she was doing in Tani's class. Even more mysterious was when she started arriving with various groups of heavy, middle-aged men wearing huge overcoats and long mufflers, who would shake Fang's hands vigorously after the lecture and disappear.

But last week, Fang Quan finally came to the office, cool and restrained as always. She looked around for stray students, closed the office door and, completely out of character, suddenly hugged Tani. Then she explained that until the two of us arrived Shanghai Teachers College had followed Beijing's policy of hiring older foreign experts. National and regional authorities believe this is the most realistic policy because young teachers are so irresponsible and don't work hard enough. When we arrived, the FAO and the faculty were afraid they had been saddled with a lazy, young goof-off. (We explained that in the U.S. the situation is exactly the reverse, because young people must compete for jobs whereas tenured faculty don't need to prove their popularity with the students.) The hug was to celebrate the letter Fang Quan claimed she had just written to Beijing reporting that S.T.C. was having a very good experience with a young teacher. Students, she said, think Tani is the most wonderful foreign teacher they've ever had.

We thought the old/young dichotomy quite interesting. Older faculty don't trust the younger faculty's academic training, that much is clear. Some of this might be a part of the general opinion here that people don't mature until they are at least 40. Some of it might reflect a realistic appraisal of academic decline since the GPCR. But many older teachers have very strong grievances against junior faculty who humiliated, tortured, or beat them during the struggles. We can't imagine how painful it must be for both generations to have to work together every day. Fang Quan embraced Tani again, and left. She never said who the strange men with the big coats were.

We have consulted with Yang and Fang about staying here next semester. Our original plan was to go and teach in Wuhan, Central China, but that has not panned out yet. In the meantime we are establishing good connections and a reputation here. Don proposed that we take the three months to compile an English primer on contemporary U.S.A. at a second-year reading level. There does not seem to be any textbook available which gives a full, balanced, up-to-date survey. Fang Quan and Lao Yang say they would prefer that Tani repeat her American lit survey as a seminar for their junior faculty, and college teachers from other campuses who will come and audit, and they want Don to give his popular lectures on American society again. However, they will have to decide which contribution is more valuable, and then let us know.

Two weeks ago, Tani caught a cold which has turned into a mild bronchitis. Lao Yang says she has got a "fall cold." People here get sick from the weather. No one south of the Yangtze River has indoor heating, so to compensate and protect against the constant cold everyone must monitor the weather very carefully. Pei Hua,

Xiao Qian, our students, and Lao Yang have all taught us to put on
jackets, remove sweaters, add underwear, knot our scarves, take off
or put on gloves, and drink hot liquid as the temperature and wind
fluctuate. We have never lived any place where so much attention
had to be paid to the weather. And we have never felt the weather so
directly, as when the cold blasts come in waves down off the Northern steppes into the lower Yangtze River valley. Particularly during
winter, everyone works out daily to strengthen their resistance to
disease. Students have their own athletic classes, and many do extra
exercises during the class breaks. To keep us well, the authorities
have arranged to have an old, very vigorous physical education instructor come twice a week to teach us calisthenics and *taijiquan*.
We hear that he begins his own practice at four o'clock every morning when the temperature is lowest, and even works out in the snow,
though people assure us it almost never snows here.

Everyone is extremely sensitive about health. Doctors and lay
people, in fact almost everybody we run into, tells us about the
power of Chinese medicine. It has become a private joke between us,
because at the end of every testimonial, without exception we are
assured that unlike Western medicine "Chinese medicine has no
side effects." Unsympathetic foreigners expand this to its logical
end and claim that Chinese medicine has no effects at all. One week,
Don's voice gave out and he got very good results using the standard
Chinese cold treatment which includes throat massages, resting the
voice, taking vitamins, and drinking herbal teas. But the herbal
tonic did not seem to help Tani's bronchitis. So Lao Yang finally told
her to go to the clinic and consult Dr. Mei.

The clinic is a one-storied bungalow on the northeast border of
the campus, just off the huge athletic field that stretches from our
dormitory all the way to the swimming pool right near the stream
bisecting the campus. We decided to go over to the clinic and meet
Dr. Mei. We walked around the athletic field, turned onto a gardened
area and walked into the clinic, arriving first in a spacious, clean, central waiting hall. We noticed a dispensary for Western medicine immediately to the left and a sign on the wall directing clients to a hall
where two doors opened onto rooms with southern exposures, one an
examining room, the other a small "injection room." We were not the
only clients that morning. All the sick people were lined up in the hall,
some sitting on a bench outside the examination room, waiting for
the doctors to open the doors. Since no one would dream of going to
the doctor alone, that involved quite a lot of people. The door opened
and we all went in; someone came forward to ask what the foreign expert would like, and we said she would like to consult Dr. Mei. While
we sat in front of a wooden desk waiting for Dr. Mei, we watched and
listened as the other sick people consulted with their doctors. A client

can choose either Chinese or Western medicine but the consultation is very similar. The doctor asks about pain, urine, bowel movements, menstrual, temperature, pulse, assuming that the sick person will accurately report all symptoms. Friends feel free to comment on the client's general health. The doctor writes the symptoms and diagnosis onto a small chart which the client, not the clinic, keeps. Depending on the problem, the doctor prescribes the medicine, and then the client and the client's friends go and have it filled. (In the case of gynecological exams, which are conducted in a separate room, the client's friends will invariably stand beside her at the examining table, hold her hand and talk to the gynecologist, who is always another woman.)

Finally Dr. Mei, who heads the college's clinic, arrived. He's tall and thin and has a kind of obvious charismatic authority; or maybe it just seemed so to us because he'd gotten such a great build-up from all the other foreign experts. Lao Yang and Fang Quan go to him because he reads English and keeps up with the international medical journals, and because he mixes Chinese with Western medicine. He ushered us to his examining desk. After a great deal of questioning and some examination, Dr. Mei suggested injections for Tani. Dr. Mei does not tell you what he thinks you should have. He asks you what you would like. For colds you can have drops for the nose, drops for the ears, lozenges for the throat, vitamins for overall strength, even eyewashes along with the standard, herbal tonic. Since this was mild bronchitis, Tani received an herbal mix and some antibiotics, with some nose drops and vitamins. The Chinese pharmacy filled the tonic prescription, mixing a variety of herbs, bones, meals, and dried flowers, on a tall pile of newpapers; then the pharmacist deftly twisted a sheet of paper into a series of cones, one cone per infusion. Chinese antibiotics are much weaker than Western pills because doctors here are afraid of overmedicating. Many people told us that their bodies are more sensitive than foreigners' because Chinese rely on natural remedies, which, the argument goes, work well but much more slowly than the traumatically effective Western drugs. The mild antibiotics Dr. Mei prescribed came in a glass tubes, packed into a cardboard box, like tubes of tempera. The sick person takes care of the medicine, so twice a day Tani took her box of tubes back over to the injection nurse, climbed up the three steps onto the highchair, and pulled down her pant leg to expose her thigh. The nurse selected an enormous syringe from a huge newly sterilized pile lying on the white tray, fitted it with a reusable needle, and administered the medicine very, very slowly. It worked, and in a few days Tani recovered.

10

Intellectuals and Power

Shanghai, November 8, 1981

*W*e entered the lives of our senior students at an opportune moment. Their sense of having been sacrificed, or "lost," is very great. But in just a few weeks many will be assigned to the schools and translation bureaus, the agencies which are all waiting to get one of the first class of "real" college-educated speakers of English in more than a decade. The feeling of having come such a great distance is leading to enormous ambivalence. In an intense classroom discussion, a student stood up to say that to him the GPCR had been distilled in an image he remembers from then: A powerful, squat, modern Chinese woman wearing a green army uniform, one arm raised in a fierce salute to show the red bandanna tied around her forearm, unfurled by the breeze, a whip held coiled in her other hand. That image of female beauty, he said, captured in a vision everything he felt at the time to be most inspiring about the GPCR. His idea of beauty had changed since then, he admitted, and so had his political ideology. But he still remembered how inspiring it had once been. The rest of the class started booing and shouting that he shouldn't talk that way to a foreign teacher. We are glad he did. His point is simply never made in our presence. This generation grew up during an extraordinary period of history. Many of them like to say the GPCR was like Nazi Germany. But the analogy is incorrect, not only because, as another student said, "no one got made into soap," but also because they were the executioners as well as the victims.

Classes 1977 and 1978 feel they were cheated out of their youth and unjustly punished for their idealism. One student said, "the GPCR destroyed the dream we had that millions of Chinese could unite as brothers and sisters. It turned our former heroes into hated foes." "How *can't* we be lost," wrote another student (who identified himself as "a man who has some feelings of [being part of the] lost generation"), "when some of the ruffians we hated and had contempt for turned into men of virtue, and the chiefs of our enemies who made the plan to slaughter our people became the honored guests?" He ended his essay, "I would weep for those who died in the battlefield, believing that they were fighting for justice!"

The movement to send down students to the countryside, which we Western intellectual radicals thought at the time was so wonderful, had quite a different effect on the people who actually went. Some of them now understand how difficult it is to farm, mine coal, dig ditches, and put up power stations. But people who accept this knowledge as a positive gain still object to the harsh way they had to learn it. Many sensitive people were tortured by what they interpreted in the villages as barbarism and sexual degeneracy. More than one student has told us that peasants have no time to think, no energy to spare for conversation, and that is what made living with them torturous. People say, as though to justify their own bitterness, that even the workers hate Mao Zedong now. The ideology of the GPCR, said one woman, was too ambitious and its promise to transform the world was ruined by selfishness, greed, and hypocrisy.

Many students tell us stories about witnessing. That is, many claim to have seen horrible things happen during the GPCR when they were young. "I remember," one man said, "that Red Guards would take someone for criticism and force them to take off their shoes and stand on a platform and clap their shoes over their head and confess their crimes. Or to make a person put a hot chain on their head and then stand outside the marketplace and strike a broken basin with a ladle to attract attention and then to confess their crimes." A young female student said: "Once I remember seeing some middle-school students take their teacher out to the broad-jump sandbox and force him to lie down and then beat him with strips of bamboo. The young people who did these things, of course, could not help feeling badly. When they did, they had to carry out psychological warfare in their own minds. They had to draw the line between what was beloved and what was counterrevolutionary."

Over and over we hear these witnesses; yet the closest we have ever come to hearing a first-hand account was from a student who asked rhetorically in one of our afternoon office sessions: "Why were the Red Guards so cruel? Because they were naive. Most Red Guards, and I was one though not very radical, were naive. *The ones who committed the worst crimes were bad people to begin with, and these bad people influenced the naive ones, and encouraged them to commit crimes. Many of the bad ones had grievances they wanted to express and felt they could take revenge on their enemies."* We often do not know: what is memory and what is confession?

The most compelling stories come from rehabilitated ex-rightists, the very dangerous class enemies our students might have tortured. One frail old man took us aside at a party once and, speaking in the most elegant English imaginable, told us he wished to tell the story of his own suffering so that someone relatively unburdened by GPCR horror stories would remember his. He had been charged by some illiterate workers of accidentally defacing a newspaper portrait of Chairman Mao. When he got to the part of the story that involved his own suicide attempt (he leaped out of a fourth-story prison window, head first and unfortunately landed on his feet, merely breaking his hips), he said that as he left the sill he had had a vision that his mother would catch him and protect him from further persecution.

The other level of GPCR experience we hear about most is the symbolic humiliation. A woman told the following story in class one day. At the beginning of the GPCR, she was in her early twenties and had just started teaching middle school. She walked into her classroom and saw her name written on the blackboard upside down. The experience upset her so much, she never completely recovered. To this day she cannot trust her young students the way she once did. People also say they felt emotionally violated when they had to wear arm bands or signs with "dirty words" written on them, like cow-demon, worm, insect. Some have horrible memories of watching crowds force their parents and older brothers and sisters to wear enormous white dunce caps covered with scrawled indictments, or suffering "on the spot criticism" struggles, even beatings. One unfortunate man accidentally caused his own parents to be physically assaulted by a neighborhood committee. He had been a little boy at the time and did not understand how dangerous his actions were to those around him.

The symbolic level did not affect everyone to the same degree. Some people were perfectly able to ignore the shaved heads and the humiliation rituals. But everyone talks about the GPCR in similar terms. Whenever they describe it, they do so in terms of symmetrical oppositions—GPCR/the present, dirty/clean, ignorance/knowledge, insanity/reason. These are the reference points students use to explain the GPCR to us.

The category of ignorance is particularly large and embraces a great deal: cadres who are not intellectuals and only got where they are now because of their slavish devotion to authority, villagers, workers, and the speaker's former, younger self. Generally what happens is that a student will come to talk to us about his or her former self and will contrast that to the present knowledgeable self after three or four years at college, that is, the one we see sitting in front of us. A similar opposition emerges when students talk about China and the West. Often they imply, sometimes even say outright, that China is ignorant, weak, dirty, backward, and undeveloped (although if you argue that China is a part of the Third World people get offended and say it is not true), while the West is knowledgeable strong, and clean. We try to keep in mind that during the GPCR the same people we talk to now relied on the reversal of this very same dichotomy, with China occupying the more dominant position—pure, clean, powerful, elemental, irreducibly moral.

The recent inversion can't help but make students very anxious because they are still convinced that in many ways China is superior to other countries. The contradiction in their own feelings leaves them baffled. If China is really superior, why isn't it also stronger in relation to the West? During the GPCR this problem did not exist. Young people could point to the power of China's masses particularly during the huge mobilizations, when millions of people dug canals and built bridges, erected new agricultural projects, put up buildings, laid down roads, and renovated many public works with nothing but raw human labor. Now the feeling shared by many people is, as one student put it, "if China is so superior, why do we still have to do everything with our hands?"

The opposite of ignorance is knowledge, which has been traditionally the monopoly of intellectuals in China, and our students are very much still within that tradition. One reason students attend our lectures so devotedly and drop by to talk with us is their need to know how the West became so powerful. They believe that knowledge is power, power is the encyclopedic memory of information, and, since we know about the West, we ourselves must be powerful. If only they have our knowledge, they too will be strong. We just cannot make them understand that in the West intellectuals don't necessarily have power, and furthermore knowledge is not encyclopedic information. Students sometimes drop by after a good lecture and say "we got a lot of knowledge out of that talk," the implication being somehow that knowledge consists of nuggets that can be mined by industrious intellectuals.

Many of them approach the study of English in the same spirit, that by appropriating the rules of grammar it's possible to "master" a whole language. The person with most knowledge of grammar "knows" the language best. In fact, as we found out, it allows the Chinese speaker of English to subdue the native speaker. The Chinese speaker becomes a metaphorical Henry Higgins, the native speaker a rather more sophisticated Eliza Doolittle. The department asked Tani to prepare the final exam for all the intensive readers, and the entire class of 1978 knew this. Both she and Don downplay grammar, and encourage their students to learn more about American culture, to practice their listening comprehension, to learn to skim, and to read more "extensively" than "intensively." Nonetheless, Tani's students started going back to their Chinese teachers to get more grammar. They were a little reluctant to let her know what they were doing. But Tani cannot teach what they want; being a native speaker, she doesn't know much grammar, and anyway she doesn't approve of grammar cramming. So they really were forced to go back to their old teachers. One session, Tani got the class to show her how they would prepare for an ordinary exam in intensive reading. They showed her how they go over every sentence, every clause, every verb, every adjective. Everything gets diagrammed. One very long, complex, sentence had given everyone difficulty. One of the study groups took it to the Chinese grammarians and were told that the sentence was wrong. So they rewrote it. The students were right in a sense. The offending sentence was badly written and the meaning was vague. They used the power they had accumulated from years of grammar study, found a weak sentence, and destroyed it. But, they also destroyed its nuanced meaning. Because even in English, the fact that a sentence is "wrong" does not mean it shouldn't be written, or that the meaning it conveys is less valuable.

There is no sense trying to change these scholastic habits. Our colleague Valerie has taught English as a second language for years in France, and knows other professionals teaching in Shanghai. She tells us very funny stories about foreign experts' attempts to change what they see as outdated Chinese teaching methods. Some have already given up in frustration. They cannot accept the obvious fact that Chinese students learn better if they can learn their own way: start with rote memorization, grammar rules, sentence construction, and then worry about conversation and shades of meaning, not the other way around. Valerie has observed that Chinese students learn to read, write, speak, and then comprehend aurally in exactly the reverse order stressed by Western pedagogy. The emphasis on grammar means students tend to neglect comprehension, but can easily construct very good sentences. They also have a habit of mouthing your words as you talk, as though appropriating the language issuing out of your mouth, or maybe mentally diagramming the sentences as you speak them. It seems inexcusably formalistic to most foreign language teachers. But in our experience, these students speak English more fluently after four years of study than their counterparts in the U.S speak Chinese.

In any case, our students are working voraciously now because the GPCR robbed them of time and because they want to stop being ignorant and weak. As a student wrote in a moving essay, "I was bitterly fooled. [The GPCR] deprived me of my youth. Because of it I struggled with all my selfishness and individualism—all kinds of bourgeois ideology. Now I understand that people ask you to be honest only so that they can easily cheat you. And they themselves tell lies all the time!"

Their histories are more complex than that because they were oppressors as well as victims. Students draw absolute lines between then and now, and because they cannot forget the part they played previously, they feel a need to retell their stories to outsiders. They want us to know what happened, even though they don't want us to know what they did. So at least in their relations with us, they keep on repeating what they want to forget, and they keep on avoiding the fact that it could not have happened without their participation.

It looks quite likely now that the GPCR will end up doing exactly the opposite of what Mao had intended; it will actually entrench scholastic habits and justify the prerogatives of the intellectuals. Mao tried to use the GPCR to undercut the historical position of the educated class in China. Before the twentieth century, the ruling "gentry" class provided the government with educated bureaucrats. Knowledge translated directly into political power in dynastic China; if a man succeeded in passing through the state examination system and earned a high degree, he would be rewarded by an appointment to a magistracy or an even higher position. Chinese intellectuals have a tremendous social legacy. Popular culture is full of images of scholar-bureaucrats, successful examination candidates, and other affirmations of the connection between bureaucratic or state power and book learning. The hangover is so great that, according to one student familiar with the culture of the very poor in Shanghai, college graduates are still referred to nowadays as "examination graduates" or *xiucai*, the traditional term for an imperial degreeholder. The Party is recruiting intellectuals now. And national exams make it more difficult to become an intellectual; once again, more "middle-class" than peasant and worker children are getting into colleges and universities. The state is reviving the arts of the scholar-gentry as national culture. Confucius's birthplace in Shandong has been renovated. Last week, a national symposium on neo-Confucian philosophy issued the following state-ment: "Scholars in China should criticize [Confucianism's] negative aspects and correctly evaluate its positive ones, to help eliminate feudal influence and construct a socialist civilization." Ten years ago, the idea that Confucianism had any positive aspect was un-thinkable.

Most students believe that they should have more power than people who don't attend college. One woman even said she thought the Party ought to be dismantled, and a ruling elite, selected by ex-amination should carry out another land reform. Student-officials would then set up local administrations, or satrapies, and develop a new, modern form of feudalism. That suggestion really shocked us. It had an uncanny resemblance to the gentry-mandarin ideal of rule by personal moral example, although our informant claimed she knew nothing about Chinese history, being a victim of the GPCR.

One day a very intelligent student read a paragraph in his in-tensive reading textbook about "progress," and commented that China should import "the idea of progress" before technology, because ideas precede facts. Students talk earnestly about "the spiritual elements" of life, a conception organized to resist the Marxist unity of theory and practice. We hear the same thing from most students: Knowledge is power, intellectuals have knowledge, intellectuals should therefore be running the government. So, to our students "modernization" means sanity, as opposed to madness; goodness, instead of the degraded rural villages; cleaniness, rather than filthy names and dirty places. It is quite possible—to return to the original image of the woman with the whip—that "moderniza-tion" will become just as emblematic or clicheed as the "Great Cultural Proletarian Revolution." But at this moment reaction against the GPCR is extremely great. And all that remains in public memory about the GPCR is suffering, despair, failure, disappoint-ment, misery, waste, and death.

Our intensive reading sections leave next Monday for their six weeks of practice teaching. Each class monitor has already divided students into seven or eight groups of three persons. Every group has a curriculum chief, who is responsible for the collective lesson plan. Members will collectively criticize each other, and the faculty advisers will evaluate the group's overall performance. Besides ac-tually teaching, our students expect to visit the homes of their middle-school students, in order to investigate family conditions and decide how to improve individual student's work. To some degree, career assignments rest on how well students perform in practice teaching. It helps that Shanghai Teachers College can send its people into the "key" middle schools in the city; that will give them a real edge on the competition for job assignments. Needless to say, the department has a stake in how well people do, so it is providing extra material, effort, and money. But even with all the aid, students are keyed up and anxious. They don't know if they will do well, or whether they will even enjoy teaching.

The class monitors are under even greater pressure because they are responsible for the classes' general discipline, and must make sure each work group gets along. Xiao Hu told us she was having a minor problem with a particular group where two students had had a quarrel and refused to work together. She is still at the stage of doing "ideological work" to mediate between them, though she may have to use force in the end. Overall, monitors prefer pressure to enforcement because force undercuts harmonious working conditions, the ultimate objective of ideological work. We also notice that monitors have recently been enforcing the dress code more strictly, too. All female student-teachers must either cut their hair or wear braids; dress is confined to low-heeled shoes, dark clothes, sturdy, but unflamboyant. The males must shave off their mustaches, cut their hair very short, and are prohibited from wearing any strange or weirdly colored shirts. The idea persists among people—not just Party members—that dress is a clue to personal morality. The government doesn't link pretty clothes to "bourgeois" morality any more, but many parents still don't want their children exposed to provocative Hong Kong fashions, wild color, or long hair and mustaches. So the teacher's dress code remains quite restrictive. Teachers, in fact, seem fated to become the dowdiest people in town.

Watching the students bring themselves up to code, we started realizing how comfortable we have become with our campus personae. Don is still a lot more gracious about the whole process than Tani, but it comes more easily when you are ethnically Chinese. Tani has just had to learn gradually how to accept her inevitable role as the foreigner. She still hates it when people patronize her by trying to teach her how to use chopsticks, and she can feel intellectuals laughing at her behind her back because she makes mistakes in speaking Chinese. But everybody has roles they must conform to. That is the meaning of dress codes, the strict age hierarchy, formal titles, and family terminologies. Tani has learned to accept her assigned role by studying the way people around her conform to theirs. Just as her section started fixing themselves up she had a long serious talk with them in class one day on the problem of dress code. It turned out that many of them disagreed with her decision to wear Chinese clothes. It was perfectly all right for Don to dress in middle-level cadre's clothes, they said, but since she was foreign she ought to dress like one, and anyway they like to see her in foreign clothes. They did understand when she explained how she hated to be stared at all the time. They said her gray corduroy suit was perfectly acceptable, as long as she occasionally wore a bright colored scarf from home. People feel more comfortable with her when she lives up to their expectations. The neighborhood people know who she is, and they don't pay any attention when we go for walks in Xujiahui. Sometimes, she envies the small, dark-haired Western women who claim they can pass as Chinese national minorities. But Tani prefers her present position to no position at all. Friends and relatives teach her what they expect from her, so she doesn't ever feel at a loss in a social situation. Xiao Hu once spent a whole conversation in Chinese talking about the "foreigner," addressing Tani directly, but as Donald's wife, and so a member of the family. We get the feeling that to Xiao Hu, Tani is two persons at the same time, the public foreigner and the private relative.

Don's experience is every bit as complex, but not as contradictory, because "Chinese-ness" is not really a category: to be Chinese here is to be human, everyone else being less than human. (The Western counterpart to that is our own parochialism in judging all non-Western cultures and humanities as less than rational, less than humane.) Gradually, Don is learning what specific categories he belongs to. He is, for example, middle-aged, a very comfortable niche in China. Even people who ask him directions on the street automatically defer to his graying hair, calling him "Master." Middle-aged people have authority and vigor. On campus Don's Ph.D. and his being a full professor in the U.S. thoroughly define who he is; no matter what the occasion, that is how Fang Quan introduces him, and since there are very few full professors at S.T.C. Don is quite a celebrity if only for that reason. We tell them that doctorates are fairly common in the U.S. and it is not as difficult to become a professor in America as in China. But by present-day Chinese standards a full professorship is about as prestigious a position as you can have. In certain situations, usually when we are off campus, visiting the commune, for example, Don may take the more passive role as the foreigner's Overseas-Chinese husband, and, as we are beginning to realize from travel experience, most officials mistake him as one of them, assigned—not married to—a young foreign expert. But on campus he is the professor from the United States. Although this flies in the face of Don's American urge to deconstruct strict status hierarchies and at times not only embarrasses him but really rubs him the wrong way, he is still more fascinated right now to discover where people intend to place him than to insist on his Westernness. A consequence of our hosts' manipulations is that Don feels a part of himself emerging that he has been out of touch with for many years, the part of him which might have been stronger if he had lived in a

Chinese community all his life. He discovers himself knowing automatically how to socialize with people, how to manage affairs with ease. He feels less isolated, more like the people around him, and definitely more touched and formed by them.

The more of the Gross legacy we uncover, the more we are convinced that our decision to conform is correct. Each week we hear new stories about the crazy American teacher with the beard, who married one of his students. All these stories come from Chinese, and we have no doubt that Gross had his own way of seeing things. But it is truly remarkable how much conflict and misunderstanding can result when two cultures meet so blindly. A bewildered female student came to the office specifically to tell us a story about how Gross had offended everyone at the farewell party the department gave him when he jumped out of his seat and started yelling "China is a gigantic prison and you are all prisoners. Your society is irrational. Every one of you is insane." We asked other students about this incident, unwilling to believe the first informant, and were assured that indeed it had taken place. Gross also griped that the farewell party was just a way of "paying him off." "They brought me here, used me, and now they want a polite way of getting rid of me," was the way he reportedly put it.

Some of the faculty have recently told us Gross's work habits truly baffled them. He began coming to class late, without a lecture. He dismissed class early. The most unforgivable thing he ever did, from their point of view, was to ruin the records of the entire class of 1977 by giving the following exam. He took a paragraph from a story, cut it into puzzle pieces and instructed students to reassemble them. More outrageous, the story alleges, he leaked the exam to his girlfriend, so she and her dormmates were the only ones who passed it. The authorities could not change his grades yet didn't want to flunk everyone in the class, so they asked him to give another exam. He refused. The crisis came, according to another student, when Gross arrived in class and stood at the podium in total speechless frustration, for half an hour—until the bell finally rang. The class elected a representative to reason with him. They asked him just to talk, to talk about anything, so at least they could listen to his beautiful, colloquial English. The student representative reminded him that on his application form he had stated that he could teach 100 different subjects, so there had to be something he could talk about. No results. The Chinese teacher in charge of Gross was caught in the middle. She told the students to be patient, but she knew something had gone wrong. Nothing in her experience had prepared her to handle such a bizarre foreigner. Gross threw chalk at students when they did not answer his questions. He bribed students with books, saying he refused to give the college administration the satisfaction of inheriting his library. But the single most outrageous thing Gross ever did, according to many students, was to curse his class by telling them that all Chinese people are like lemmings running over the cliff into the sea.

We don't know what *really* happened. But the significance of the conflict is easy to see. Gross and the college never broke the cultural barrier. Neither side could comprehend the other's point of view, or learn from it. Isolated, lonely, and unable to speak Chinese, Gross hated not knowing what things meant. But to learn, foreigners have to give up some parts of their Western personality. Gross couldn't do that, either because he wouldn't or because he just didn't know how.

Lao Yang says the department wants us to write the sophomore reader on contemporary U.S.A. after we get back from the winter break. Tani will also give faculty seminars on the history of American literature. The reader will be a challenge, since we'll have only twelve weeks in which to get it done. Upper authorities had to approve our staying on for a second semester. But the department made the decision about the textbook.

11

Modernism

Shanghai, November 11, 1981

Last week we saw a fascinating film by Yang Yanjin, a relatively young director at the Shanghai Movie Studio. Most Chinese films lean heavily on complicated plots. *Xiao Jie* (A Little Alley) broke this and several other current cinematic conventions. The plot was simple. During the GPCR a young male worker met a teenage boy in an alley. They became pals. Then the worker discovered "he" was really a she—when the Red Guards cut off her "bourgeois" hair she was so ashamed that she disguised herself as a boy. The worker tried to console her by stealing a wig. Unfortunately the revolutionary opera troupe which owned the hairpiece caught him in the act, beat and blinded him. By the time he gets out of the hospital the young woman has vanished.

By using innovative cinematography, Yang transformed this simple encounter into something special. The first scene began in the present. A film director (actually Yang playing himself) sits with the blind worker encouraging the man to relate his story, which the movie conveys through a series of flashbacks, a relatively new technique in Chinese films. Since Yang also refused to use an omniscient narrator, whenever the story reached a turning point he shifted from technicolor to either black and white or sepia, to emphasize shifts of time or point of view. The beating sequence was particularly dramatic. The camera recorded the action objectively, until the belt buckle smashed the hero's eyes. Then Yang subjectivized the entire scene by cutting to psychedelic color explosions, followed by a totally blank screen with a voice-over.

What intrigued our students most was that Yang refused to provide a denouement. Boy never did find girl. When the story reached the present, the director-in-the-film asked the protagonist how they should end their story/film. They considered three possibilities, offering the audience in effect three endings from which to choose. In one, the worker will recover his sight but find his beloved smoking, dancing, and wearing a provocative dress at a drunken bash hosted by the decadent children of a corrupt, high cadre. In the second outcome, the worker will remain blind, but discover that the woman is now married to the film director. In the third, the woman will find him on a train and decide to devote her entire life to caring for him. As each narrative possibility unfolded, the male character remained fundamentally unchanged, while his female opposite showed her essential malleability—decadent socialite, professional matron, model worker. Quite a number of our female students said that none of the three incarnations rang true, and so for them the end was the least convincing part of the film. But they still found themselves fascinated by Yang's technique.

What struck us most was the way the film examined some of the basic dichotomous categories of Chinese culture. In one excellent scene, the hero and the "boy" go to gather herbs for "his" sick mother. They ended up laughing and rolling around in the grass. That puts pressure on the "boy." So "he" begins to question out loud the oppositions of up and down, in and out, old and young, and finally male and female. During the GPCR the rebels reversed these fundamental categories of Chinese experience in order to challenge inherited habits of dominance. Down overcame up. The young prevailed over the old, and students made teachers their prisoners. Outsiders invaded the inside; and, at the very deepest possible level of violation, women turned into men.

This horrifying cultural inversion showed up in two other moving scenes. In one, the heroine stands at a mirror touching her shaved head. A long stationary camera focused on her double image as she began binding her breasts before slipping into her male disguise. Accidentally she catches sight of her sexless reflection; she smashes the mirror and falls down on the ground moaning like an animal. In another scene set in the period before she decides to disguise herself, she takes her violin to a pawnshop where she encounters a gang of Red Guards. One of them, an exaggeratedly demonic looking man, snatches her large-brimmed, feminine hat uncovering her shaven head, the sign of a bad-class background. To further prolong her agony, he throws the hat into a men's toilet room. This forces her to walk helplessly up and down in front of the door, eyeing her hat, but unable to step over into the sexually forbidden boundary. Many of these scenes were shot either with a distorting lens to emphasize the height and ghoulish appearance of the Red Guards, or in sepia, which Yang usually associated with abuse of the heroine. This allowed him to draw an effective line between the present order and the pathology of the past.

Yang's concern with gender as a way of showing the GPCR's assault on the "natural" order of things turned up again in the polarized image of female aggressor and female victim. We knew the militant image from *The Red Detachment of Women*: belligerent pose, hawkish eyes and painted eyebrows, sturdy legs planted on the earth, muscular arms with sleeves rolled raised in an operatic-style attack. In *Xiao Jie*, the Red Guard opera singer whose wig the worker tries to steal was the uniformed revolutionary woman with a whip, and the film did everything possible to discredit this vision of female militance. Instead it promoted a protagonist who looked like an Audrey Hepburn waif, a helpless victim, and made repeated references to female virginity, purity, and rape, by drawing attention constantly back to the victim's shorn head.

The four modernizations policy has revitalized the feminine woman. Magazine and television commercials link pretty, passive, decorative women directly to consumer goods. Our male students argue that while prettiness is still not as important to them in a prospective wife as good character and salary, they wish it could be. One older woman student claimed the vision of a fragile, feminine woman evoked strong emotion in her, because it reminded her of her ruined youth. People consciously associate the trend toward images of feminine women with their feelings of having been "raped" by the GPCR and deprived of their political innocence. Everyone knows Chinese women cannot look dainty like an Audrey Hepburn, even in Shanghai. Life is much too hard to allow that kind of frivolity, though several of the students said they were willing to go along with the charade for the duration of the movie. Also many men and women see in the filmic image of the pretty, delicate, helpless woman their own hopes for an easier future, just as the rape victim represents the horrors of the past.

The Boston Museum's exhibition of American paintings arrived just recently in Shanghai. It includes a few modern works, and students keep asking us questions about abstract art and modernism. To their question, What does it mean? we keep replying that modern art does not *represent* anything. This does not help much, because all students assume meaning comes out of realistic representation. Their next question is, if the paintings don't "mean" anything, why do we call them art? The gulf between Western abstract expression and what our students expect from art—representation, meaning, moral message—is very wide. We have tried to draw parallels between Zen-influenced Chinese paintings, a kind of expressionism, or calligraphy, a very abstract art form, and contemporary Western painting. One of the students particularly interested in art history made a similar argument; but his point that calligraphy is an abstract art did not convince the rest of the class. People rejected his comparison on the grounds that Chinese characters, no matter how you "abstract" them, still convey their intrinsic semantic meaning. We also have problems trying to explain Faulkner's *The Sound and the Fury* which has drawn a great deal of attention lately. The "Quentin" chapter just appeared in translation in the popular, intellectual journal *Dushu* (Study).

Several things, we believe, stand in the way of our students accepting modernist premises. Chinese socialist realism expresses many of their deeply felt assumptions about style and the significance of art. Now that they are able to study a whole range of styles, many still prefer nineteenth-century realism. Much recent Chinese literature has been built on the convention of realistic narrative. So the audience prefers novels and films to be heavily plotted, to have characters who represent moral qualities, to include meaningful conflict and provide a proper resolution at the end. Some came out of *Xiao Jie* shaking their heads, not knowing what to make of a film without a proper ending. Most basic of all, the world that produced Einstein, Picasso, and Faulkner is so different from the China of today that it is hard to explain why modern painting and novel do convey "meaning" to Americans without being representational.

When we first arrived on campus we were surprised to find a color-chalk rendition of Picasso's face, a short biography of the artist, and a copy of his "Les Demoiselles d'Avignon" on the fine arts students' blackboard. To us, "Demoiselles" broke the representational tradition in the West by initiating Cubism. We wondered what the painting signified to our students. So one day Don asked a group of his students why the display had been put up. One thoughtful man admitted that the painting really meant nothing to him; he'd assumed that it was there because it is a famous Western painting. Nevertheless, certain modernist techniques are currently being adapted. Yang had obviously been influenced by Western cinematic concepts of time, and that was what had inspired his decision to try and jolt his audience by withholding the denouement. The recent popular novel *Ren ah ren* (Ah, Humanity) incorporated a kind of watered-down "stream of consciousness" narrative about the GPCR. But these are still exceptions. People are investigating "modernism" and are extremely interested in it, yet they still have no real way of understanding it.

Significantly, the graduating seniors at the Shanghai Academy of Dramatic Arts gave a performance of Ba Jin's *Family* this year. We do not know who chose the play, the students or the authorities. But Ba Jin, one of China's most famous pioneers in the modern colloquial literature movement, wrote *Family* as a novel during the period of cultural upheaval known as the May Fourth period. The play adapted from it is a comprehensible, heavily plotted realist story, and several movies have been made from the novel. Most literate people know the characters and stories as intimately as they know traditional novels. *Family* is one-third of a trilogy that covers the history of a whole cast of characters all related to each other—and in this regard, as well—the novel reflects earlier, dynastic fiction. Set in the 1920s, *Family* focuses on the evils of the old Chinese family system. Subplots abound. The main one follows three brothers of one branch, much in the style of Turgenev. The adaptation we saw was not too successful, because it had to leave out so much of the novel, but we enjoyed it for a number of reasons. It intrigued us to hear the older, May Fourth language being spoken on stage. Also the acting style was half operatic and half naturalistic, with main characters giving highly expressive, romantic performances, while minor roles were simple caricatures. Seeing the play reminded Don of reading the novel when he was a boy in Shanghai in the 1930s. The fatalism of the novel had been an unquestioned part of the life of his social class then.

The May Fourth Movement was the modern anti-Confucian cultural movement which began in 1919 and continued to influence intellectual and literary attitudes until 1949. The movement's most prominent characteristics were its attack on traditional Confucian scholasticism and its use of Western fiction as a means of exploring new, revolutionary personal habits in a highly psychologized, contemporary, colloquial style. We bring up this historical event because we want to make a point about the borrowing between cultures, which applies to the May Fourth period, but also holds true for contemporary China.

At the heart of the May Fourth aesthetic lay a Chinese interpretation of Western romanticism. Romanticism in the West was fundamentally a reaction against classicism, and it celebrated emotion as a means of criticizing abstract, universal reason, just as it emphasized human feelings in order to damn objectivity. Western romanticism also encouraged the new bourgeois distinction between the public and the private. At the turn of the twentieth century, Chinese intellectuals borrowed from Western romanticism, but under completely different circumstances. Confucian culture had never emphasized a Western kind of objective reason. It made a distinction between the inside and the outside, but this had little in common with Western bourgeois ideas about public and private. Most importantly, traditional Chinese society had never provided the kind of individualist subjectivity celebrated in Goethe's *Sorrows of the Young Werther.* But when Confucian culture collapsed, disinherited Chinese intellectuals seized the subjectivity of Western romanticism and tried to use it to construct new identities. Similar derivation can be seen in the May Fourth women's movement which appropriated Western feminism and the Western female personality ideal as a way of rebelling against the traditional Chinese definition of women's roles. May Fourth romanticism in China gave way eventually to Marxism; in many cases, the same people who made internal revolution by reading and writing Western fiction repudiated the new bourgeois subjectivity they had helped to create, and turned instead toward the Marxist unity of theory and practice.

We are not saying Chinese intellectuals distorted Western romanticism, any more than Californian Beat poetry distorted Japanese Zen Buddhism. Ginsberg and Ferlinghetti used the Japanese ideas they discovered, in a very specific, unique American context. Their Zen enlightenment made it possible for them to overturn the heavy weight of the conformist, middle-class, consumer society of the 1950s—all with the fragile weapon of poetry. Still, it would not be correct to say the Beat poets "understood" Japanese Buddhism. Intercultural borrowing begins because something in the *borrowers'* culture makes alien practices appear very valuable, not because what is being borrowed has any extrinsic, unchanging transcultural value or meaning. The borrowing goes on all the time. Yet in spite of it, cultures never really penetrate each other.

It is the second week of November and we can already feel the cold wind blowing in from the Northern steppes. People warn us that the really cold weather won't arrive until December. Peihua gave us a serious lesson in dressing last week. The orange and black nylon long johns go over the white cotton ones; then add the regular shirt, two sweaters, and a woolen jacket. When you go out of the house put on the big woolen coat. The really cold weather must be very, very cold, because even with all our layers now we feel chilled a lot of the time. Finally we understood why we had to buy jackets several sizes too large. Fortunately, the foreign expert building will get steam heat, starting mid November. None of the classrooms have heat, so the authorities have put a small coal-burning Franklin stove in our office.

Life in China is not easy. The weather is harsh. There isn't the selection of fruits and vegetables available that we are so used to in California. Shanghainese are privileged, compared to other Chinese; but even they must stand in long lines for food, grain, and to board the bus. People have heavy schedules. The supportiveness of social relations makes everyday life more bearable. But life is much more serious here because it takes much more of an effort to live.

12

Socialization

November 16, the Chinese women's volleyball team won the world cup from the Japanese. The previous day they had smashed the American team in a game we happened to see because we were having lunch at Peihua and Mingzhang's that Sunday. Mingzhang and Peihua say they don't approve of TV, and we thought it was awfully strange of them just to switch it on right in the middle of our meal. But if they hadn't, we would have missed something very important. The following morning the atmosphere on campus was incredible. We had never seen the students so keyed up. Both sections of intensive reading (even Don's relatively unflappable senior men) interrogated us good-humoredly, but ruthlessly. Had we seen the game Sunday? What had we thought? Would we be watching the final game between China and Japan that evening? Fortunately somebody had pulled Tani aside earlier and given her a preview of what was to come, because her reading section refused to do anything until she promised to clarify her position. Drawing on clues provided by the first student, Tani told them that because of the circumstances (her husband and all the Chinese relatives were rooting for the

P.R.C. team), she had not been able to say anything. But in her heart she had been cheering for her "own" team. The students applauded. Tani had managed to come up with exactly the response they had expected. "We knew you must have been feeling very awkward," one student sympathized. They all said that they had thought of Tani during the game. It must have been uncomfortable for the American teacher with the Overseas-Chinese husband to watch her own team get slaughtered. Of course, no one had to ask Don where his sympathies lay. They automatically assumed he would be rooting for the Chinese side; the alternative would be unthinkable. They just wanted to know how it felt to him to see "his" country overcome what had been up to that moment touted as one of the best volleyball teams in the world. Tani asked her students how they would feel if the Chinese team upset the Japanese and won the world cup that evening. They said they would know that "Chinese virtue had triumphed."

China and Japan fought a hard, close game. Finally, the Chinese broke the tie in overtime. The victory had barely been announced when students started running out of the lecture halls where they had been watching the game on TV and onto the athletic field in front of our dorm. A spontaneous demonstration erupted. A microphone appeared from somewhere. Class leaders and department student representatives leaped onto the stage and made up slogans about the virtue of hard work. Someone read a telegram the student body was sending to the victorious team in Tokyo. A huge crowd of deliriously happy people milled around the field, half listening to speeches, but sometimes just standing up, suddenly, in the midst of a group of friends to let out a happy yell. Reserved female students were inexplicably throwing firecrackers at each other, and then laughing like lunatics. A woman from the athletics department got onto the microphone and teased the men, urging them to work harder so they could catch up with the women. A class monitor tried to give a speech. He shouted weakly, shook his fist, then convulsed the whole crowd when he got everything mixed up, threw himself off his speech cadence, and ended up giggling uncontrollably. A representative of the foreign languages majors seized the microphone and cried, in English "Long live the women's volleyball team of the People's Republic of China!"

This is the second time student enthusiasm has really startled us; the first was during the media blitz on reunification with Taiwan. Then students had become so excited they insisted on making up sentences about Taiwan during their conversation drills. Both incidents revealed unexpected depths of patriotism in our students. But they also showed, in a larger sense, how emotional they are behind all the correct deportment we generally see. One rather cynical working-class student told us it was exactly this quality in "middle class" college students that he distrusted most, their cheap easy passion, because it makes them so easily led around by the nose. Look what happened to them during the GPCR, he said. Workers, who have their own way of seeing things, he claimed, usually size up situations a lot more realistically than the pampered, overheated scholarly intellectuals. He is probably right about the students. But coming from American campuses, we just can't help falling in love with their maniacal pursuit of learning and their wildly passionate ideals.

American stereotypes—the withdrawn, dehumanized Chinese engineering student; the impassive Oriental hiding out in myster- ious, urban, American Chinatowns; the passionless, blank, inverted Other, to everything comprehensible, rational, and Anglo-Saxon —are nonsense projected through the filter of nativism and racial fear. Watching the students go crazy after the game, we looked at each other and started laughing. Shanghainese have a truly Mediter- ranean temperament. Their impulsiveness and their insistent need to touch when talking to you never seems to be quite contained in- side the reserve demanded by good manners in China. And it is quite true that in many situations Chinese can be very reserved. Par- ticularly on formal occasions or around superiors, people act with exaggerated politeness to stress their own relative insignificance. At those times people expect to act out a position based on hierarchical status, self-derogation, and self-consciousness. Their actual feelings might not be reflected at all in their behavior, but what is more startling than the politeness is the degree to which it masks "hot" feelings inside.

We've adopted Xiao Qian's metaphor to explain this change- about: Chinese are like thermos bottles—cold on the outside, hot on the inside. One way people express their heatedness is by talking at length about their personal feelings. People talk about themselves in an incredibly sophisticated way. With the big exception of sex, our friends and students seem unself-conscious about their inner feel- ings, or at least their inhibitions are formed and expressed in ways that are not familiar to us. Perhaps this is due to the present genera- tion's exceptional experiences during the GPCR. Young people grew up trying to purge their "thoughts" of all sorts of bourgeois flaws by writing confessional diaries, talking seriously to friends, commit- ting the words of Lin Biao and Mao Zedong to memory. All of these reinforced a kind of facility with self-analysis. They are still ex- pected to write "self-criticism" as a routine part of their cur- riculum, and many carry on long, intimate correspondence with friends, keep diaries, write poetry, and engage in self-improvement regimens.

Still, a great difference between Americans and Chinese (at least those of the 1960s generation, on both sides of the Pacific) is the matter of being looked at, and looking at other people. One day, all the foreign experts—Valerie and Anne, the older British woman, Don and Tani, and Nelson, our most recent arrival from Scotland—were outside doing *taijiquan* with our teacher. Immediately a crowd gathered, and a photographer from the college newspaper arrived to take pictures of us. This kind of thing makes Tani, Valerie, and Nelson feel very awkward, until they looked around and realized people were either looking or being looked at, all around them. Two students were boxing nearby, a man was teaching another man a martial art, some women were throwing a javelin, a group of students were playing volleyball; and they all, not just us foreigners, were being watched by scores and scores of onlookers. No one else seemed the least bit embarrassed or self-conscious.

In the West, we modify our behavior because we fear that while people might not be looking at us, they do see us and probably disapprove. When this kind of self-consciousness turns into paranoia, the troubled self becomes deluded that someone or something is actually controlling it. The conscience or "super ego" monitors behavior from the inside. We are not saying Chinese have no inner prompter. But the cultural convention of staring and being stared at seems to release people here from the feeling of being trapped inside themselves, because it does not make room for the famous privacy or individual space Western upbringing constructs and Western psychiatry reconstructs.

Contemporary Chinese grow up looking and being looked at. Tani did not. So many ordinary patterns of behavior here seem quite pressuring and oppressive to her, sometimes just plain rude, because people ignore the culturally defined space she assumes belongs to her, that is, her privacy. She winces sometimes when she is in a situation where someone else happens to be losing his or her privacy to the group. When she calls on a student in intensive reading others give the answer under their breath. If the person standing up answers incorrectly, everyone feels free to correct the error out loud. This is not common in an American college classroom. And in a sense the Chinese response is kinder, since no one is left sitting alone on the hot seat for long. But to Tani it is subliminally irritating when the class refuses to acknowledge the individual enough space to make a mistake. We interpret the constant connection of students with each other as an extension of this habit of looking and being looked at, and it helps us grasp the cultural particularism of what we in the West insist on as individual privacy.

Anne, the other British foreign expert here, gave a talk recently on loneliness in American fiction. Afterwards her students wrote little essays that Anne shared with us; we enjoyed them as another expression of the basic psychological differences between the West and China. One student wrote:

> The feeling of loneliness is universal. Almost everyone feels it at some time. Babies will cry if their mothers' absence has been found; aged people will look gloomy if their children have little connection with them or they come only for any reason except the passionate, emotional one. Lovers will lose heart if their sweethearts seem to be eccentric from them. All these feelings can well be classified by the term, loneliness. The difference is only that you will find a lot of people who are ready to help you, talk to you, console you, accompany you or even become your step-parents or adopted children. That is because we have so many people in our country.

Most students define loneliness either as having no relatives or having bad relations with relatives. But they all saw their own form of loneliness as a universal feeling, just as they assume all people love nineteenth-century realist novels and insist Tani must root for her "own" volleyball team. Many essays offered pragmatic ways to get rid of loneliness. One said the government should punish children who desert or neglect their parents. Another pointed to a new government policy which helps young people to meet each other. One person said he thought the government made people lonely. Another simply wrote, "As I'm young, I have no idea of loneliness." Someone else claimed:

> I think there is very little loneliness in China in 1981. But I'd like to say something about myself in 1977. I graduated from middle school in 1977 and unfortunately I was sent to the countryside which is several hundred miles from Shanghai. There I had to go to the fields working together with the peasants so during daytime I didn't feel lonely. But at night especially when I went to bed I was always thinking of my family. Since I was born I had never left home to stay alone. And every night we had talked about everything we did during the day or watched the TV. But in the countryside I had nobody to talk to. Luckily I entered college in February 1978, and that ended my loneliness, which lasted for about four months.

The next followed in a similar vein:

> There are various kinds of loneliness in China today, but none is serious I think, except the loneliness of the child. At the first glance it seems unreasonable, however it does exist more and more, and is neglected. Because of birth control, each family can

be allowed to have one child who is usually ignorant of brotherhood and sisterhood. The child spends most of his time playing by himself. The contact with other children is not permitted by the parents for fear that their child might be hurt or injured. Though in the kindergarten or the primary school the child might have a good time, yet once at home loneliness overwhelms him (or her). In spite of the fact that the parents love their child, they don't know what the child needs. Thus, the generation gap widens, and the child hides himself up. The best method to stop loneliness of the child is seemingly to have more than one child in each family. But the population will increase at the same time. I don't know what effects this. Maybe to make parents aware of what their child needs will do, but who knows.

One afternoon last week, Ruifeng, the wife of Don's other cousin Minghui (Minghui is Mingzhang's younger brother, and we visited them in Wuxi not too long ago), arrived at our dorm with her son, Xunda. She had come to Shanghai from nearby Wuxi for a few days, "on outside assignments" as they say, and is staying at her mother's place here in town. She came to invite us, together with Mingzhang and Peihua, to dinner with her family. Since Liberation, urban women no longer lose contact with their natal family after marriage. Daughters bring their own family connections to their marriages and continue to rely heavily on their mothers for support and affection. Under the old regime, a daughter married into her husband's family and was perceived as "belonging" to them, so her relations with her siblings and parents might easily erode over time. In any case, no one expected the natal relationships to be maintained. With the new shift in emphasis, kin language can no longer cover all the possibilities. When Don asked around how he should address Ruifeng's mother, no one could come up with the correct kinship term for a relation between the self and the cousin's wife's mother.

Ruifeng had arranged the dinner to confirm our kin relationship. Since kinship still provides the grid of most social interaction, one very old and sure-fire means of establishing a connection continues to be *tanqin*, finding some remote family relationship and celebrating it with a meal. No family can possibly maintain all the connections a large network offers. Which relationship you acknowledge and cultivate depends on the personalities involved and what you can offer each other. And in a *tanqin* situation no one tries to disguise strategic concerns. In this case, they need to send children abroad for study, and did not hesitate to let us know that. One cousin saw Tani admiring a baby and jokingly offered her the child to take home as an adopted daughter. We did not feel at all offended by the gesture and in fact wished we had the power to help out. Kinship is a language we are gradually learning to speak; and there are many ways of saying no. We enjoyed the dinner and the wealth of social possibilities the hosts offered us.

They received us in a very beautiful room, decorated exactly like our foreign experts' apartment, with the same lacquer-brown woodwork, a white ceiling, pastel yellow walls, all very clean and tidy. The beds had new cotton bedspreads; the deep maroon curtains were clean and pressed. A glass bowl on the fireplace mantle provided an accent, as did an inobtrusive, purple lampshade and a Western-style landscape painting. But to get to that lovely room, we had to climb a seedy staircase and pass through a dark hallway crowded with cases and boxes, and studded with the old belongings people hang on the walls with hooks to keep them off the ground. The room we ate in later had also deteriorated. Its yellow walls were faded almost gray; water stains had rinsed the pigment out in big, obvious swatches, and had buckled the plaster underneath. Exposed woodwork was cracking into powder. Over the bed hung a nondescript sketch of the young couple who occupied this room and who had carefully displayed a large number of family photos on the mantlepiece, far away from the damp, decaying windows. Both rooms had some solid, modernstyle rosewood furniture.

Ruifeng's mother and other family members received the two of us, Mingzhang, and Peihua in the renovated room, treating us to tea, candies, and special Shanghai cookies. As we sat in the beautiful, freezing cold room, still wearing all of our outside clothes, including the gloves, talking, joking, noshing, and waiting for the dinner, the children came in and out of the room to greet us. The eldest grandson climbed up on his granny's knees, while the younger ones played on the carpet. The adults talked about the children, their personalities, how badly Ruifeng and Mingzhang had spoilt Xunda, how lucky these children were having so many cousins, how well they got along with each other, and their school work. Adults reasoned with children, hugged, and petted them constantly, reprimanded then gently, and praised the littlest one when he shared pieces of his orange with his cousins. One of Ruifeng's brothers arrived and she introduced him by name. But no one ever bothered to introduce any of the daughters-in-law who sat everywhere dandling the children on their laps.

Ruifeng's widowed mother has enormous authority, commensurate with her age and social status, and makes no apology or allowance at all for her near total deafness. We think she has another daughter besides Ruifeng and five sons, one of whom is a pathologist doing graduate work at U.C., Davis. Of the other four sons, three are married and have jobs, the youngest, a victim of the GPCR, is both unemployed and unmarriageable. All of the sons live with their families in the same building as their mother. This second generation already has seven or eight children of its own. Originally the family rented the downtown, three-storied house from the Frenchman who had it built for his family. After Liberation, the renters stayed on, and as the family grew each son and his wife took over two rooms. Partly we suspect, because the autocratic mother decided to keep her family of sons together, but also because of the housing shortage. When people cannot find rooms elsewhere they simply have to subdivide what they've already got. During the GPCR, the mother told us, the Red Guards confiscated most of her fine furniture, but bits and pieces have recently been returned by the government.

When we moved to the other room for the banquet, all the sons disappeared to do the cooking. All the daughters-in-law sat with us around the table, each holding a grandchild. Not one of them said a word throughout the entire meal, except to coax the children to eat. Only Ruifeng, her mother, and the guests talked, mainly about Chinese family relations. Don remarked that he thought Chinese children had an easier time growing up than American kids, since Chinese children always had their cousins to rely on. The hosts agreed half-heartedly. After a little pause, Peihua said politely that the old family really was "feudal," and that she felt young people should break away from it. Our students say the same thing, however we had never heard it from a middle-aged person before. But not too many people have ten siblings, as Peihua does. People often condemn the old family for favoring sons over daughters, undercutting the ambitions of young people, making them too dependent on their parents' protection and authority, and for being itself a hotbed of "contradictions" or conflicts, since so many people have to live so closely together. (A very severe student of ours argues that the contradictions in the Party actually developed out of the Chinese family system. Since Chinese custom encourages old people to oppress young people through the family system, he argues, old politicians feel it is natural for them to dominate the country and refuse to give up their power to anyone younger than themselves.) Our impression is that the patrilocal, patrilineal corporate "family" or *jia*, has gained strength since Mao's death. This seems quite evident in the news media which tend to discredit powerful female role models and to reaffirm the effeminate ideal. At the end of the banquet, the sons who had been cooking came out of the kitchen to chat with us briefly.

In spite of the attacks on it for nearly a century, and more recent competition from the *danwei* (work unit), *jia* (family) still occupies a central place in everyone's social life. We've talked with other foreign experts about cases in which foreigners have been tricked and cheated by local people, even by their own students, and we suspect now that our experience here has been greatly determined by our family connections. The Shanghai academic grapevine is pretty efficient. The percentage of people attending college is very small, and many of them already know each other from middle school or professional associations. Besides, foreigners are always an interesting topic of discussion: Mingzhang has teased us every once in a while about the things he's heard about our lectures. And of course, we know almost everything there is to know about poor Mr. Gross. So inside the Shanghai academic community we are known as very well-connected people. We have to conclude that Tani has never been approached by an unscrupulous student for that reason. She is not just another foreign expert, but the wife of an Overseas Chinese, and a daughter-in-law, a sister-in-law, a cousin, and an aunt inside the Luo (Lowe) family. Our relatives and Chinese friends never tire of telling us reasons why we absolutely need the protection of "relatives and friends" (*qingqi pengyou*) as our buffer against the outside world. They don't have to say, because it is so self-evident, that having relatives and friends extends the circle inside of which *guanxi* operate.

The term *guanxi* describes social connections based on concrete, reciprocal exchange of favors and goods among family members and others. In a sense, *guanxi* is the way people organize relationships outside the *jia*, transforming strangers into kin by extending them favors and incurring obligations. All pseudo-family ties are cemented by this process. And ideally all relations between people should have a familist overtone. A Chinese doctor usually does not try to intimidate patients through a show of professionalism. Patients play on the familist ties between parent and child, making the doctor a parent through *guanxi*, usually giving the latter food or gifts. In return, the doctor is supposed to treat the patient's entire being, including feelings and fears which Western doctors tend to consider "psychological" and hence not a part of their responsibility. This kind of relationship cannot develop unless both sides accept the obligation to give and receive concrete favors as tokens of the *guanxi*. Unfortunately, *guanxi* and family ties also make it virtually impossible to fire workers even though the government has recently given managerial cadres the power to do so. If you fire an irresponsible worker, his relatives will visit you to try mediation, and mediation failing will harass you. In an extreme case, the worker might even stab you. All this would happen, because in firing a worker you are violating not only a business contract but a human relationship or *guanxi*.

This also applies to shopping. If you have no previous *guanxi*, (perhaps you neglected to give the clerk at your local grocery a piece of candy or a new year calendar), your chances of getting what you want are pretty slim. When mothballs come on the market once a year, there is a frenzy of *guanxi* reaffirmations. People give cigarettes, generally, in exchange for good cuts of meat. Gifts must be given to obtain better quality goods sold in the government stores. The more powerful the recipient, the more expensive the gift. The government campaigns against *guanxi*, which so easily degenerates into outright corruption. But it is extremely difficult to rise above such a fundamental social pattern. Life in China requires "relatives and friends," relying on them encourages *guanxi*, and since social life exists in a world of scarcity, the system easily sinks into bribery, hoarding, "back doorism," nepotism, and worse. Until the Party proves once again that it can rise above *guanxi* itself, reform will fail. And that rests, in turn, on how long it takes China to recover from the GPCR.

13

Media

*P*hotography is the rage now. Everybody wants to rent or borrow a camera at least once, to take photographs of the family. We've also met a number of young men who are turning photography into a serious hobby, and are showing their work in local photo contests; like the display we saw in Suzhou last weekend or the one that's going on here at the campus right now. (Photography contests seem to draw as many or more enthusiasts as stamp collecting, a quasi-official, intensively competitive hobby among middle-school and college students.) Many institutions—the city government, a factory, a school—sponsor photo contests and display the winning photographs in the glassed display cases that you generally find in any *danwei* or garden. The public bulletin board with its photo displays is so much a part of the Shanghai landscape that the American consulate has had them installed along the wall around its compound, trying to one-up the city authorities by displaying glossy color photographs of the moon walk, and other attractive propaganda images.

This is not a painting, but rather a photograph imitating the "mountain-water" genre of Chinese painting taken by Di Feiwan, a student at Shanghai Teachers College. The photo won first prize in a municipal contest. (Di Feiwan)

Prize-winning photographs inevitably fall into two categories, either highly stylized shots of natural scenery, or imitations of conventional Chinese landscape painting adapted to the medium of photography. Every once in a while, a high-speed action shot of women dancing, or muscular men doing the hundred-yard dash will also place. But, the one thing we have never found displayed at the contests, is an unposed "candid" shot, of the kind most common in the U.S. Without exception, Chinese artists and viewers expect photos to be posed, formal, and public. To some degree this emphasis, particularly the preference for photo-landscape, parallels work of nineteenth-century Western photographers who also began by imitating oil landscapes. In the Chinese case the tendency to copy from medium to medium derives out of a more general cultural insistence on narrative perspective, and the current assumption that everything—from political ideology, to social psychology, to literature, to how people dress—must reinforce a single, consistent point of view. In the Western world photography has developed its own conventions and styles, no longer relying on other media for clues. And we suspect that inevitably, as the camera pushes its intrusive way into popular Chinese perception, the temptation to use photography as a substitute for Chinese-style ink wash landscapes will eventually be abandoned. In the meantime, Chinese photographers continue to take formal landscapes that look like painting, and people "sitting" woodenly for posed portraits.

In her book *On Photography*, Susan Sontag says the photographic image breaks reality into little pieces. By now, the West is so used to the surrealism of the snapshot, that most of us are not even aware of how thoroughly it has shattered our world; we seem already to have incorporated the effects into our personalities.

The Chinese are still resisting that pressure. They find the ability of the lens to "distort" or select parts of "reality" quite irritating. They expect to put as much of themselves into a photo as possible, and they don't like anyone, especially tourists, to snap up little pieces of them. Conscious of this preference, we always ask politely for permission to photograph people. Sometimes we get it, but more often people politely turn us down.

Once, visiting a garden in Suzhou, we spotted some peasant women in colorful headscarves who were also enjoying the gorgeous surroundings. They made such a lovely photo that we went over to ask their permission to shoot. The women didn't appear to understand the Common Language (*putonghua*). But a man standing nearby came over and asked, "Why do you want to photograph them?" And in response to our rather naive answer, that the women were "beautiful," he said unbelievingly, "They aren't 'beautiful,' they're just peasants." The man's remark conveyed a sense of the cultural dichotomy between urban and rural, the definition of what is beautiful and which parts of reality ordinary people feel ought to be photographed. By the time we'd absorbed his lesson, the colorful peasant women had disappeared down the path.

How a people communicate meaning differs culturally. In China, the written ideograph or "character" has always dominated and controlled meaning—how people understand, think, and communicate. Unlike the abstract signs that make up our alphabet, ideographs communicate at several levels concurrently. Many ideographs are indeed pictures and obviously intended at one time to represent visual reality pictorially. This earliest function has been even more reduced lately, as the government simplifies the script further and further to ease the labor that must go into learning to read. Ideographs also function like any other written system, in the sense that people read Chinese for its meaning. But, in addition, the ideograph is also the basis for a sophisticated calligraphic art, which is enjoying a terrific revival currently. So the ideograph is at once pictographic, semiotic, and calligraphic, and can communicate at all three levels. Inside a Chinese cultural context, each level reinforces the others. Right now the photographic image, with its own distinctly multiperspectival, surrealist attitude is being introduced on a mass scale, as the technology becomes popular and available to even the hobbyist. The photo image here will probably remain a simple affair for some time, merely recapturing the likeness of family or a familiar scene in order to reinforce memory. The obtrusive Western advertising image, on the other hand, invested with all sorts of power, motion, and appeal, will inevitably put pressure on older Chinese perceptual categories.

Since the end of the GPCR, more advanced, potentially dynamic, advertising has proliferated. The rigid, severe political billboards of ten years ago have been replaced by a pretty young woman's face surrounded by a few butterflies and bees endorsing a soap, a facial cream, or toothpaste. A progressive couple holding a beautiful child proclaim the virtues of the new family planning policy. These advertising images merely reinforce the verbal message. As Americans we see them as straightforward and narrative. But Chinese friends have already started complaining about their overtly seductive implication. Chinese ads haven't yet begun juxtaposing or contrasting one image over another, because audiences are not used to the mixed, loaded interplay of meaning characteristic of Western image communication. You do not find things like the famous Levy's rye bread ad, which juxtaposed a picture of the bread with the image of an Indian chief to suggest that all Americans should eat "Jewish" rye. There aren't any ads yet where a sign and a different image are linked to form a third level of signification. Since Chinese consumers have been exposed to only one-level advertising, where an appropriate image is properly contexted by the message, those who read Western magazines find themselves extremely vulnerable to the flashy, powerful, semisurrealist ads in them.

Chinese brand names have developed without pressure from the West. In the U.S., corporate names are sometimes attached to particular commodities, like Coke and Frigidaire. We also have animal brands which enhance the image of a commodity. A man who drives a Mustang or a Couger gets the sexual power of the giant cat or wild horse, along with the car. In China, animal brands are common, but they do not enhance the intrinsic quality of the product. Most Shanghainese prefer Flying Pigeon bicycles over such other brands as Flying Deer, Sea Lion, and Phoenix. Phoenix has been the symbol of fortune for millenia, so not surprisingly it turns up on other commodities like cigarettes. We are using a Flying Fish typewriter to write you this letter, but there are also Flying Fish handkerchieves. Since people love butterflies, they can buy Butterfly cosmetics and Butterfly sewing machines. Traditionally, Chinese conferred favorable meaning to everything double, so we find Double Butterfly jackets, Double Horse textiles, and Twin Cat blankets. Panda wine and Panda condensed milk seem to borrow product recognition from the characteristic Chinese animal. The color white evidently enhances a brand, so there are White Cat washing detergent, White Rabbit cream candy, and Big White Rabbit powdered milk. We have also come across Golden Cock biscuits, Seagull shampoo, Peacock socks, Bee and Honey soap, and Lion toothpaste. Our particular favorite would never sell in the U.S.—White Elephant battery lights.

There are several ways to explain China's heavy reliance on animal brands. Since the state rather than private corporations controls commodity production and circulation, one wouldn't expect a heavy reliance on advertising brand names to sell. But Chinese thinking has always drawn a correspondence between animals and human activities. In *taijiquan*, one parts the wild horse's mane, stoops to spread the white crane's wings, grasps the tail of the bird, and so on. Brand names fall back on a cultural reservoir of animal or animistic images drawn from folklore, poetry, and language association. The important difference, so far as we can tell, is that these images do not attempt to enhance directly the value of a commodity or to sexualize it. You don't drink Big White Rabbit milk in order to look or act like one.

Chinese filmic image also comes framed inside the older, more familiar, fictional narrative. Films have big plots which gradually unfold to deliver definitive, moral messages. The audience transfers its novel-reading habits to the screen and expects a film to be novel-like, the more subplots the better. Coming from the U.S., we know the filmic image's potential to break older narrative framework and rely on the sheer intensity of audio-visual effects themselves. But so far Chinese films do not have the imagistic impact of recent Hollywood films. Someone we know attended a special screening of Francis Coppola's *Apocalypse Now*, at the Shanghai Movie Studio, and was absolutely horrified by the intensity of the film. Generally, Chinese filmgoers expect the plot to unfold in one, forward-moving direction. They find excessive use of flashbacks upsetting. We are accustomed to Hollywood films and tend to find Chinese movies too slow and not visually stimulating enough, precisely because they still subordinate the essential property of the film, its audio-visual image, to the older literary convention of fictional narrative. Cinematographic properties are used to convey literary narrative. We don't mean to deprecate these films, because once we do get into the narrative we often find them absorbing. It is simply that our perceptual habits have been formed by substantially different filmic and literary conventions.

Television is the most popular luxury item in China today. Since Chinese TV production remains limited and the studios cannot shoot enough film to fill two nighttime channels and both day and nighttime weekend television, the networks use a lot of foreign footage dubbed in Chinese. The evening program begins at 7:00 and consists of the domestic news, read by a newscaster sitting in front of a map of the P.R.C. This is followed by 15 minutes of foreign news, primarily dubbed-over news clips supplied by foreign governments and television stations. At 7:30 viewers often get Western documentaries. One night we saw a German film about horse breeding. This is followed by the Chinese equivalent of Western soap opera, maybe the story of an ideal courtship between a factory worker and a People's Liberation Army officer. One night we saw an excellent Beijing acrobatic opera, based on an episode from *Journey to the West*, a traditional epic about the adventures of Chinese Buddhist pilgrims to India. Recently, one of the Shanghai channels has been running a very popular Japanese samurai film, and a Hong Kong *gungfu* serial. Both of them are a lot more violent than the usual Chinese fare, and parents including Peihua and Mingzhang have started worrying about the effect this will have on their kids. But obviously Chinese television has not taken over and dominated channels of communication as has happened in the U.S. Nor does advertising play a central role. American TV's most effective programming is the expensive commercial with its fast-action montage. Chinese commercials, sedate and straightforward, have a long way to go before they shape popular imagination the way Western ads have.

So far, communication of photo, advertising, filmic, and televised images has not overturned the traditional narrativity of the ideograph. In the West, publicity image, sustained by corporate capitalism, has all but taken over our definition of reality. But the Chinese still prefer the formal portrait to the photo snapshot, the unilevel reinforcement of advertising sign by an appropriate image, the filmic narrative of a novelistic plot, the straightforward rebroadcasting of other media on the TV screen. We suspect Chinese image communication will never match America's powerful, multiperspectival media, partly because narrative is so fundamental to not only Chinese culture, but also to the communication of political ideology.

Monday evening, we went to a modern dance-drama performance called *Fengming Qishan* (The Phoenix Returns to Mount Qi), based on an ancient legend about the fall of the Shang and the rise of the Zhou dynasty. The performance combined many styles, including Western ballet, modern dance, and traditional folk dance. As usual, the dances used representational pantomine to act out the heavily plotted narrative. We didn't enjoy it at first, but after a while the narrative pulled us in. Everyone else in the audience sat in a trance, thoroughly enraptured by the innovative genre, which had been forbidden fruit just a few years ago. Everyone, that is, except for Lao Gu, the driver. Lao Gu is a traditional opera buff. At each change of scene, he reopened his program notes and poured over them once again, in a losing battle to interpret the peculiar spectacle unfolding before him. Hybrid performances do not interest him. Then, in the course of his ruffling, he inadvertently discovered an ad taken out by the Shanghai People's Television Factory. He stared at it incredulously. "What is this page of advertising doing in a theater program?" he grumbled to Don. Lao Gu represents many contemporary Chinese for whom realities are self-contained, internally consistent, and who see no obvious connection between a dance drama and television factory.

14

Generations

Shanghai, December 5, 1981

*T*uesday, Mingyao came to see us. He is in Shanghai from Baoji, "on outside assignment" for a few days. (Though they seldom get vacations, people often travel "on outside assignments" for their work units.) Mingyao spent his childhood in the interior during the Second World War. After the war, he returned to Shanghai and eventually completed his dental training in Beijing. In 1961, on his father's recommendation, he volunteered to resettle in Xian. Before that time, he had always considered himself a Shanghainese: he spoke the city dialect, ate Shanghainese food, enjoyed its semi-Western culture, dressed in city styles. Moving to Xian meant leaving all this behind. Mingyao thought of himself as a pioneer. Probably his motive for going was a mixture of loyalty to his father and political enthusiasm. Many progressive, patriotic, well-educated young people decided in the idyllic post-Liberation period to contribute their lives to socialist rural reconstruction. In the late 1950s and early 1960s, young professionals particularly volunteered to settle down wherever the government sent them, often in areas which previously had no medical or technical personnel. Mingyao stayed in Xian for many years. Then he moved to the small, nearby railway-junction town of Baoji to join his wife, who was a gynecologist, also a native of Shanghai. They now consider themselves provincials. They still love to come back to Shanghai when they can arrange a visit, but they no longer consider it their home.

Mingyao is heavier and sturdier and looks much older than his younger brother, Mingzhang, even though the two are only separated by eleven months. He speaks more directly and uses colloquial phrases we never hear in Shanghai. It also amused us a great deal to listen to him order his younger brother around, scolding him for his city sensitivities, boasting about the hardships real people in real places like Baoji take as part of daily existence. The difference between the country brother and the city brother impressed us. But we also are so used to sophisticated, indirect Mingzhang that we probably exaggerate Mingyao's rusticity by comparison. Clearly Mingyao knows more about the China outside the big cities. He enjoyed talking about rural life with us, and analyzed current problems without rhetoric, very honestly, concretely, pragmatically within a genuinely Communist framework. (He was still praising Stalin, for example.) All in all, his sturdiness impressed us because we never see it in the people we know here.

The interior of China exercises a real fascination over us. We have yet to get very far away from Shanghai, or see a real peasant, or a real village; so we have never, Tani keeps telling Don, seen the *real* China. Mingyao makes us feel humble, because he has lived and worked in the "real China" for so long. He is the sort of person we identified with and romanticized before we knew about the darker realities of the GPCR, and we still idealize what he has done with his life. He genuinely serves the people. Now we speculate a lot about what Don might have become under similar circumstances. He might conceivably have been molded into the kind of person Mingyao is, a determined, strong-willed man who has internalized great discipline and accepted hardship as a part of life. Or Don might understandably have broken under the pressure. As Mingyao talked we both automatically began comparing life in Baoji with our own very pleasant northern California lifestyle back home. Mingyao keeps up with the world from small, remote Baoji. He studies English, Russian, and Japanese. He has been reflecting on the lessons of American history, and after asking us to compare Lincoln's assassination with Kennedy's, he asked us why, in our opinion, North Americans had lost the pioneer spirit. Mingyao prizes this "pioneer spirit" very highly, and suggested that probably the only people in the U.S. who could still match the nineteenth-century settlers were the people of Alaska.

One night, several weeks ago, Mingzhang and Peihua had invited us over for dinner and Mingzhang told us a story he'd heard at work that day. A man went to consult a fortuneteller who had a reputation for truly uncanny prognostication. The man asked if his plan to go to the U.S. would be successful. The fortuneteller said he didn't think so, and refused to change his prediction even when the client said he had already managed, after a great deal of difficulty, to get a passport and visa. A few days later the man was at the airport just before boarding his flight to San Franciso. He entered the customs inspection and there the officials uncovered the gold he was trying to smuggle out of the country. They revoked his passport, thus proving the prescience of the fortuneteller. Mingzhang is a wonderful storyteller and after relating this piece of information, he winked and said he for one definitely believed in fate. But Peihua laughed and said, "the hero seizes the opportunity at the right moment, and acts with decisiveness." Mingzhang and Peihua love to gently pull our legs, and tweak our noses sometimes, and there is no doubt the story is apocryphal. But it circulates because of what it says about people's real lives. People do have a feeling that fate determines what will happen to them, if not in a superstitious sense, then with the same sort of certitude that Americans believe in the "power of positive thinking" or "where there's a will there's a way." Some of this comes from the way people are raised, by the rule of parents. That Mingyao would go to Xian and Mingzhang remain in Shanghai was not decided by the state, or primarily by themselves, but by their patriotic father. Our students sometimes tell us with great melancholy that they have fated lives because the college authorities are at this very moment deciding where they will work upon graduation, theoretically for the rest of their lives. So the mark of the hero, what our students love to call "the great man," is to seize the moment fate has determined for one.

Like so many educated Chinese, Mingyao is a passionate patriot. His own sense of determinism or fate was formed by his historical experience working with farmers and railway workers, and he has firm and very educated ideas about the problems facing the country. He listed the most pressing ones: (1) the absolute necessity of a population control policy, even if it contradicts the peasants' desire for large family; (2) economic modernization, which from his point of view requires a Stalinist-like work discipline; (3) educational modernization, by which he means not just the accumulation of knowledge, but developing a truly scientific attitude and methodology; and (4) the persistent problem of replacing unqualified middle- and low-level cadres with qualified intellectual cadres. Coming from a very intelligent, experienced Chinese who has worked in the interior, where changes proceed at a very slow pace, we appreciate the value of his judgment.

We invited Mingyao, Mingzhang, and Peihua to have dinner with us the next evening, and as the brandy flowed we answered his questions about America, and he ours about China. Then the conversation shifted to more intimate topics, and Don and his two cousins reminisced about their common grandparents, Third Uncle and Aunt Ruth, Fourth Uncle, and their respective fathers. Someone mentioned Minghui, the youngest of Don's male cousins in this branch, and we told them about our visit to see Minghui and Ruifeng in Wuxi, and the dinner we'd enjoyed at Ruifeng's mother's apartment. Mingyao seemed quite pleased with Minghui's career as a mid-level administrator in a modernized plant in Wuxi. Don had the same compelling feeling most Overseas Chinese have when they meet close relatives, that stretching across cultures and manners, historical accidents and the power of fate, the threads of kinship tie the Chinese family together. And for us, as we realize increasingly, relatives open a level of China which travel, acquaintances, and friends do not provide. And for that we are very grateful. Mingyao invited us to come and visit him and his family in Baoji next spring, when we plan to do some traveling. He told us that foreign tourists never go to Baoji. We leaped at the opportunity to see a nontourist part of the Chinese interior.

Because Chinese families divide more strictly into generations than American families, we socialize almost exclusively with the middle-aged relatives, those who had, for the most part, already matured before the GPCR. When we compare their experiences with those of our students, we understand what people mean when they talk about the generation gap. At the heart of this gap lies a paradox. The middle-aged generation—between Peihua and Mingzhang's age, and people in their sixties now—enjoyed a much more relaxed, unpressured maturation, because at that time the population was half its present size, and also the general atmosphere in the country was more optimistic then. Now enormous pressures have emerged, like overpopulation, which younger people blame on their parents. Reaction after the GPCR has led to the reinstatement of older, more conservative habits, along with a general anxiety about China's slow pace of modernization. All of this has placed greater pressure on the young. The revival of intense academic competition, unemployment, sudden restrictions on family size—all of these affect primarily the young. Our students' generation just now establishing families claims that the worst of the impact will hit the generation even younger than themselves, that is children the age of Mingzhang's son, who were impressionable children during the worst violence and confusion of the GPCR.

Articles like the one in a recent *China Daily* express the growing concern of parents and school administrators over the intense pressures placed on kids to succeed:

Schools and family pressures are seriously affecting the "healthy growth" of more than 60 million Chinese middle-school students. In a report on recent investigation of youngsters in ninè middle schools in Beijing, the magazine *Chinese Youth* said teachers and parents are driving the students so hard "on the narrow path leading to colleges and universities that most teenagers are out of breath." [Yet] fewer than 10 per cent of China's middle-school graduates can go to colleges.

Several of Don's cousins worry that their children might not pass the college entrance exam. So Minzhang, for instance, has hired two private tutors to teach his son English and math after school. Parents like Mingren who live in Nanjing, or Ruifeng's mother whose youngest son spends all his time at home for want of anything to do, have only to look at those of their children cheated out of even secondary education during the GPCR, in order to tighten the already highly disciplined regimen of the younger children who may still have a chance.

A look at the admissions test to Fudan University's graduate program in American and English literature illustrates what we mean. A hopeful candidate takes two rounds of exams. The extensive general exam aims at eliminating most competitors, since Fudan's graduate program has only six openings, and college seniors from all over China, including one from our campus, have qualified to take the first round this year. The general comprehensive consisted of six three-hour tests: (1) compose a short essay on how Chinese ought to treat and understand Western literature, using classical Chinese; (2) general examination in a second foreign language, other than English; (3) political education; (4) English and American literature—outline the plots of *Vanity Fair, The Scarlet Letter, Forsyte Saga,* and *For Whom the Bell Tolls*; comment on the Transcendentalist School; identify five titles and comment on them, for example, *The Canterbury Tales, Utopia,* etc.; and write a short essay on Augustane literature; (5) translations from English into Chinese, and Chinese into English; (6) basic theories of phonetics and grammar.

Our student had used three textbooks to cram for this ordeal: something written by a William Long, an outline of English Literature translated from the Russian into Chinese, and a brief historical outline of American literature in Chinese. It took him two months to memorize all the necessary factual information. He did not read any literature. Not because he didn't want to; but even in Shanghai he could not obtain all the relevant titles.

By the time of the second round, only twelve candidates, including our student, had survived. The second round mercifully took only two hours. In the first hour, candidates wrote on one major twentieth-century writer of his or her own choice. Our student chose Hemingway's *Old Man and the Sea*, which he had read in Chinese, for lack of the original. He listed works by Hemingway, talked about his style, his themes of violence and death, and the "optimism" of the mature Hemingway, which the *Old Man and the Sea* "expresses so well." The second hour required candidates to comment on the sonnets of Shakespeare, Milton's *Paradise Lost*, some obscure work by Lamb, and *Brook Farm*. Though he made it to the second round, our student was not among those finally selected.

The vital old professor who gave Tani such good advice about cracking the whip came over for dinner last week. Luo Qinsheng is head of the department's English teaching group. Now that the graduating class of 1977 has gone off to practice-teach, he spends most of his time traveling around the city to the various laboratory schools, overseeing their ideological small-group discussions. Luo has a "typically" crisp Cantonese personality, even though he has never been to Canton in his life. The notoriety of the Cantonese is amazing in Shanghai. "Oh, yes; he's a Cantonese, you know," people say when we mention Professor Luo, in somewhat the same way as blue-blooded Bostonians used to refer to the Irish. Luo began studying English as a boy at the Public School for Chinese in the Shanghai British concession, and spent several years teaching there upon graduation. His ending up on the S.T.C. faculty must have something to do with the Party (we never ask people directly about their Party affiliations), since he, Yang, and Fang founded the foreign languages department here together in 1961. He apologized for having no college degree, which is clearly beside the point because he speaks English as fluently as a native. Luo is a widower, living with one of his adult children, and spends his spare time reading his favorite nineteenth-century novels by Dickens, George Eliot, Thackeray, Mark Twain, and Conan Doyle.

Luo is one of our guardians. He always seems to know what we are doing and what we need to know. When we first arrived he came to discuss students' attitudes with us, and now that our students are practice-teaching he allowed us to question him about the next stage in their career. One part of his job is convincing graduates to accept their job assignments with enthusiasm, requiring in many cases a great deal of convincing. He counsels the disappointed parents of students who have not gotten what their parents wanted for them, he consoles students themselves, he can review assignments, make allowances, and decide on punitive measures when unavoidable. Graduates can always, as a last resort, refuse their assignments, but most do not because the penalty is no reassignment for another five years. Luo's position means he meets with students' families fairly frequently. People still receive professors with great pride, particularly when Luo makes courtesy calls on the sick or dying in the student's family. In this regard, he does what the class monitor does on behalf of the section but at a higher, more prestigious level. The faculty is concerned that the GPCR undercut respect for middle-school teachers, and they are trying to revive the middle-school teacher's status. They are increasing the time they spend with students' families and extending their responsibilities farther into the homes.

After dinner we invited him to our apartment, where Luo sat erectly in the center chair, as guest of honor, smoking cigarette after cigarette with enormous satisfaction and sipping on the turbid, green tea we had prepared for him. Never in the course of our conversation did he mention it, but he had not escaped his stint in the "cowshed" during the GPCR. All intellectuals of his age were "herded" into prisons called "cowsheds," and humiliated or punished. Like many foreign visitors, we have enormous respect for Luo's generation. Their stamina and persistence simply amaze us.

Several nights later we invited Lao Yang and Fang Quan for dinner. It seems natural to put the familiar *lao* (old) in front of Yang's name and just as appropriate not to do it with Fang Quan. Students kid Lao Yang and say she's an American. Anyone who speaks a foreign language develops a foreign persona, and it's true Yang has acquired American mannerisms with her English, whereas Fang Quan is definitely more British.

During dinner we talked about the college. Fang said we had no way of imagining the amount of change that has already occurred on campus in just the last few years. The college has always been independent-minded. To break its spirit the rebel mayor of Shanghai dismembered it during the GPCR, and gave pieces of the campus to other schools. It has taken the administration five years to retrieve everything and begin reforming teaching methods. Yang talked mostly about the daily operations which are her responsibility. She said she and Luo would soon be evaluating student teaching and preparing the senior class for its job assignments. Fang Quan has little to do with this aspect of teacher training. She is the long-term planner and does a lot of traveling, "on outside assignments," to teachers' conferences, and to Beijing to confer with the Ministry of Education. Both look forward to a rise in the English proficiency level of incoming freshmen over the next five years, as the current S.T.C. graduates take over middle-school foreign language instruction in Shanghai.

When we entertain guests, dinner is served in our communal dining hall, so everyone usually ends up joining the party. In the course of one conversation our older British colleague, Anne, decided to shift the discussion to something she found more interesting. So she initiated a rather one-sided conversation about her own lifelong desire to be a man, illustrated with portraits of all the different people she had never been able to become because she had been born the wrong sex. (The punchline was, "Who wants to be a *woman diplomat* like Claire Boothe Luce, for Christ's sake.") At the end of her rather sad monologue, she asked Yang and Fang "Haven't you always wanted to be a man, instead of a woman?" Both of them rather rudely started laughing. "Why, Anne," Yang said bluntly, "I have never thought about it before." Fang added in her exquisitely modulated voice, that she hadn't given the idea too much thought, either. Educated women of Yang and Fang's generation come from upper-class backgrounds, and have more authority in a relative sense than Anne's did in the West. The prestige attached to education made it possible for them to get jobs, if they could obtain a college degree. While we can be most certain that both women have encountered resistance from male students and colleagues because of their sex, Yang's reaction to Anne's question also underlined some basic differences in the experiences of Chinese and Western educated women.

In China, women never give up their female networks as the price for a career. Men expect to get most of their emotional support from other men; and women, no matter what work they do, are closer to their female relatives, friends, and colleagues than, in most cases, to their husbands. All women keep up contact with classmates they had as far back as grammar school. Professionals have strong relationships with other professional women and with their own female relatives. Women also develop pseudo-kin relations, where an older woman "adopts" a younger one. This has been traditionally known as a *gan* (dry) relationship. Yang practically treats Tani as her pseudo-daughter, supporting, praising, criticizing, protecting, and gently pushing Tani around. At first we assumed this was a feminist alliance. It is not. The link is neither particularly conscious nor particularly political. It is the natural extension of primary kinship into the workplace where women are still seriously disadvantaged. Yang and Fang's laughter was part embarrassment, part incomprehension at Anne's self-hatred. This particular element of sexual politics does not play a dominant part of Chinese women's experience.

15

Political Ideology

Shanghai, December 13, 1981

*P*olitical ideology plays a central role in Chinese life. It defines national goals, monitors social transformation, and intimately affects the daily lives of the people. Right now, political rhetoric is not as important as during periods of mobilization, like the GPCR. People are either painting over old slogans, "Long Live Chairman Mao," "In Work Style Learn from Dazhai," or "Down with Prof. X X," or just letting them gradually fade away. We almost never see a portrait of the Chairman anymore. The Party has promised there will be no more mobilization campaigns, to the enormous relief of everyone we've ever met. But none of this means that politics has retired from center stage. Ideology remains the dominant social language, and its core is still Mao's emphasis on revolutionary will.

In light of the GPCR, the Party has been reassessing Mao's personal importance. Although one article in the *Beijing Review* ("The Causes of the Cultural Revolution" by Zhu Yanshi [September 14, 1981]), admitted "Comrade Mao's mistake in leadership is the immediate cause," the June 27, 1981 Party Resolution on Certain Questions in the History of Our Party still insisted that "Comrade Mao

Zedong was a great Marxist and a great proletarian revolutionary, strategist and theorist. It is true that he made gross mistakes during the 'Cultural Revolution,' but, if we judge his activities as a whole, his contributions to the Chinese revolution far outweigh his mistakes. His merits are primary and his errors secondary" (*Beijing Review*, July 6, 1981). The Party has launched the four modernizations policy but the present attitude toward Mao might very well change again, if the four modernizations fail to deliver.

Political discussion takes place in journals, newspapers, political education departments, and Party conferences; but it also directly affects our students. The college administration no longer admits students on the basis of class origins, but ideological consciousness is still one of the important criteria. While they are in college, all students are required to take courses in political economy, Marxist philosophy; and Party history on a pass/fail basis. A political instructor and a class monitor, both members of either the Party or the Young Communist League, supervise the students' political lives. They lead by persuasion, encouragement, moral exemplar, and when necessary, by fiat. Everyone from the students and department typists to the deans participate in small-group political discussion each Friday afternoon. At these small-group meetings, participants discuss such Party and government documents as the June 27, 1981 Party Resolution, the economic report of Premier Zhao Ziyang before the current National People's Congress meeting in Beijing, and so on. At the end of their education, when students receive their job assignments, political attitude as well as academic performance are both weighed.

We've encountered a whole range of student opinions on politics, from the upright to the disaffected, and we have learned to discount both extremes. Students who try to impress us with their ideological rectitude come off as phony. Yet, no matter how cynical the others claim to be, they still strike us as highly idealistic and politicized, because our American concept of what constitutes the political is so much narrower. Many people say the present generation of students has a distinctive psychological make-up. Grammar school indoctrination in the 1950s raised their political sensitivities to an unprecedented height. Disillusionment in the GPCR broke their tendency to hero worship, but not their habit of defining experience through politics. In general, students now approach issues of doctrine with one primary concern in mind: How does it affect me? What can I get out of this? Deciding how to take advantage of changing political circumstances requires a high level of sophistication. And that impels students to study political documents.

The government is fully aware of this. We found the following fascinating official assessment of the present generation of college students, in *China Daily*, (December 12, 1981), which though written in a different rhetorical style confirms our own experience at S.T.C.:

> Researchers from the Research Institute on Youth ... went to Beijing, Shanghai, Chengdu, Hangzhou, Nanjing and Wuhan. They found all sorts of trends in the thinking of students, from dynamic to confused. Some had extremist and even anti-socialist views ... Compared with students in the 1950s, students nowadays have many weaknesses, such as in the firm belief of the four basic principles [i.e. upholding the socialist road, the people's democratic dictatorship, the leadership of the Party, and Marxism-Leninism and Mao Zedong Thought], in discipline and collectivism, and in public moral concepts.
>
> However, they have some significant strong points which compare favorably with their forerunners thirty years ago, such as they can think for themselves and don't indulge in blind worship; they want and seek highly-developed democracy and culture; they are realistic, and are sensitive to new ideas which they can readily absorb.
>
> The mainstream of students have the following common desires:
> — They wish to build China into a rich and powerful country. . . .
> — They support reforms and demand that the Party's style of work be improved. . . .
> — They want to promote democracy and lively exchange of ideas. . . .
> — They are concerned about their future and want to be of use to the country. . . .
> University students' main problems are the following:
> — Some students who want China to be prosperous and powerful are not clear what road to take, and want to ape Western ways.
> — Some who feel dissatisfied with the Party's unhappy tendencies exaggerate the dark side of things and tend to break away from Party leadership.
> — Some yearn for democracy but cannot distinguish between capitalist and socialist democracy, and thus tend toward liberalism.
> — Some are impatient to make a name for themselves and tend toward individualism.

This August, Hu Qiaomu, leading Party spokesperson on ideological and cultural matters, gave a 30,000-word-long talk on "The Tendency Toward Bourgeois Liberalization," to define the current policy on culture (*Red Flag*, No. 21 [December 1, 1981]). Western press has recently headlined it as an attack against the intellectuals and a return to Mao's 1942 Yanan talks subordinating literature and art to politics. But we have to disagree with that interpretation. The gist of the talk was on the need for "correcting the 'Left'-leaning thinking, while fighting against the social trend of bourgeois liberalization." And near the end of the talk, Hu stated: "The basic points are: literature and art are reflections of man's social life and life is the only source of literature and art." We believe the proper context for Hu's criticism against bourgeois liberalization is the political trends we have indicated in the earlier part of this letter, namely the needs of the Party to recoup its ideological position after the disaster of the GPCR without losing control of the problems facing young intellectuals. In this sense, Hu's talk is not and cannot be a return to the Yanan forum talks on art and literature.*

Beyond the definitions of left doctrinairism and bourgeois liberalization, the Party has also been making an effort recently to infuse daily life with socialist ethics. Personal conduct, moral example, and ethics have traditionally been the core of Chinese political culture. Personal ethics is the test of ideology, since belief should properly blossom into correct conduct. Not only the government, but families as well have always instructed children in the intricacies of kinship and social obligations, by pointing out models for emulation, and by encouraging moral reflection, enforcing the notion that others have an obligation to watch over you. We frequently hear older people bemoaning the decline in the moral conduct of the young since the GPCR. Most think the government is not doing enough to enforce ethical conduct.

Part of the current campaign is "the five stresses and four beautifuls" (*wujiang simei*). The five stresses are on proper decorum, manners, hygiene, discipline, and morals. And the four beautifuls concern mind, language, behavior, and environment. Beautification of the mind means cultivating political ideology, moral character, personal integrity, and upholding Party leadership and the socialist system; beautification of language means using and popularizing polite language; beautification of behavior means observing discipline, working hard, concern for the welfare of others, and safeguarding collective interest; and beautification of the environment means paying attention to personal hygiene, sanitation at home and in the public places. This strikes most Westerners and many of our Chinese students as a peculiar

---

*In late 1984, a leading spokesperson promised the Writers' Congress that the Party would let a hundred flowers blossom and a hundred schools contend, in order to enable art and literature serve the people. This is a further step toward relaxing control over cultural expressions, though the provisor, that art and literature are to serve the people, could be an important qualification if they are found later to be "not serving people."

combination of scholasticism and Boy Scout catechism. We see it as an integral part of the long-lived Chinese tradition of the officially sponsored moral exemplars, the constant linking of political ideology with ethical conduct.

The government has also launched morality curricula in the schools. *Beijing Review* (December 7, 1981) reported that since August, primary schools in Shanghai have been emphasizing courses on morality, imbuing the post-GPCR students with love of Party and country, proper personal behavior, and self-discipline. Meanwhile middle schools are introducing their students to Marxism-Leninism and Mao Zedong Thought. The article continued with the following story:

> The principal and teachers [of] Shanghai No. 1 Normal School noticed that children found it easy to abide by the rules of con- duct when they were with others, but were more lax when they were alone. At the suggestion of the principal, the students held a discussion on "When I am alone." They talked about how to over- come the temptation to give in to weaknesses when no one is watching, and about proper behavior for a child by himself. These discussions exerted a good influence on the children. Once, after a math test was graded and returned, 5th-grade stu- dent Li Fen found that the teacher had not noticed a mistake he had made. When he picked up his pen to revise the answer, shame flushed his cheeks. He thought, "I should be honest, when I'm alone," and asked the teacher to lower his mark.

The longer we stay in China, the more clearly we feel the power of this pervasive social morality. If you think long-time resident Westerners in China can escape its effects, consider the following exchange between David Crook and Jack Steele. Crook wrote a let- ter to the editor of *China Daily* several days ago, which criticized the national binge after the Chinese women's volleyball team beat the Japanese team. He pleaded for "friendship first, competition sec- ond," and criticized the manner in which the Chinese sportscaster had emphasized national competition during his coverage of the game. Steele, whose credentials as a friend of China reach back even farther than Crook's, countered Crook's letter in a subsequent issue of *China Daily*. Filling two long columns, including a capsule history of sports competition, Steele concluded:

> Winning may not be everything, but losing is not the object of play- ing a game. As to "Friendship first, competition second," it just isn't the way the world of sports is made. When it takes the field these days, China puts making friends and winning in world com- petition on an equal footing. Good clean play and determination to

advance in sports is the way things are done now. Smiling and shaking hands with a member of the opposing team who just stole the ball from you and booted it in for a score simply isn't the way it's done in the big time.

Reading these well-intentioned but peculiar letters makes us hesitate to stay here longer than our one year.

16

Maturity

*C*hinese society favors older people. The language uses expressions like "old" and "young" to make statements about the value of seniority. It's almost more accurate to say that ageing itself is a seniority system with perks, benefits, and power. Xiao Qian and Xiao Hu are *xiao* or small, young, junior, because they are under 40. The term *lao* as in Lao Yang implies experience, endurance, persistence, and the maturity only people over 40 have supposedly had time to accumulate. Students never call Professor Yang, Lao Yang, as we do, because it is a familiar term; but they all tell us they admire her because she actually is all the qualities which add up to *lao*.

Older people are troubled by many of the changes that have occurred over the last decade. They complain about everything from the decline in the quality of young people's handwriting, and the general lack of manners, to the confusion surrounding generational distinctions. They claim that mature people do not get as much respect as they once did. There is a great deal of truth to the claim, we suspect, partly because the generation gap challenges conventional thinking on ageing. "Generation" itself is not a completely accurate gauge of people's real experience, in the sense that our students, for example, don't really qualify as *lao* but their experiences in the GPCR have made them something more than *xiao*. Confusion not withstanding, people still use the terms *lao* and *xiao* as normative categories, even when they talk about such mundane practical issues like lining up for the bus.

The bus crisis has gotten a great deal of attention lately, even in the foreign press. People never line up anymore, as they used to do in the 1950s. Even worse, when the bus doors open, before the old people can step off, horrible, tough, young *a fei* or teddy boys shove their way on, bashing and trampling everybody. It's an interesting point, because what makes people mad is not just that they are getting trampled, but that it's very young boys who are the perpetrators, turning a violation of common decency into an offense against the seniority system. It makes us angry, too. We have started protecting old men and women by leaping in front of them like a shield to stick our elbows into the thug's bellies—they never expect it from a foreigner. At least we get a few licks in before we get stomped.

Even so, if you look at Shanghai social conventions from an American's perspective, older people still command a phenomenal amount of respect and power. Americans see ageing as a time of failing powers and feel pressured to hold onto every sign of youthful vitality. In China, the older you get the more secure your personality and social status become, the more extensive your *guanxi*. Our students may criticize the older generation now in power, yet, when it comes to a meeting or dinner, younger people always sit quietly and modestly, while the older people do the talking. We noticed this in the way people treat us, as well. Don is 53. His age is a real asset here, because everybody agrees that 50 is the prime of life. Attitudes toward Chinese women Tani's age, 31, seem closer to the way older Americans look at people in their late teens—awkward, very much in need of guidance, unsteady, barely capable of adult life.

Partly that is because people stay younger longer in China than in the U.S. Shanghainese pamper their children. When kids hurt themselves or just try to do too much and burst into tears, grown-ups almost always come to the rescue. We have never seen a child scolded in public. Adults don't have the attitude that children should be allowed to go on crying because it toughens them up, or that kids who get hurt should pick themselves up and stop crying to show how grown-up they are. People "oversupport" their children, from an American perspective. Mothers, but fathers, too, cuddle children all the time, and carry on long conversations with them, but so do siblings, grandparents, aunts and uncles, adult friends, and even friendly strangers at times. Consequently, children do not consider themselves children only in relation to one, exclusive set of parents, but live in a world made up of many adults who rank almost as highly on the seniority scale as parents do, like aunts and uncles, grandparents, grand uncles and aunts, teachers, the head of the school teaching group, the Party secretary at their parent's *danwei*, and so on.

When children leave the family their social connections expand to include more fictitious kin, such as schoolmates who are either older or younger "brothers" or "sisters," and later workmates. Part of childhood training involves learning how to address all these people correctly—*ayi* (mother's sister), *niangniang* (father's sister), *bobo* (father's older brother), *shushu* (father's younger brother), *jie-jie* (older sister, or honorific for all older girls), *didi* (younger brother and honorific for all boys younger than yourself), and so on into minute details that are gradually becoming extinct. Each term is a model for teaching the child how to act in its relations with specific relatives. Even people the child does not know receive fictive kin-name-terms according to their generational age (Tani is usually *saosao* because of her generational position as Don's wife, although her age makes this a very funny designation sometimes), and gender. Several times on buses we have seen a friendly older woman approach a younger woman and offer to help with a child or the bundles. The young woman instructs her child to call the helpful stranger *ayi*, which gives the child its clue as to expected behavior, and is an honorific term for all older, nonkin women. We even heard a woman say to her toddler once, as the two stared out of the bus window together, "look little brother, see all the aunties and uncles." She had transformed a crowd of strangers into potential relatives for her child.

Maturing really does take a long time here. Beginning with infancy and childhood, slipping into an intermediate period around age seven, when the child becomes *taoyan* or troublesome, and proceeding into a heavily masked puberty which people have only recently, in the twentieth century, designated under the category "youth" (*qingnian*). No one expects to have a Western-style independent young adulthood. Very little overt rebellion goes on. People in their early twenties do not look forward to experimenting with sex, drugs, liquor, or travel. As late as their mid-thirties, people of both sexes usually dress and sometimes still act like a dependent child. In the presence of a superior, like an older brother or mother or father, people automatically infantilize themselves as a gesture of respect for a superior. But convention also insists that young people should be sheltered from making choices for themselves. Parents, teachers, older siblings, Party authorities all take the anxiety out of existence by sheltering "young" people from stress. Many parents prefer to cook, shop, run interference, and find "back doors" for their children in the struggle for advancement. A Chinese-American friend of ours told us a story about an overseas P.R.C. student who attended a university in the U.S. The student, a man in his early thirties, had no difficulty unpacking his own suitcase. But at the end of his stay he had to call on his host to repack it, as it was the first time his mother had not been there to do it for him. As a consequence, it really does take people years to reach maturity or *lao*. Maturity means that you are married and have children of your own, who in turn expect protection from you.

We're not sure exactly what impact things like Shanghai's generation gap will have in the long run. But Chinese culture has never made a sharp distinction between infancy, childhood, teenage, and adulthood. The American pop notion that there are biologically determined stages of human development, each somehow fueled by automatic changes in sexual libido, does not find a very tolerant audience here. We lent a very *lao* friend of ours a copy of Gail Sheehy's *Passages* to try to convey how differently Americans view the process of maturation. She returned the book to us in bewilderment. She told us directly that she didn't like it, and apparently fearing the worst asked if it had been very influential. We suspect Sheehy's rather cavalier sexual attitudes probably upset our friend. In a general sense, the idea that sex—not moral development, not ability to apprehend "spiritual" matters, not even the basic capacity to act like a decent adult person—underlay American ideas of what maturity meant, probably made her unwilling to believe our claim that *Passages* had been a best seller. Our friend didn't know what to make of Sheehy's "developmental stages" either, since contemporary Chinese society still prefers to divide the span of a human life into specific positions based on concrete social relationships—beginning with the one between the parents and children, ending only with the death of one of the people involved.

Since they do not see biology playing much of a part in social maturation, parents stress what really matters, that is, molding and training. Chinese parents mold children to conform to pre-established "child" roles. Maturity consists of simultaneously mastering the position of the child in relation to your own parents, and demonstrating your ability to train the next generation into being children. No matter how old a person is, he or she remains a child in the eyes of parents and such metaphoric "parents" as the Party secretary or professor. People expect to receive parental guidance and criticism until their parents die. Individuals grow old and mature inside a continuum, stretching in many directions, rather than in a staccato rush of "stages," the first necessarily completed successfully before the next can be initiated. Social positions actually undercut biological age. That is why the category *qingnian* (youth) is used commonly, rather than "puberty", a sexual term, or the American "teenager" that carves a special niche out of youth when our society allows "hormones" to "rage" and children to rebel. Chinese youngsters shade quietly from childhood into "youth," their sexual maturation virtually ignored. The generation gap really does present a problem in this context. Mostly, people still assume that a positive moral value attaches to intimacy between the generations. How should individuals train their own children if all they can anticipate from them in the end is an effort to extricate themselves from parental control.

We do not want to idealize Chinese social customs. They succeed in preserving more continuity of experience, but they also press people too tightly, leading to exaggerated responsibilities which oppress everyone. Parents feel they must provide for their children until they are simply too feeble to go on. Children struggle to live up to not just parents' but also grandparents' expectations. In their old age, parents feel it is the obligation of their children to serve them in every way thinkable, from giving money to literally feeding them. Since generations don't split off to lead individual lives, intimacy means everyone in the family constantly meddles in everyone else's affairs.

The consequence of all these demands can be extraordinary ambivalence, as illustrated in a story that circulated all over Shanghai recently. A middle-aged couple had several children. They also had to take care of the husband's aged, quarrelsome, unattractive mother who was very old and in her dotage. One evening the mother became quite ill. Taking advantage of this opportunity, the middle-aged couple slipped some sleeping potion into her food and when she fell into a deep slumber, they wrapped her in a blanket and took her to the crematorium where they told the attendant she was dead. Unaware and overworked, the attendant agreed to slip the old lady into the fire, to save the cost of a funeral. This is a composite of the many versions of the story we and our colleagues heard from our students. Many informants said that while they could understand why the couple might want to kill off the burdensome old mother, they naturally could never absolve the couple from the crime of matricide. Mostly people talked about the story as though it had actually happened. When we took our questions to Peihua, she snorted. No one could possibly get anything but a very stiff, very cold cadaver past the crematorium attendants. She knew. She was a doctor.

The point of all this is, nonetheless, that contemporary Chinese society emphasizes the connections between people, not the "stages" unfolding inside people, and draws on a range of "natural" connections from kinship to pseudo-kinship, and on to other compelling relationships between people of the same age, same gender, same language, same district, same school, and so on. People always belong to some sort of group and are never left alone for very long. When a girl or boy enters college, she or he is immediately sought out by senior students who graduated from the same district middle school as they, or, in the case of national universities, who came from the same province or town. Older students take care of the younger ones, just as older siblings might. More obvious political collectivities such as the class section are also very important, because, in spite of internal competitiveness for grades and materials, the sections do become genuine communities. There are political officials, like the monitors and class officers, but over the years students classify themselves, so every section has its own sluggard, genius, clown, beauty, counselor, and so on. People get stuck with class nicknames, like "Fatty" or "Camel." And every section develops its own personality or esprit. We agree with the general consensus, for instance, that '78 section I is old, critical, dominated by men, and very demanding. Class '78 section II is seen universally as much more daring, imaginative, young, high-spirited, and feminine. Class '80 section I is too passive, '80 section II is a little better; but every section has a character, and since the sections stay together for the entire four years of college a great deal of mythology can develop to reinforce their characters.

In general, sex is submerged into this social framework, so mostly overt sexual codes don't surface in people's daily behavior. This seems particularly true in college. Male and female students do not socialize with each other. They sit together in the same home room, and we've kept our eyes open, but we just don't see anybody flirting. This may have something to do with their heterogeneous ages, and the fact that a sizeable number are already married. But even hand-holding is rare, married couples not excepted. We would love to know what goes on beyond our gaze. The dean told us that love affairs have been officially forbidden on campus because everyone's energy should go into study. He seemed to imply that something powerful had made it necessary to impose strict rules. And we did hear a story about a boy from another college in Shanghai who got several girls to sleep with him, before one of them reported him and had him expelled. (Sexual crimes are punishable in a variety of ways, expulsion from school or work unit, primarily. Ordinary, conventional people consider promiscuity as something between a crime and a mental disorder to be treated by incarceration in a juvenile prison. Rape on the other hand is punishable by death.) It might be that people just don't want to tell us stories about sex because we are foreign teachers and new here. People also know that Americans have very different attitudes toward sexuality in general (and this is one point on which they do see definite cultural differences).

One day two extremely young women visited our colleague Anne to be briefed about American sexual habits, before the two left to study abroad. They had come to her rather than the two of us because of all the foreigners Anne is the oldest, and presumably the oldest is the wisest about everything. Their question was: If an American boy approaches one of us and asks for sex is it considered good manners to turn him down? ("Since we don't do that sort of thing in our country!") It would seem that most people find it easier to talk about political discontents than to discuss their intimate sexual feelings with strangers. Only one boy has ever brought up sexual matters during an office-hour visit, and that was a gory "true" story about a girl who got tricked into becoming a prostitute by a street gang. We classified the story as a political "darkness" story (there really is prostitution in China) rather than a sexual one. On the other hand, a young female student caught up to Tani one day on the road and asked whether Americans talked about sex openly with each other. She had seen an American magazine, she said, and had been struck by how boldly sexual the ads were, so she had become curious. She blushed when Tani replied that it was not uncommon for ordinary "workers" to talk about their intimate sexual lives with each other.

Curiosity aside, our experience has been that students live very chaste lives. The regulations, dress code, study schedule, and constant emphasis on social responsibility do tend to put a damper on things. Other people have not found this to be the case. We met a foreign expert teaching at a provincial campus, who claimed that when she arrived in China several years ago students lined up outside her office to talk about sex. She said that she and several other other experts held impromptu, segregated sex education classes to accommodate them most efficiently. During the thought liberation movement of the late 1970s the general atmosphere, by all accounts, was looser. It could also be that the pressure to ask foreign experts about sexual matters has relaxed; after all we are not the first foreigners to teach at this school.

Young people in Shanghai do talk a lot about alienation. But with their very different upbringing and because of their culture's emphasis on making "natural" connections with other people who are "like" you in some way, students have a difficult time grasping the ideological tension in the West between "the individual and society." (Obviously individuals don't *really* exist outside of society, but in the West we have developed an ideological position which glamorizes the supposed opposition between the individual and society.) Students say they experience many sorts of alienation, between government and people, ideology and experience, the older and the younger generations, and between different political positions. But the characteristically Western notion of individual alienation simply is not a part of their experience. Many students find romantic individualism exciting. They identify with great men and great women in Western history, like Napoleon or Lincoln, or Harriet Beecher Stowe. But their approach to social life always puts the ethics of social relations at the very center of human value and expectation. Rather than personalizing ethics as a matter between oneself and a god, the Chinese tradition emphasizes the importance of the human moral-social bonds.

Confucian teaching stressed Five Bonds—between subject and ruler, father and son, husband and wife, elder and young brothers, and friends. To be an ethical person one learned to live by the standards set by the different bonds. Childhood training consisted largely of teaching children how to live properly with others. The system was so important that one could almost consider interpersonal relations a religious obligation. Even now, China remains a polity of moral persons rather than one of universal, transcendent laws. Schoolchildren learn about ideal social relationships between parents and children, children and the Party, brothers and sisters, and so on. When our students romanticize Western individualism as the solution for Chinese problems, we always feel skeptical. We don't think they know what they are talking about. We see their interest in individualism as a projection of their discontent, for no matter how individualistic they claim they want to be, underneath, everyone of them still expects the full support of Chinese social relationships.

Nonetheless, Shanghai society clearly felt under stress. Almost anyone will tell you that relations between people were better in the past than they are now. And the last thirty-five years, especially the terrible disillusionments of the recent past, have made new relationships between people and new ethical systems quite necessary. Post-GPCR Maoist thought and neo-Confucianism are very different. But each still stresses the problem of ethical conduct. We were aghast by the similarity between the neo-Confucian injunction that the moral person should "be vigilant over the self when alone," and the fifth-grader Li Fen's realization "I should be honest when I am alone." Both approach personal conduct from the norm of social gaze. Our point is that Westerners assume they are in a profound sense always alone, except perhaps in front of god. Existential solitude is a premise for Sartre and Heidegger. When Chinese intellectuals turn to existentialism, which they call "humanist morality," you can see an apt illustration of the difference between China and the West.

Last spring, the Shanghai Youth Academy of the Dramatic Arts gave ten performances of Sartre's *Dirty Hands*. We've also found out that at about the same time a Fudan professor came to S.T.C. to lecture on existentialism. Quite a number of students are looking for alternatives to socialist morality; existentialism seems to provide new, key concepts, and besides has the glamor of coming from the West—even if the students read more into it than they get out of it. So we are constantly discovering intense pockets of interest in Sartre among the senior students. And we keep on getting papers like the one Tani received on Kozinski's *Being There*, in which the student had used the novel plus a quasi-existentialist vocabulary to explore ethical problems.

Don got a truly magnificent existentialist essay, or should we say projection.

> Man . . . is without any support, reliance or relationship whatever with other individuals or society. Nevertheless, man as a sort of social existence has to be in society's yoke, no matter how hard he tries to escape from it. . . . Existentialism defines that man cannot in the least choose his social status, nor his being . . . but he may choose a way in which he faces them. Existentialism speaks highly of an individual's will and says that things become what man wants them to be. . . . To live is to struggle against one's destiny, to make a free choice of oneself, though this struggle may be a failure. . . . It is not up to man to decide the degree of cruelty the world exercises on man, of injustice life has for man, and how to this fate which God has arranged for him. All he can do is to decide to do, and he should readily challenge life and find his joy in doing so. This should be a living principle for man. . . . "Man is his own creation."

The essay is not so much an accurate description of existentialism as a mixture of leftover Maoist voluntarism and a keen sense of what fate means to a young Chinese. It is an honest, genuine, moving essay and communicates a real sense of the author's experience of suffering.

So-called existentialism attracts our students because they need a personal ethic. Some students make existentialism into a private religious feeling. It allows them to cultivate moral development within set, fated situations. It is extremely private, and it also seems to be reassuring to this particular student that his failure was not in vain. He sees Sartre as a philosopher who accepts failure, perhaps echoing the moving poetry of the ancient author of the *Li Sao*, as a way of teaching, of remolding the self.

Existentialism suggests itself to some Chinese intellectuals because it allows them a quietist form of self-aggrandizement that fits well with their sense of importance. That is why no one seems too interested in surrealism. Resisting students' desire to use existentialism as a way out of Chinese problems, Don goes around pouring cold water on them. "Never mind existentialism," he argues, "Sartre isn't that important any more. If you really want to understand the West, you have to understand surrealism. That is the art and aesthetic of the modern West." Don really believes what he says; but we also know surrealism completely upsets current Chinese sense of narrativity and moralism. Besides, surrealism cannot be easily incorporated because its intent is so completely outside ethics, human relations, religiosity, and hyper-emotionalism. Chinese students just cannot project their own needs through Western surrealism. So they really have to learn to confront it on its own terms.

Each of us tries in our own way to communicate to our students the difference between the two cultures, forcing them into unfamiliar ways of seeing and cognition. None of that "one world" stuff for us.

17

Two Worlds

Shanghai, December 28, 1981

Both of us received requests from our intensive reading students that we visit them over the practice-teaching period. Since no one ever tells us what to expect from trips, and we really have no way of finding out beforehand, Don wasn't too enthusiastic. He enjoyed his seniors very much. But he had all the sophomores still to teach, plus his new lecture series, and the plans for the textbook he wanted to mull over, on top of our "foreign expert" duties, so he kind of forgot about the invitations. Tani wanted to go and had committed herself to the trip but kept on procrastinating. Somehow, six weeks passed, despite a growing crescendo of hints. Having held her tongue for weeks, Lao Yang finally abandoned indirection and told Tani straightforwardly that no matter what else happened our students were expecting us and we were obligated. Don and his large entourage of department and FAO officials drove off in Lao Gu's sedan, on the day of his visit, to be met by an equally large entourage at the West Shanghai Municipal Middle School, one of the city's most important key middle schools.

Metropolitan exams select the very best students to attend key schools. Needless to say, many of these come from college-educated families. Don was interested in the new emphasis on key schools and educational excellence so he grilled his students about the emerging competitive system in the middle schools. They explained that college-educated parents expect their children will need outside help to make it through the college entrance examination, so they begin tutoring kids at home from the very early grades. As the children get older it is not uncommon for such families to hire private tutors as well. This hot-house forcing, plus the intense competition and priming in the classroom pays off. An average of 70 percent of the graduates from the key school Don visited enter colleges and universities, another 20 percent go on to technical institutes. This is in stark contrast to the nationwide average, where only 10 percent of all middle-school students enter college, and college students constitute less than 1 percent of the total population. Everyone is very sensitive to the class implications of this kind of an educational system. One of Don's students said quite frankly that the middle-class educational environment gives key middle-school students clear advantages over children from a working-class background, but that he saw no way of producing scholastically superior students without resorting to the key school system. As everyone was quick to point out, district resources are also being pulled into the key schools which adds to the boost the more heavily middle-class student body gets.

West Shanghai Municipal has science labs, basketball courts, and a faculty of 90 classroom teachers, for a student body of approximately 800. The school restricts class size to 45, as opposed to ordinary schools were class sizes of 60 are not extraordinary. Don was struck by the billboards he saw outside the teaching buildings, in the courtyard. Competitions seemed to exist for everything, students receiving prizes for excellence in their hobbies as well as their studies.

As he showed the professor the school grounds, one of Don's students remarked that he found middle-school students around the age of fifteen most intellectually curious. At that age students start asking questions after class, though not as a rule in class. Younger boys and girls either seem to have no opinions or are too shy to approach the teachers.

"Now that you've taught here for more than a month," Don asked, "what strikes you as the most important thing you've learned?"

"Previously," one student replied, "we had to study very widely. But teaching is more like pouring a large quantity down a small funnel into a medium-sized bottle." Don agreed that that sort of summed it all up. Then all his students insisted Don give them pointers from his own long teaching experience.

Tani visited two schools. Her own group of '78 section II were practice-teaching at 51st Shanghai Middle, a key school for the near-by Xujiahui district, where Mingzhang and Peihua's son studies. A strong connection exists between S.T.C. and No. 51 because the husband of one of the department's faculty has an important position at No. 51. A greeting committee composed of the principal, a few older teachers, and some minor Party authorities as well as a group of Tani's students met her in one of the home rooms. A minimal brief-ing ensued. Then, as the last of the officials stepped out the door, the class of 1978 section II swarmed out of their chairs and started mak-ing rude remarks about being polite, teasing Tani, telling her she had looked terribly uncomfortable during the briefing (pure imagination on their part), and insisting she must have been bored out her mind by the briefing (admittedly true). It's difficult for us to know how to take this group of students. We heard once they got so rough on a teacher that she started crying and ran out of the classroom. They do love to embarrass people. They are the ones who mock-innocently revealed the *guanxi* between S.T.C. and No. 51, right in front of the No. 51's Party branch secretary, who looked enormously pained by the whole group of them. They are definitely more daring than section I, Don's intensive readers. But when occa-sion demands they can be as ingratiating as any class.

When she acceded to Xiao Hu's repeated requests to visit her at the North Shanghai Municipal Middle School in the predominant-ly working-class Zhabei district, Tani had had no idea what to ex-pect. Xiao Hu only said she wanted her foreign relative to see her teach a lesson. The car drove from No. 51 out into one of Shanghai's previously most notorious slums, up to a new, spick-and-span, key school, the inevitable blackboard and chalk greeting at the entrance. Tani, the unflappable Xiao Qian, Lao Yang, and Professor Luo were ushered immediately into the back of a fairly sizeable, beautiful, newly built classroom. The whole faculty, the entire Party branch, and Xiao Hu's own classmate teaching group, filed behind them. (Later someone explained why so many people had attended. The faculty said that if the English teachers were going to be there they thought the entire faculty should get a chance to see the foreigner. And the school Party secretary and staff said if the faculty showed up they should too. So everybody came.) Down in front sat the 45 middle-school students, each with a pair of earphones. Lao Yang and Professor Luo took out their notebooks.

Suddenly, one of the young students shouted, "Class rise!" and in strode Xiao Hu. It was a cold, cold day. Everyone sat stiffly, feet already freezing on the cement floor of the elegant, unheated room.

Xiao Hu was wearing an enormous, fuzzy, gray turtleneck sweater. She looked nervous and fierce. "Good morning, class!" she barked in English. "Good morning, teacher!" the class shouted back.

Xiao Hu smiled only three times the entire lesson. She slapped transparencies into her projector, stabbed the pictures with a nastily pointed lecture stick, mouthed the dialogue numbly, snapped the machine off, and drilled her frozen students. They must have been as nervous as their teacher, surrounded by authorities, observed by the first native speaker of English most of them had ever seen up close. Only much later did we understand how much hard work had gone into this visit. Xiao Hu and Xiao Qian had put weeks into convincing N. Shanghai Municipal's authorities to let the foreigner come. The school had never had a foreign visitor before, so every contingency had been discussed, including security—just in case.

By the end of the lesson, the audience had lapsed into a near coma from tedium and the cold. Only Lao Yang and Professor Luo still scribbled in their notebooks. Xiao Hu dismissed her exhausted students. She and the rest of her teaching group took their guest into the language lab and asked for tips. Xiao Hu, tired but triumphant, disregarded the enormous crowd of officials and students waiting to shake the foreigner's hand, and put both her arms around Tani's waist and asked delightedly for criticism. Tani said she should smile more and relax, but reassured her that teaching takes practice.

In the car back to college, everyone criticized Xiao Hu: She had a terrible accent; she didn't use the article "the" properly; she allowed a student to respond incorrectly; her speech rhythm was too Chinese; and some of her sentences were unidiomatic. No one excused her for being tense and nervous. They had no excuses, for they assume that teaching should be hard, exacting, and tense. Xiao Hu might never become a great teacher. But she certainly has determination. She wanted her distant foreign relative teacher to observe her lesson, and she got her way.*

Behind all the drilling, memorizing, testing, and group criticism are some basic attitudes about learning. In Chinese, there are expressions like "it will come gradually" or "the student was influenced without even knowing it." People assume that students will learn, no matter how difficult the subject matter or how untalented the student. The belief persists from earlier times, when learning was still primarily normative. Confucian learning sought not so much to teach students quickly, but to make sure they

---

*Later, after returning to the U.S., we got a letter from Xiao Hu informing us that she had been assigned a job as a translator.

absorbed the ethical content. So "good" teaching sped the acquisition of moral knowledge. But the quasi-religious nature of at least the elementary stages of old learning also meant it could be gotten in spite of bad teaching. People now still assume good teaching should involve a personal link between teacher and student. Our students believe, as we do, that it's best to learn a foreign language from a native teacher. But they extend this from language learning to the presumption that foreigners possess an inner knowledge of English. Prolonged, direct, personal contact influences not only the learners' ability to speak, but their personal qualities as well, since all learning should affect one's character. (People are scandalized by stories about brilliant college students who turn out to be bad individuals, the implication being that with so much education, they have no excuse for moral failings.) All approaches to learning emphasize patience and endurance, and give students an almost passive faith that no matter how difficult the subject matter, given time, they will all master it.

Our students have endured our foreign teaching method, cultural-historical emphasis, and personal idiosyncrasies for almost four months. Finally we are beginning to make some headway. Don's lectures on contemporary U.S. society—politics, economics, social class, private life, media and communications, advertising and consumption—have been going well, and even the sophomores are beginning to see that the lectures present a consistent, overwhelming, undeniably different reality. Different, that is, from what they had expected in the beginning. Now when he talks about the United States as a capitalist country, or a First World nation he does not hear his students switching their minds off. Best of all we have both been gratified to hear that students are beginning to admit how different their world is from the West we have been describing to them.

Last week Don decided to give a lecture on modern art. His course material, coming on top of the Boston Museum Exhibition and the general interest among intellectuals in Modernism, has sparked quite a lot of interest. He got some oversized art books with colored illustrations from the fine arts department, and lectured to a highly charged, tense, excited student audience on the historic shift from Impressionism to Surrealism, and how this change can be related to other media besides painting, such as photography, the film, and the novel. The students were fascinated by the prints Don used for the lecture, particularly Ernst and Dali. Many of the older students had read about these artists but had never seen their work. Yet what really shocked them was that they found their curiosity overwhelmed by a deeper revulsion. "Where is the beauty in modern art?" one very brilliant student asked Don after the lecture.

These paintings, she continued, might illustrate experiences very different from their own, and through prolonged contact with it they might even learn to know it intellectually. But she doubted they would ever genuinely feel it. It simply was not beautiful, she said, neither to her nor to anyone else at the lecture.

"Modern art," Don repeated, "has abandoned mimetic representation. It is not interested in the aesthetics of 'beauty.' Isn't honesty and integrity of expression more important than the representation of beauty?"

Having delivered such a successful lecture on modern art, Don decided to follow up with a reading of Beat poetry. He selected Allen Ginsberg's "A Supermarket in California" and parts of "Howl." He read each poem out loud the first time in a quiet voice and explicated all the obscure references and difficult phrases. Then he read the same poem out loud again, but this time giving it a dramatic rendering. The audience finally grasped what a different world Ginsberg lived in, and how completely different from themselves was the audience he sought to influence. The student who had been troubled by the problem of beauty in modern art came up to say she had understood what the lesson was about.

Similar epiphanies are happening among Tani's students, as well. Not too long ago an average, not too talented student caught her in the hallway between periods. He said he had finally understood through her analysis of Dos Passos that American writers simply associate images differently from Chinese writers. This insight had then led him to realize that *USA* probably had one meaning to Chinese readers, and another to Americans. Now he wants to know more about American social life, so he can begin reading *USA* more from an American point of view. Students who come to her for office-hour discussions catch on even faster. They came originally to confirm their fantasies about the West, but have stayed on to confront the problem of cultural differences. Recently, in a very intense office discussion they focused in on the difference between Ginsberg's "Howl" and William's "Red Wheelbarrow," which Tani had explicated in lecture several days before. "Ginsberg is relatively simpler to understand than Williams and other modernists, since the one thing Chinese readers can hang onto in Ginsberg's poetry is its obvious passion," one boy said.

"You can easily feel what he feels," another person said, "because the emotions are so strong. He is angry, he is alone, he is unhappy. Williams's poem is more difficult for us. You asked us what the poet meant when he said, 'so much depends.' What does depend on this image? Without any explanation, the poem would have meant nothing to us, because it hasn't any emotion."

Eventually the conversation moved to the problem of didactic literature. "When we first started talking," another student said, "I thought no fundamental differences existed between cultures. I thought art was universal. I rejected the idea that when we borrow from another culture we borrowed what suited our own purposes. Now, it is a problem in my own mind. I see that twentieth-century Western painting and novel are really very different from our own notion of what art should be, that it should be beautiful, and what it should do, namely to instruct us. Western art in this century is not that way at all. I honestly don't like modernist novels. I don't understand them, but I am very curious about them."

Another got right to the point: "For the past thirty years we have thought of literature in terms of didactic purposes. That is how I always read a novel. I look for a character, David Copperfield or Jane Eyre, who can teach me some moral truths. I want to know how to live my life, what is the value in living. I have read Dostoevskii, but I don't like his novels because they are too realistic. When I read that sort of fiction which describes hardship or cruelty, I feel uncomfortable. There are writers in China now, who are raising the question of what we should write about, what we should teach through our literature, how we should teach it. But their answers are not especially enlightening. When I read, I either want to learn something of a moral nature, or I simply want to escape from the real world into a dream, into a fantasy."

The first student said she felt the moral focus of Chinese "feudal" literature was actually good. "In our society, though our cultural, material lives are inferior to the West, we actually conserve many moral patterns which make our lives meaningful. Even so, we have been through many terrible experiences in the past ten years, and frankly I have little desire to read about them in fiction. We know such things exist. We have experienced them firsthand. Why read about? I cannot imagine a literature which is not fundamentally didactic."

Yet, Tani feels that many of her students are indeed shifting from the question "what moral lesson can I learn from *Jane Eyre?*" to "why do Ginsberg and Faulkner write the way they do; what's so important about the red wheelbarrow; and what sort of vision of America does 'Howl' or *The Great Gatsby* express?"

Don's open lectures on Western civilization have also been arousing interest. He usually gets between 70 and 100 auditors, most from the foreign languages department, and others from the history department and from nearby colleges, plus an old retired professor of jurisprudence who studied at the Sorbonne many years ago. This week a couple of very polite, male history majors came up to ask Don to drop by their dorm after lecture to meet their friends.

Don welcomed that. We've been quite curious about other students on campus, and Don wanted to find out whether history majors here have a better grasp of social and cultural contexts than the language majors.

The students took him to their dorm—a clean, narrow, but very crowded oblong room with four double-decker bunkbeds along the two walls, and a row of tables running down the center. A dozen eager, polite, deadly determined students inquired about his health, and finally, having finished all the politenesses and formalities, began grilling him: What did Don think of Wittfogel's *Oriental Despotism*? Are there any good comparative studies of the West and China? Could he compare Indian to Chinese development? Don was delighted with that question since our experience with the language majors has consistently been that they refuse to see China as part of the Third World. How are Chinese young people different from American youths? What about a comparison of the two groups in the sixties? How important is Marxist historiography in Western academia? How do Chinese students compare with American students? How much do most Americans know about the GPCR? What happened to the Black Panther Party? After an hour and a half, they asked Don to return for another meeting and cover more ground. Clearly the history students are substantially better informed and more theoretically and analytically sophisticated than the language majors.

The second meeting took place in a large classroom with about 40 or 50 students attending. How would he criticize E. H. Carr's *What is History*? (A previous foreign expert had criticized it severely.) Compare the training of historians in Britain, France, and the United States. Explain your own approach to history. Why do American Sinologists emphasize the importance of bureaucratic society in pre-modern China? What about the problem of accidents and coincidences in history? A few students even made polite, but firm criticisms of some of Don's answers, which impressed him a great deal because he's gotten used to the foreign language students' kid glove treatment of "their" foreign experts. On the way home he queried this attitude, and the student escorting him said that he felt history majors were generally more intelligent than language majors. And across the board in all departments, the seniors and juniors are smarter than the younger students because the former lived through the GPCR.

A couple of weeks ago we had an opportunity to look at the world our students inhabit reflected though the prism of a movie called *Ke cong he lai* or *Whence Came the Guests*. It made us feel uncomfortable for it showed a whole range of stereotyped foreigners. The story was set at the Canton trade fair. Most of the assorted

Europeans, Arabs, and Overseas-Chinese characters in the film represented unattractive but innocent businessmen. A few had come on a mission of industrial espionage. The plot called for the male police chief and his upright female detective to discover which of the foreigners are the spies. The plot was terrible and the acting an affront, but we did learn a lot about how Chinese filmmakers stereotype non-Chinese.

There was a stereotype to offend each one of us. The story's chief suspect, a tall, thin lecherous Scot called McGregor, had a gorgeous, sexy secretary to take his dictation. Since he is such a rotten fellow he propositions her, and strangely when she turns him down he starts crying like a baby. After that encounter, McGregor either works too hard making money or sits around in the bar drinking (what else?) Scotch. Needless to say, our colleague Nelson who actually is a Scot found this characterization unrealistic and foolish. Kathy, the beautiful secretary, who turns McGregor down, ends up disgracing herself anyway. She falls in love *at first sight* with another man; unable to contain her passion she immediately slow-dances with him (gasps of horror from the audience!), and later that evening kisses and hugs him (more gasps). Tani took offense at the exaggeration, and the way American women are always blamed for what Chinese perceive as Western sexual excesses. Don got his, when a group of Overseas Chinese with long, greasy hair and circa 1940-style zoot suits entered the picture, diamond rings on their little fingers, conniving endlessly with each other about how to cheat people in a series of sneaky business speculations. Fortunately for international friendship, all the inscrutable foreigners turned out to be innocent. The culprits were Guomindang agents sent from Taiwan.

We suspect the tendency to stereotype foreigners and other out groups might be even stronger in China, where manners, costumes, and behavior attitudes indicate one's position and status even more than in the U.S. You would never find an important Chinese person in public, dressed in their society's equivalent of blue jeans or jogging shoes. In order to establish genuine contact, foreigners have to circumvent some very unflattering stereotypes. But, like everywhere else, it's possible. Don has a Caucasian aunt who spent years teaching English in China. Once, when her children were playing with some other kids, Aunt Ruth overheard one of the kids say, "Do you know the foreigner living in that house?" "That's no foreigner," countered a second kid, "she is Mingde's mother."

Sometimes we foreigners simply compound the problem. We know a certain Mary K., a very strait-laced American liberal-feminist in her early forties, who teaches at a technical institute in the city. Recently, Mary invited some of her foreign expert friends to join her and a group of her students for a Christmas party. They all gathered in her hotel room and enjoyed the cookies and punch which she had arranged. Then Mary passed out song sheets so everyone could sing carols. Many Chinese guests already knew the old songs like "Jingle Bells" and "God Rest Ye Merry Gentlemen." However, Mary had carefully purged the lyrics in the version she handed out. So instead of a song about merry gentlemen, the words of her song sheet read "God rest ye merrie gentlefolk." "Christmas" had become "Marymas"—as it should, since really the mass belongs to the Virgin Mother rather than the Child. The more discrepancies they discovered in the lyrics, the more polite her Chinese guests became. Finally, out of sheer desperation apparently, they started giggling helplessly like little children. We only heard the story because Valerie attended the party and came over to ask us whether Chinese people always act so ridiculously at parties. We told her they did not any more than Western people acted ridiculously at Chinese parties, and interpreted the giggling as the result of polite people being confronted with completely inexplicable demands. Perhaps, in this case, giggling signified their terrible anxiety, since there were no clues to help them explain what Mary had done and what she expected them to do under the circumstances.

Before she could expect her Chinese students to understand the significance of American feminist liturgical reforms, Mary would have had to explain the following: (1) the patriarchal roots of the Christian liturgy; (2) how popular culture in the U.S. has been changed by the consciousness-raising movements of the 1960s and 1970s; (3) the objectives of Western bourgeois feminism; (4) the dilemma of a woman who is at once a feminist and a Christian; (5) the underlying contemporary Western assumption that people's sexual identities are the most important part of their personality make-up; and (6) the meaning of this specific Western feminist reform in a society like China's, where people see the "women's problem" in a totally different context. No wonder Mary K. confused her guests.

The morning of December 26, Don's intensive reading section sent a large delegation to our dorm with a huge Western cake. They admitted that the FAO had alerted them to the fact that the next day was Don's birthday. The following morning, Xiao Qian arrived with a card signed by Xiao Shen and himself. Around 3 P.M. Lao Chen the FAO chief brought over the official *danwei* cake frosted with whipped cream. After supper, Xiao Hu filially arrived with her contribution, a small birthday cake she had bought at a downtown bakery. And that is how we found out how many cakes an Overseas-Chinese full professor, 53 years old, merits. Don happily ate a piece from each.

18

Children

Since the intensive reading students returned from their training at the key middle schools, they have been using class discussion time to talk about domestic life. Generally they agree the trend toward child-centeredness has accelerated. Parents in their late twenties to early forties tend to swaddle and pamper their infants. Peihua says, in her experience as a pediatrician, parents are not using their common sense as they used to and tend to rush children to the clinic for minor stuffy noses and imagined illnesses. Among younger parents the view prevails that childcare centers are dangerous in two senses: attendants are illiterate and therefore a "bad" influence, and the children sent there catch too many colds from each other.

In most young Shanghai families both parents work, so finding good childcare has emerged as a major problem. Very few people make enough money to hire babysitters. Parents who either can't get into a daycare center, or refuse to subject their child to unknown dangers there, turn to relatives. Overwhelmingly couples prefer the wife's mother, rather than the husband's mother, because bringing the latter into the picture runs the risk of setting up the old explosive confrontation between husband's mother and wife. Maternal grandmother taking over the childcare appears to be relatively commonplace. (Official encouragement aside, grandfathers take very little part in raising young children, and do not as a rule do any housework. As one middle-aged woman we know said firmly, old men are simply "incorrigible." Sometimes they agree to do some cooking after they retire because they have spare time and need a hobby; and it gives them a good way of embarrassing their wives. Men who cook feel entitled to criticize the food their wives served all those years.) Young couples agonize over the problem of childcare, because having grandma around constantly means she will meddle more in the couple's intimate life. The trade-off is the security of their only child. Since Shanghai's inadequate housing means young couples often begin married life living with in-laws anyway, the desire to protect the child by remaining where they are, in grandma's house, sometimes conflicts with the desire for a separate living space.

We wonder how grandmothers raise these children. Several of our adult female students have told us they feel the effect having been raised by grandmothers. Such a great gap separated the very old-fashioned expectations bred into them by the older women, from the modern ideas about women's social roles taught in schools, later. Interestingly, everyone can agree on one thing: children today are spoiled rotten. According to our friends, relatives, and students, the present child-centeredness is a very recent phenomenon. In the fifties and sixties, the government encouraged large families. Child rearing continued to focus on hierarchical distinctions and the separation between parents and children. We discussed this older pattern with a man in his early thirties, who told us that when he and his brothers and sisters were children, their parents never took them to the movies or to adults' parties. Children then didn't expect their parents to include them. He said he had had a very nice childhood, an evaluation we have learned to expect from people of his generation. He spoke uncritically about the simple facts of his childhood: ingrained respect for parents and teachers, strong discipline, a settled sense of knowing his place. He did not complain about the repressiveness of family life, or even unfair fathers, teachers, or authorities, as one might have expected, given his generation's anti-authoritarianism during the GPCR.

One thing this man and many other students have criticized is the complex, almost institutionalized way their generation had learned to depend on their parents for success in later life. One woman said that when she was young, her parents expected to help their children get into a key school, qualify for a good university, find a high status job, and select a "good" spouse. Parents who objected to all the interference still had to do it; otherwise, they genuinely disadvantaged their own children. Other students have commented to us that since parents habitually did these things, children ended up being too dependent on adult protection and authority. When our classes argue that they were overprotected by their parents, the implication always seems to be that this coddling led to naiveté and that is why they failed to see through the rhetoric of the GPCR. This shifts the blame backward a generation, and encourages young adults in their habit of using the GPCR as a substitute for analysis, a way of explaining away all problems.

These memories of generational dependence form the context for what everyone claims is a new problem: the generation gap. We asked students to describe the generation gap, and they said it had originally begun during the GPCR when they were teenagers. Many of them said they suddenly felt they no longer had anything to say to their parents and avoided being seen on the street with them. They felt they could only confide their inner feelings to other young people. We told them that in the U.S. we *expect* teenagers to go through that "stage." But they were so intrigued by their own exceptional experience they weren't really interested in what was happening to teenagers in the U.S. What concerned many of them was the possibility that their own children might perpetuate the gap. One day during a class discussion of child rearing, a woman said that she had a six-year-old son. Now she worries that when he gets to be fourteen or fifteen he might refuse to walk down the street with her. Everyone laughed sympathetically. One male student in his late thirties who is married but has no children yet, told her she'd better stop worrying since it's probably inevitable. He felt, on the basis of his own experience, that boys feel alienated from their parents for a few years, but when they grow up they eventually begin to love and respect their parents again.

When our own students talk about their childhood relations with parents, they almost never mention their fathers. We have asked several male students whether they'd ever felt any sense of competition with their fathers, and they inevitably say no. Like previous generations, this cohort says "parents" but means mother. Once Tani told an older male student that some Western psychologists diagnose the relationship between Chinese fathers and sons as an ambivalent mixture of dependence and aggression. Not strangely the student rejected the idea, arguing that Chinese family life is determined by material conditions in the country and so one could not extrapolate from Western theory to Chinese circumstances. The notion that the Red Guards had committed crimes out of resentment against "the father" struck him as even more absurd, although he felt hatred had definitely been a factor. The hatred had had nothing to do with the father, however, since it was directly connected to social injustice and the need for revenge. Another pattern familiar to Western observers does persist, in the sense that fathers, while not necessarily representing unjust authority, do play a regulatory role in children's lives, whereas mothers tend to have closer, more emotional relations with both sons and daughters.

Another class discussion recently raised the issue of sibling rivalry. A man told a story about his own experiences in a large family. The moral of his story, which included long digressions on the inevitable fights between brothers and sisters, was that order of birth determined personality type. In his old-style family, the oldest child received all sorts of extra attention until the second arrived. Naturally the mother then turned her attention to the infant. The consequence was that the eldest ended up with a pleasing, balanced personality because he or she learned early to be independent and become responsible for younger siblings, which although a burden also trains the elder in virtues like patience, understanding, and so on. Needless to say, the class loved that, since they all knew who in his family had been the first-born. But they also agreed with his generalization that the second child, especially if a son, is likely to have an "incomplete" personality, because he learns to bully the elder brother at home but cannot stand up for himself at school. In terms of birth order, first turns out best, the second is almost always the worst, and the rest are mediocre.

Many people, particularly young men, endorse the idea of a large family and regret having to limit births at all. We have run into several who argued that they see no reason why they should suffer for the sins of the parents' generation. And it's true that concern about population control is pretty much limited to middle-aged people. Young women and men seem reluctant to discuss the issue. When we push them they say the new policy is bad because it will produce a generation of single, spoiled, unhappy children. Several have said outright that they consider the government's policy repressive and intend to have at least two children, no matter what the penalties. In Shanghai it costs about Y50-60 a month to raise an infant; a nursing mother needs fresh fruit and vegetables, supplementary milk powder, and extra protein. That's not even counting the pregnancy itself and the costs of the infant's clothing, daycare, and other necessities, which soar without the government's subsidies. And since urban people have no way of supplementing their incomes as rural people do, we suspect their plans will change later. Not only that, several women we know who have had a child say that the experience of giving birth was so horrible and painful that they would consider having a second only in the event of an emergency. From their point of view, the government's policy actually protects them from the continuous pregnancies encouraged by the husband's family.

What stimulated general discussion of these issues—children, child rearing, childhood, and the changes in socialization practices since Liberation—was a story one group of students told in class about their practice-teaching experience. This group had gone to visit the home of a student who had impressed them all as being an intelligent and well-behaved boy. When they arrived they found that at home he turned into a real tyrant. Most appalling, he used things he had learned at school to humiliate his illiterate parents in front of the guests.

We found the story fascinating because it reminded us so much of family complaints about Minghui's precocious four-year-old, Xunda, the most undisciplined, rambunctious child we have ever met in China. He insists on being the center of attention, screams and whines. When he thinks the adults are not paying attention to him, he does spectacular stunts like pulling the tablecloth and all the dishes down on his head, or purposely pushing the typewriter off the desk. He has terrorized his parents and older sister. The family makes no secret of its disapproval of this behavior. Mingzhang went so far as to spank Xunda one day when Ruifeng came to Shanghai for a visit, figuring apparently that the prerogatives of the older uncle included disciplining nieces and nephews. When we visited in Wuxi and saw Xunda at his most destructive we had diagnosed the problem as hyperactivity. Ruifeng's story about how the teachers at the daycare insisted Xunda was such a compliant, intelligent, helpful, well-disciplined little boy did not seem convincing either. After hearing our student's version of the bad child/good student story we had to reevaluate Xunda. But we found it interesting for another reason. People often tell us that before the GPCR middle-school teachers had a lot more status than now, and children would use teachers to undercut parental authority. Apparently, even kindergarten teachers have more influence in China than in the U.S.

Students are talking about these issues partly because an awful lot of them are looking for marriage partners (people marry to have children, and expect to conceive as soon after marriage as possible) and because of the general shift in their attention following their disillusionment in the GPCR. All their lives they had been taught to "serve the people," or attend to the affairs of other people. Love, marriage, individual children were parochial and "selfish" concerns. Now they have turned inward to love, marriage, and children. Both men and women have inflated expectations of marriage, in spite of clear evidence around them that love marriages often do not succeed. All our students are intensely concerned with love. Recently they have been telling us they even approve of divorce, reasoning that in a society where divorce is easy to get, love must be thriving; why else divorce your spouse. In their search for love, people encounter many hardships. Men complain that the women are too conservative and look too hard at material factors before considering "spiritual" ones. One male student said he suspected women did want love and passion, but since they kept their feelings so well hidden he couldn't really say for sure. The few criticisms we've heard directly from women revolve around husbands' conservatism and their "feudal" expectations that even a very well-educated wife should sacrifice her prospects for a better career in order to take over childcare, housework, or just save the husband from embarrassment.

Quite a number of auditors come to our lectures, and most of the time we don't even know who they are. But last week after a lecture which seemed even more crowded than usual, Fang Quan took Tani aside and introduced her to two young teachers who had just returned from three years' government-sponsored graduate study in Canada, and had dropped by to see how a successful foreign teacher introduced foreign materials and teaching methods.

The two of them teach at a new cadre-training institute in Jiading, a suburb outside Shanghai, preparing candidates to study abroad and giving refresher courses to English teachers. Both are in their mid-twenties. Tani took them to the office to talk about their experience. Both Ms. Wang and Mr. Chen said they had faced many of the same problems with older students that Tani had encountered at first. Precisely because of her foreignness and by using a little old-fashioned hype, Tani has showed senior students that a young teacher can be good. According to Wang, young Chinese teachers face a far more severe problem. First, they must convince their teaching group of older, more experienced colleagues that the new foreign methods acquired abroad really are sound, before they can even try them out in the classroom. The language students tend to be even more conservative than the faculty. Ms. Wang said several told her to her face that they consider her "method" ridiculous and inappropriate. They refused to sit in a circle and speak English to each other. They don't like to invent conversations or play communication games. They insist on taking conventional exams. Several just don't attend her classes at all, preferring to audit the older professors' lectures on intensive reading and grammar instead. Since the older professors at the center don't care whether they speak English or not, all the students have to do is memorize twenty new vocabulary words a day and they can pass with flying colors.

Talking to the young teachers about their years abroad also reinforced our own analysis of the way our students learn. Chinese and Canadian ways of approaching knowledge differed in a number of substantial ways, according to Ms. Wang. The most profound in her opinion was that Chinese students usually have little desire to ask questions. It is not a matter of having burning questions in mind which they learn to repress, but rather that in their own experience questions do not form a legitimate part of classroom learning. Both Wang and Chen said that for them the most difficult part of Canadian university life was the examination requiring students to "analyze" a problem. It took them a full year, with the help of tutors, before they felt confident analyzing. Both felt exhilarated once they'd mastered it and realized they both had had the necessary ability all along, they just had never been asked to do anything like it before. As returned students, they told us, they feel it their duty to impart the skills of analysis and questioning to their own students, and gradually lay the basis for a genuine modernization in education.

Tani has been correcting exams all week. Students were asked to write an essay on the historical significance of one of the assigned texts. Tani had given them supplementary lectures analyzing the general backgrounds and social contexts of their assigned readings. These lectures were then made available to them in mimeograph form by the department. Students do not get a grade for this course, but are required to take it as an enrichment program, partly because they already have all the units they need to graduate. But also, we suspect, because the administration did not want to run the risk of another Gross "foreign" exam disaster.

About 70 percent of the students could not demonstrate ability in using the lecture material. One student explained later that while the lectures fascinated them when they were listening, once they left the classroom they could not repeat what Tani had said, because nothing in their previous intellectual training had prepared them to retain these analytical concepts. When the exam time came around, they did what they knew best. One student ignored the exam question altogether and wrote about Ben Franklin, North America's leading sage:

> Of all the readings we've got, Benjamin Franklin's autobiography interests me the most. I could not help reading it three times successively without a break. Why? First of all, the language of the prose was plain enough for a Chinese student like me to understand, though at times it was profoundly salty and engagingly humorous. The most important reason, needless to say, is that its content strikes me as unusually significant. Unlike most other readings which seem to me were talking about

something which had happened on another planet or in our country in the future, what Franklin tells us in his autobiography is quite familiar to me.

Interestingly enough, like Franklin, I once made up my mind to be completely virtuous, too. In order to live without committing any fault at any time, I compiled formidable lists of "do's" and "don'ts," such as "respect all people and speak humbly," "do not say anything that is not absolutely necessary," "do not be fussy." But no matter how hard I exacted of myself, I could not defeat my old bad habits. In the end, concluding that some faults were an indispensable component of my nature and certain accomplishments were beyond attainment, I gave up my attempt.

Now, Franklin's autobiography shows me that there was nothing wrong with my intention, which was quite similar with that of the great man. What spelled my failure was method—I had no method at all. I was too ambitious to try to break all my bad habits at one stroke and require the contrary habitude of virtues all on one morning, unlike Franklin who fixed on just one of the virtues at one time and would not proceed to another until he had mastered the one he was engaging to attempt. Otherwise nothing could be achieved, as my failure had proved. Now, certainly, I would follow Franklin's examples in every details, if I would resolve to be a paragon once more. But, that's only "if."

It should be made known that my attempt was made six years ago, during the so-called "Great Cultural Revolution," when everyone was somewhat mad or unreasonable. Now, it seems to me to have no obvious reasons to apply myself to those effort-consuming and little-benefitted tasks again. I found a ready answer to my unwillingness in Franklin's autobiography: "Such nicety extreme as I exacted of myself might be a kind of foppery in morals, . . . a perfect character might be attended with the inconvenience of being envied and hated; and that a benevolent man should allow a few faults in himself to keep his friends in a countenance." And, what is more, some of Franklin's thirteen virtues seem to me to be something of superficiality and cunning tact. It seems to me as if Franklin was not inculcating people to be moral, sincere at heart, but to be nice in appearance. [The student was referring to Tani's lecture notes here and seems to be pressing to find a flaw in "his" writer that is not too damning.]

Anyway, in China, where its agriculture and industry are backward, its way of life is simple and humdrum, and its people, relatively speaking, naive and Arcadian, Franklin's autobiography is still timely. I suppose, to most of the pleasure-oriented American young people, Franklin's maxims might be regarded as out-of-date, dry and affected. But, in China, humility is still reputed to be something of top morality. A self-important person, though extemely intelligent and capable, may not be applauded

by common people, especially by those in power. But in America,
a friend of mind who is living in that country now told me, one
has to talk big, has to sell oneself; if you remain humble and
modest, you probably will be looked on as a dullard, good-for-
nothing fellow. If only I could have a complete copy of Franklin's
autobiography and translate it into Chinese for my countrymen.

This student and all the others who genuinely fell in love with
Benjamin Franklin could not be shaken from the belief that there
were virtues expressed in the *Autobiography* that had nothing to do
with the author's social, cultural, and class background. Like all
moral exemplars, Franklin transmitted virtue across time and space.

With few exceptions, students insisted on texts which they
believed gave them the best moral instruction. Further, they had tried
to unravel the "true meaning" of the story only after reading it from
beginning to end at least three times—without pausing to eat or
sleep. Some said they were so moved by their story that they wept
when a character wept, felt anxious when the character was in
danger, and laughed when the character was happy. Tani cannot explain this for sure, but guesses it may be a conventional response in-
dicating that literature exerts a very strong influence on the reader.
Other exams claimed the chosen story turned out to be the best the
students had ever read, the most beautiful, the most moving, the most
instructive, and so on. Only a handful grasped the notion that pre-
Modernist fiction is, as one of them put it in her paper, "chosen and
selected," or, as Tani had explained in lecture, ingeniously constructed out of the narrative conventions of American bourgeois
culture.

The exams also illustrated another habit of Chinese intellectuals the tendency to approach literature as a formal set of verities
which may be read directly back into the world, or "social reality."
One student did this in a remarkably moving essay interpreting
Sarah Orne Jewett's "A White Heron," and probably spoke for many
of the class majority who claimed that of all the assigned readings
they enjoyed Jewett's the most. The essay stated that the little girl
represented the older class, the boy the rising professional class
(nothing remarkable here), and the animals and plants represented
"traditional morality." The story was "good" precisely because it
was sentimental and made the reader feel badly that the traditional
morality of the plants and herons had come under attack. Students
also generally assume that reality and its "reflection" in literature
are objective, stable, rational, and orderly, and for that reason most
of them stayed far away from the Modernist fiction, though they
have begun reading it with great interest. Only a handful of the
poorest students reverted to turn-of-the-centry Chinese literary

thinking to insist that Harriet Beecher Stowe's "tract for the age" or "call to the age" had, teacher's lecture notwithstanding, really caused the Civil War.

The concern with morality and truth caused some difficulty for many students who chose Twain's "The Story of the Bad Boy." The short satire on middle-class moralism of the horrible "Sid" sort shows wicked, boisterous, nasty "Jim" smoking and drinking and routing all the "good" people, while hypocritical "James" never gets anywhere. Satire is very difficult to grasp in a foreign language. Yet the language problem seemed quite secondary to the students' moralistic reflex, which made it simply impossible for them to accept the possibility that Twain might reject the "traditional morality" of James and Sid.

> The theme of the story is what was the outcome of the bad and the moral people. In accordance with the development of society [reference to lecture notes] Mark Twain through the description of Jim reflected the fact that the morality of the society had gotten worse. Bad persons had been left unpunished, while the moral and honest ones were bullied by evil. The wicked got profit from their immorality and misconduct, while *the honest got cheated and were left in poverty. The purpose of this story was to tell the reader that traditional morality had died and the present society was different and faced a precarious future.* [Italics added.]

Everyone just assumed that James, the Sunday school prig, stood for the good people caught in the decline of traditional morality.

The exams also showed an amazing talent for cliché. One way Chinese students absorb English is by memorizing phrases. Once the students master basic grammar, they begin committing to memory hundreds of maxims, slogans, sayings, and proverbs. This is the way Chinese necessarily learn their own language, particularly the written script. And it seems to work very well here. Clearly, our students here speak English a lot more fluently than students at an equivalent level university in the U.S. speak Chinese. Yet when you combine an English studded with out-of-date clichés with literary hagiography the result is an essay like the following:

> About Emerson's "Self-Reliance." Self-Reliance is a slogan we Chinese are familiar with. Yet this is the first time that we know it as a slogan first put forward by R. W. Emerson. Born in a family with its elders as ministers for eight generations, Emerson preached the gospel of love and self-reliance for more than forty years . . . In the matter of style, the piece is just like Francis Bacon's in a way. It is a series of reflections and meditations

rather than finished treatise. It has always the spoken tone. It is extremely noted for nuggets if not beautiful and forced expression of deep and practical thoughts. We may easily find in it the striking sentiments expressed in the style of proverbs. Let us further illustrate our point. When we are reading the piece we find the course of thought is not rambling or disconnected, yet it makes its impression chiefly by the sense and meaning of each idea as we come to it, by the illustrations or the figures, by the interest of each elements, in short, rather than by the round of completed thought which it presents. This kind of expression has one great advantage at least, for it gives us Emerson's thought about self-reliance with the utmost sincerity and genuineness, and permits him to say exactly what he wants to say and exactly how he wants to say it. . . . Sometimes we feel that the meaning of the sentences are not quite clear, yet we still feel that something very beautiful has passed this way. So actually what we feel and enjoy is not its concrete words or even its meaning but the abstract piece itself. Therefore, Emerson can well be regarded as the friend and aid of everyone who will live in the spirit. Nonetheless, we think it necessary here to utter a word of caution to those who have or will read this piece. We have heard and said ourself so much praise of Emerson and his wonderful piece that we are likely to think that everything he said must be accepted without qualification, and we may be misled by some of this extreme statement. "Self-Reliance" is full of expressions which are excellent to stimulate our thought and our character; but we cannot always accept them literally and proceed to carry them out without thinking. When Emerson says "hitch your wagon to a star," the man who goes out in the road with his vehicle and tries to do this literally will waste his time in futile effort. . . . Taken in the right sense, this essay remains as a whole a magnificent call to study living. Such is Emerson and such his piece, "Self-Reliance." No wonder when he died, with him departed the most shining intellectual glory and the most potent intellectual force of a continent.

The papers quoted here come from the B to B-minus range. The A papers compared well with undergraduate papers at U.C. Davis, or S.F. State. They expressed a reasoned, personal opinion and dealt with genuine, historical material, rather than spurious moralizing. Some even wrote on Modernism and clearly had grasped the point of Tani's lectures. Roughly 30 percent of the exams showed command of lecture material, a genuine achievement.

Finally we are leaving Shanghai for our winter vacation, which begins in two days. That, on top of the exams, has kept us quite busy. We've been in Shanghai for over four months and it's beginning to seem very familiar to us. Now we can't wait to get into the interior and see the "real" China. We will go directly to Guilin in the southwest, where we will spend five days. From there we fly to Chengdu (five more days), continue on to Chongqing (three days), sail down the Yangtze gorges to Don's hometown of Wuhan where we will spend a two-week Spring Festival with the Luo relatives, returning to Shanghai by boat.

19

The Interior

We're finally here in the "real" China: Wuhan, capital of the interior province of Hubei.

We left Shanghai for Guilin two and a half weeks ago, on a tour Lao Chen and the FAO started setting up in mid-November. Since we are foreign experts attached to the S.T.C. *danwei* we travel through the communications circuit set up by the FAO precisely for our sort of people, rather than through the China Travel Service which handles tourists from overseas. In November, Lao Chen sent a letter notifying the FAO units in each of the cities and provinces we planned to visit, when we expected to arrive, and what sort of accommodation to arrange. The officers from each of the FAO units on the list would meet us at each destination. Xiao Qian accompanied us, literally to pay for our trip; since Chinese bureaucracies have no automatic internal credit system, payment must be in cash unless branches have made prior agreements to bill each other, a far more tedious maneuver than bringing cash. After a long conversation with Don about the American credit system, Xiao Qian began referring to himself as the "human credit card."

Xiao Qian also carried the all important *danwei* letter of introduction in his pocket. We realized the importance of the letter the chilly evening we got to Guilin after twenty-four hours on the train, and found a deserted station, a moonlit parking lot, no one to meet us, and consequently no idea where we had been scheduled to spend the night. Since no one answered the phone at the local FAO office, we woke up the taxi driver asking him to take us to the nicest hotel in town where we used the letter to get rooms. We never did make contact with the Guilin FAO. Had this foul-up occurred during a peak summer period, our trip might have begun disastrously. Later, when we got to Chengdu, the very efficient FAO cadre there said she'd been extremely worried when Guilin claimed they'd never heard of us and in response to her query had no way of confirming our time of departure from Guilin. Apparently the Guilin FAO either never received our original November letter, or had misplaced it.

Guilin is a dirty, messy place when compared to Shanghai. It's picturesque: elegant two-storied, wood and concrete buildings painted different soothing, cool shades of aquamarine, all irregularly faded, line the long main street through town. The filth comes from Guiliner's apparent indifference to public places. We looked into people's courtyards where we found, as we expected, that their homes were as clean as any in Shanghai. But people in Guilin have dirty habits. They spit on the floors in restaurants. They leave the toilet without flushing, even where directions have been painted onto the stall for their convenience. Children squat casually and crap on the downtown sidewalks. Everyone feels perfectly comfortable throwing paper, orange peels, bones, garbage into the road where it collects in heaps. A disgusted local we talked to said that actually the townspeople have been complaining to the authorities for some time about the sanitation problem. But ever since the GPCR the government refuses to use force. Typical contemporary Chinese contradiction: People hate the draconian sanitation campaigns, but also complain bitterly when the government does nothing to clean up after them. "Catch-22," as our students like to say. Joseph Heller's novel has recently been translated into Chinese.

We went to Guilin to see the famous limestone mountains and caves. During our three days' stay we discovered how Chinese tourists viewed the eerie, beautiful stone formations. At the entrance to each well-known grotto we, inevitably the only foreigners present, stood in line with the rest of the people to buy tickets for the tour conducted in Chinese, and each time it was the same. The guides never mentioned natural science. We still don't know the answers to simple questions like how old are the formations, what are their geological composition, what formed them, how long people have been coming to see them. The Chinese tourists wanted the local guides instead to *xiangxiang*, two different   Chinese ideographs which sound the same but together mean "to think in terms of similarities." To *xiangxiang*, the guides tell stories about how a certain mountain peak resembles an old man or an elephant, another unmistakably a camel, others crouching lions, or a cock halfway up the hill. Inside the caverns, the stories explain the rock formations or shadows cast by an artificial light hidden inside the limestone—two old men playing chess, a woman instructing her two sons, a basket of fruit and vegetables. The Chinese tourists came not so much to "see" the rocks as to hear them described in this kind of narrative. Once we were trailing along after a tired, grumpy guide whose feet hurt and who had been giving a peremptory *xiangxiang*. When her description finally got too thin, people began muttering and one man said that he could not appreciate the scenes unless she gave the complete narration. These magical stories are part of China's "feudal" mentality and will probably have to give way in people's imaginations to scientific analysis before China's leadership can claim its people are "modern." That seems very unlikely right now. We encountered local resistance one day as we were floating down the Li River looking at mountain peaks with a very rustic, local guide. Halfway through a story, an unappreciative Chinese tourist complained he couldn't see the resemblance the guide was describing at all. He would just have to learn how to "see" better, snapped the irritated guide.

Instead of encouraging the naked eye to view nature, the traditional narrative form makes nature an extension of storytelling. The story names the formations. The narrative convention domesticates the mountains and caves, giving people a way to comprehend the "thing." Narrativity is a much more basic Chinese way of understanding than we have realized. We see a link between this popular form and our Shanghai students' resistance to "plotless" Western Modernist novels. It also struck us that *xiangxiang* is symptomatic of China's basically spatial world view. China may not be a universal empire, *tianxia*, anymore, but it's still a familiar, domesticated place. Now something our students used to tell us about patriotism makes more sense, that being Chinese means "living in the 'mountains and rivers' of the place called China."

We took a small, two-propeller plane from the worn limestone spikes of Guilin up into Sichuan's high western plateau, and stepped out into a different world altogether. Sichuanese speak a different dialect, wear a distinctive provincial style of clothing, eat different food, and have local customs of their own. Even their history has a distinct regional tradition. During periods when a dynastic house failed to centralize China, Sichuan's provincial capital, Chengdu, frequently became the seat for one or another monarchical restorations. Chengdu is as old as Periclean Athens. For better or worse it has an intense social life (a great deal of violent, bloody struggle took place here during the GPCR), and though thoroughly provincial, cannot be considered a backwater.

Our first night in town we walked over to the older district of the city. There we found a game shop, and sat down at one of the heavy wood tables, ordering a plate of smoked rabbit meat and big rice bowls of beer. Over us, hanging from the rafters, were rows and rows of pressed duck and wild game. A chubby, friendly clerk sat at the open door of the shop selling hares wrapped in string bags piled on the table in front of her. A slogan on the wall asked patrons to pay attention to sanitation, and Chengdu is far cleaner and tidier than Guilin. That didn't stop the patrons from depositing the bones onto the floor.

Chengdu is a settled, sophisticated, cultured city. Government modernization efforts have broadened boulevards and built tall apartments. But the city still has shops, lanes, alleys, shrines, and temples left over from other centuries, even millenia. The city map showing the new main arterial network did not reflect at all what our senses encountered as we walked. Xiao Qian laughs at us, because we like old things, and it is a little silly. But after the slightly sleazy charm of Guilin, Chengdu felt confident and culturally proud to us, and we just associate that feeling with age and tradition. Instead of friendly black-marketeers, we ran into people like the grizzled old country man, head bound in his white turban sitting next to us in a well-known Chengdu noodle shop. He leaned over to ask with satisfaction, already confident of a negative response, "Is America as prosperous as Chengdu?" Then the old geezer motioned expansively around the crowded restaurant, "Have Americans got this much pork to eat?" His sense of the outside world was pretty vague. America was just a faraway rich place. But the recent economic boom in Sichuan has given the old man something of his own to boast about, without reference to anywhere else. Nowhere could people consume as much pork as the wealthy peasants around Chengdu at old lunar New Year's time.

We also felt for the first time since arriving in China that we had finally found the kind of people we knew so well from GPCR posters. Except for the sprinkling of national minorities, Chengdu people dress conservatively. The city is just emerging out of the terrible economic crises of the GPCR, and people seem either not inclined or just too careful with their cash to buy rouge, lipstick, hair perms, nylon blouses, and colored glass jewels that Guiliners love. Young women in Chengdu still braid their hair. Their fathers still wear the Sichuan peasant's white cotton turban, and squat against the buildings smoking rough tobacco in their small, long brass

pipes. The peasants around Guilin tend to be small-boned, short people who dress primarily in bright glowing blue, the women of all
ages binding their little braids with bright red thread. The peasants
coming to Chengdu have a more aristocratic bearing. They stand up
very straight, the women dress in black and gray colors, pants, padded jackets buttoned conservatively on the side; the men
swashbuckle through the streets draped in their heavy fur jackets,
their high boots, and turbans, even in the relatively warm weather
of late December before the snow. Among the crowds of local people
stalk tall Tibetans wearing animal-skin headdresses, knee-high moc-
casins, and huge padded robes, orange glass beads strung across
their chests, dirks thrust into their belts.

We think Chengdu is one of the most romantic, exciting places
we've ever visited and thoroughly intend to come back here as soon
as we can. The local FAO had arranged extensive tours of all the old
historical monuments, and told us stories about the destruction
during the GPCR. Much of the Ming dynasty architecture is gone
now, and only luck preserved the nearby Leshan Buddha (largest
stone image of the Buddha in the world), the Divine Light
Monastery, the Wang Jian Tomb, and various other relics. But even
with all the damage, we spent days sightseeing. We tend to be attracted to sites that have particular historical significance. So we
found the Wuhou Shrine, a temple complex of no architectural importance most significant because it told us even more about the
role of narrative in history. The complex has been rebuilt many
times over the centuries as a way of honoring Zhuge Liang, loyal
minister to Liu Bei during the ancient struggle to restore the Han
dynasty, seventeen hundred years ago. Now it exists to commemorate the folk tradition one can read in the great story cycle
The Romance of the Three Kingdoms. The shrine itself consists of a
series of larger than life-size statues of the romance's heroes, their
sons, grandsons, and chief attendants. The guide who conducts the
tour tells stories about the statues, adding all sorts of imaginary
details, such as the "real" height and weight of each hero. Narrative
backed by physical monuments transforms apocrypha into cultural
truth. It didn't matter to us that the images were not really antiques,
and the shrine itself had been rebuilt many times. It kept us aware
of the living tradition all around us.

Even now Chengdu seems to take its political life more seriously than either Guilin or Shanghai. We saw more political cadres in
our hotel than foreign guests, more *ganbu* in one place than we've
ever seen outside official functions. Many had obviously come to the
provincial capital "on outside assignments" from the outlying
districts. People on the street seem a lot less willing to approach
Tani than in Guilin. We took this as a probable sign that foreign is

still associated with danger, and that ideology still has a compelling role to play here. On our way over to the railway station to catch the train to Chongqing, lugging our bags and typewriter, we were a little shocked when a young man suddenly emerged out of nowhere and seized Tani's bag. He announced he was a volunteer security man, "serving the people" by protecting holiday travelers from thieves and helping them to board the right trains. After he pointed them out, we noticed other security men helping passengers in the congested station, crowded with travelers on their way to visit relatives for the Spring Festival, the old lunar New Year. The man put us on the train and answered all our questions in a heavily political language, telling us repeatedly that it was his duty "to serve the people." And he certainly was serving the people. But no one in Shanghai would ever use such terminologies in conversation, without a great deal of ironic comment. On our campus such a slogan appeared only inside the clinic refrigerator that lights up when you open its door.

We've become pretty adept at spotting Shanghainese in any crowd of Chinese. We don't even need to hear their dialect anymore. There's something about the way they dress and stand and gesture which make them stand out. Guilin people are soft and slow and curious. Chengdu people are dignified, formal, elegant. Once in Guilin, while waiting for a cave tour of *xiangxiang* to begin, we noticed a honeymoon couple in the crowd some distance away. The woman had on a tailored pants suit, and a big, gawdy nylon scarf wrapped around her neck. Her new husband's pant legs were creased, his Western-style jacket had a handkerchief tucked into its pocket and every hair on his head had been oiled into place. The two of them kept questioning the people around. Then the woman pulled a private camera out of her new plastic handbag. That clinched it. "They are from Shanghai," we told Xiao Qian. Xiao Qian stared at us. How could we know? Look at them, we said. Xiao Qian went over to make sure. We were right, they were speaking Shanghai dialect to each other. What we didn't tell Xiao Qian was that he is every bit as obvious in a crowd. He asks more questions than people from other places, walks faster, is more abrupt and determined in his bearing. And he keeps declaring loudly that provincial people move too slowly. We love it. Xiao Qian and the other Shanghainese we see on the trip remind us of New Yorkers stranded in Baton Rouge, La.

We had put Chongqing on our itinerary in order to visit the newly opened Dazu Grotto, an excellent example of religious carvings from the Song dynasty, which lies some distance out in the countryside. The hilly Sichuan farmland outside of Chongqing is nothing like the rich plateau surrounding Chengdu. As we drove along the rocky, bleak highway, we talked to Xiao Qian a little about poverty. His yardstick was the northeast, and he said that from his point of view the area we were driving through was poor, but by no means impoverished. After a while we saw what he meant. But it also made us think more about the experience of travelers in China. We are getting close enough to rural China to see it, but not to know it. But we're not the only ones, it turns out. We spent some time talking to one of the guides in Chengdu, who claimed that most city people have little idea what village life is really like. They know it's tough, poor, and still wrapped up in customary beliefs, but not much more. The attitudes of urban people toward villagers vary. In Chengdu we'd met people who were moderately sympathetic but just said, in answer to our questions about folk practices, that they really didn't know what went on in the villages, except that it did not seem to have changed much over the years. On the trip to Dazu our driver seemed to feel active hostility. He'd drive up behind farmers bent over under heavy loads and horn them to death. Xiao Qian on the other hand gets along with everyone, the driver as well as the local peasants. We generally leave him to do his own exploring; once we arrive somewhere, he always goes off to talk his speedy Shanghai dialect to whoever will answer him. Others have a resigned attitude in the face of the great difference between urban and rural society.

We get glimpses. As soon as the car arrived at the hotel, we rushed out to see the first of the distant hill grottoes lying in the fields. It was late afternoon and the sun shone very yellow on a group of tourists from some other province, and a local guide holding a staff and for once not doing *xiangxiang*. Rather he was lecturing them about the lives of the statues. "This is *guanyin*, the goddess of mercy, surrounded by a group of worshiping officials," he said confidently. "The officials were sent to our area by the Central Comittee (*zhungyang*) of the Tang dynasty. And this *guanyin* is very sensitive and intelligent, just like Premier Zhou [Enlai]." Standing there, eavesdropping, we received an object lesson in the ability of Chinese culture to co-opt the present into the past.

We visited the major grottoes the next morning and were struck by a similar feeling. The carvings wind along the cliff face of a small gorge at Mount Boading, each a huge rectangular tableau between 75 and 125 meters high, covering up to 100 square meters. They are the single most fantastic sight we've seen so far. We stood staring up at carvings of the good people being rewarded by the Buddha and the saints, and the bad, wicked people tortured by the demons, appreciating the force of images and their power to compel obedience to concrete orders: be filial, multiply, honor the bonds between monarch and subject, between father and son, between husband and wife. We didn't say anything to Xiao Qian; but we wonder if the carvings and the other incredible monuments, images, and paintings we have seen on this trip have had the same sort of impact on him. Something about traditional Chinese culture is apparently slowing down the rate at which the nation changes to adapt to modern life. That is why the GPCR tried to destroy the old. And Xiao Qian has benefited very concretely from the struggles of that period. Yet there are many problems surfacing now that were not so apparent then. The GPCR did not obliterate "feudal" attitudes. What it did was to destroy many old objects of remarkable, irreplaceable beauty. Those lost things probably had the same awesomeness and power as what we have seen, in many cases more. And now we, and probably Xiao Qian, confront what remains with new awareness and regret.

20

Hometown

*T*he Luo (Lowe) family came originally from Guandong province, but sometime in the seventeenth century an ancestor migrated to Jiangxi province, where subsequent generations prospered as farmers and shopkeepers. Don's great-grandfather passed the first level of the imperial examination system and became a petty official at the local yamen or government bureaucracy. His son, Don's grandfather, converted to Episcopalianism, later anglicizing his name and moving to Wuchang (one part of present-day Wuhan), in Hubei province. He worked most of his life at a missionary school as business manager. That is why Don's native language was Hubei dialect and everyone considers the Luos Hubei people. The reality is more complicated. Chinese friends always ask where Don is "from," since place of origin has such significance to Chinese, and he loves to answer by saying: "My great-grandfather came from Jiangxi, my grandfather came from Wuhan, my father came from Shanghai, and I come from San Francisco. So I'm a native of Hubei."

Wuhan sits at the intersection of the Han and Yangtze rivers right between north and south China, and is actually the combined cities of Wuchang, Hankow, and Hanyang. Ever since the Three Kingdoms period (third century A.D.), its geopolitical location has meant it played a key role in any effort to centralize the empire. That was what made it strategically important to the Western imperialists in the late nineteenth and early twentieth centuries. As we wandered around the old customs building that stands on the hill sloping down to the ferry boat connecting Hankow to Wuchang and stumbled across some Victorian-style bank buildings just behind our hotel, we were reminded of Wuhan's old status as a treaty port. And it has been important periodically for other reasons as well. The 1911 Revolution broke out in Wuhan. Mao Zedong made his famous swim across the Yangtze River right under the bridge. Local Red Guards fought particularly bloody battles in Wuhan, and during the early stages of the GPCR factions armed with spears, knives, nets, and grenades inflicted a reign of terror on the city.

We arrived in Wuhan in the dead of winter. The local FAO officer took us to Hankow and registered us in a hotel. Aunt Meixin and the rest of her family had met us at the wharf. They all left Wuchang, where they live, after setting a time for us to meet them at Aunt Meixin's dorm at the Hubei Institute of the Arts. Xiao Qian continued down the river for Shanghai, hoping to arrive before the New Year. Over the following fourteen days we did almost nothing except eat and talk to relatives; passing, because of the cold and hilarity, something close to what we imagine an old-fashioned New Year holiday must have been like. We did take an afternoon to visit Don's old family home in Tanhualing, formerly an exclusive, elegant, bicultural neighborhood. The old Luo family compound stands in the middle of Wuchang's former missionary district, hidden behind a high brick wall. The front garden has disappeared. Shafts and small factory buildings cover the hill in the back, where a small pavilion once stood. The house itself was partitioned into apartments during the GPCR and several families still live there. Fourth Uncle had alerted one of the present tenants of the building and she graciously led us through the aging, wood building; even with the partitions and the sooty coal burners, the house felt spacious, a reminder of how comfortable and elegant it must have been at one time. We stood in the attic and looked across the wall to the other foreign-style buildings still standing in the neighborhood. Don thought of all the stories he had heard about his grandmother, her fierce looks, philanthropy, and pious Christianity, and his grandfather who ordered things out of the Sears and Roebuck catalogue for the local missionary Boone Academy, and took his caged canaries out walking every morning.

The Wuhan Luos are provincials. Not because they took a principled stand like cousin Mingyao and left their sophisticated urban

Don with Fourth Uncle in a back alley of Tanhualing, Wuchang. (T. E. Barlow)

lives to help modernize the rural interior, but just because they live in Wuhan. They all work there, eat the regional food, speak the Hubei dialect, and make jokes only Hubei people really understand. They endure the enervating heat of the summer (when according to Aunt Meixin it's so hot people only have enough energy to lie on their cots and eat watermelon), and the debilitating cold of the winter. Don's father's generation all went to Christian schools and learned English and Western music. Their children did not grow up in that peculiar treaty-port world, which disappeared with the ownership of the family house after 1949. What remains of the

Wuhan Luo's "bourgeois" background are the stories about Grandma, the Tanhualing house, the boys playing pranks, the beautiful girls, a musical strain that runs through many of the children, and an unfortunate leaning toward evangelical Christianity in some of the older generation. The younger people are all between the ages of twenty and forty, and look browner and tougher than their parents. One of them swam the Yangtze River with a rifle strapped to his back, to emulate Chairman Mao. Several became factory workers and never finished school. All of them speak the deepest Hubei patois. Even the youngest of this generation was sent down to the countryside when their parents had to leave for stints at reform camps for intellectuals and cadres.

Soon after we arrived in Wuhan, the temperature dropped and it began snowing. Every morning we awoke, dressed warmly, and took the cold ferry trip across the Yangtze from Hankow to Wuchang, then walked to Aunt Meixin's dormitory. She and Uncle Ding have five children. One now lives in San Francisco with Don's father, having arrived there only a week before we left for Shanghai. The other four children are all married and have families of their own. Everyone else, Fourth Uncle and his wife, their four daughters who work in nearby towns as doctors and technicians, as well as Aunt Meixin's children and their spouses and children—all came by to see us. Uncle Ding had saved extra coal ration so he could keep the room warm. Aunt Meixin had hung new curtains and used her cotton coupons for new bedspreads, so the room was fresh and clean. We sat all day and almost all night, going out only to use the privy, eating, talking, smoking, swapping stories. Grandchildren slept. Someone went home to kill another chicken. A local English teacher dropped in to see Tani. One of Aunt Meixin's music students walked over in the snow to wish us a happy New Year. A distant relative came with his adopted son, and we heard all about the various family rifts. We posed everyone for pictures. Uncle Ding went shopping for more food.

New Year is now officially called the Spring Festival, but in Wuhan they still celebrate it the old way. We ate, and ate, and ate; at least two huge meals a day and then snacks. We requested dog meat for Don to try (and then had to listen to endless teasing jokes about how they'd "butcher your dog, if you'll butcher mine"); deep-fried fermented bean curd dipped in hot Sichuan pepper sauce, called "reeking bean curd" for obvious reasons; the fluffiest, lightest fish balls we've ever tasted anywhere; steamed pork covered with glutinous rice powder; Yangtze River fish and home-grown poultry; delicious eight-precious rice pudding drenched in light lard; dried fruit, mandarin oranges brought down the river from Sichuan, melon seeds, sour plums, candy wrapped in paper, Shanghai chocolates. Occasionally we made courtesy calls on a relative, but mostly we stayed inside with the food and company.

Sometimes the family would tell us about life in the really rural parts of Hubei. One daughter spent six years in the villages during the GPCR. When you "go down" to the countryside in the interior, you really go down. The first thing the peasants did when she got to their farm was to caution her about local customs. A young woman must never sit on a bamboo carrying pole or step over it, because men put the poles on their shoulders, and women's menstrual blood contaminates the men causing all kinds of pollution and illness. Rural children are far more filial and obedient than city children and according to the Luo's have more secure lives consequently. But rules are harsh and strict. Peasant households include married children, and daughters-in-law still suffer the rule of the mother-in-law. All women marry to perpetuate the patriline. Communist Liberation penetrated into these areas, redistributed the land, and rationalized land utilization. But beyond the mythology of Chairman Mao, peasants cared very little about politics. Theirs is still a world of customs, tradition, and obedience.

Aunt Meixin's children do not talk about peasants the way you might expect from a family previously so well connected to treaty-port society. They went down to the villages when they were still teenagers, and to them the rural world remains a familiar, unthreatening place, for all its harshness, maintaining a level of social virtue—peaceful, authoritarian families, the rule of the father, filial obedience, loving loyalty—impossible to find in the polluted cities and towns. Another of Don's cousins spoke proudly about the year of hard labor she had put in before the older villagers accepted her, when she could begin her work of modernizing local customs. Even after proving herself, the changes the village elders allowed her to make were not big. She taught sanitation; villagers accepted that when the benefits became obvious. She also gave knitting lessons. These, she said, were probably her most popular innovation, since sweaters are not only relatively inexpensive if you use synthetic yarns, but were easy for the younger women to produce in their spare time, easy to care for, and of course beautiful looking. Another innovation, making silk padded jackets with the buttons running up and down the front rather than along the side, also made a big hit in the village. Some of the peasants they befriended during the GPCR still occasionally come by the dorm when they are in Wuhan, to call on Aunt Meixin and her daughters.

Aunt Meixin keeps insisting that Wuhan people are sophisticated and urbane, but our senses tell us otherwise. The boundaries of the city seem more permeable, and the line between peasant and city people less easy to define. The streets are filled with broad, brown faces. We've seen fights several times. Once, two bicyclists ran into each other on a side street. In Shanghai, the riders probably would have yelled and cursed each other, then ridden off. In Wuhan, the first man said to the other, "You blind idiot, didn't you see where you were going?" The second replied by punching him in the eye. Hubei people are certainly more aggressive and less sophisticated than the Sichuanese. The stereotypical Hubei man speaks his mind, but you can't count on either his modesty or his veracity. Don has learned an old proverb, which describes the treachery of the local Hubei provincial: "Heaven has a bird with nine heads, and the world has the Hubei native!"

Part of this tough urban spirit comes out of the fact that Wuhan, unlike Chengdu or Guilin, is an old industrial town, its history stretching back to the late nineteenth century. The equivalent of Wichita maybe, in the sense that it's an industrial city in the middle of an agricultural area. The people are brash, muscular, sturdy, tough. They eat hearty stews when they can. Their clothing takes into account the harshness of the weather. And they swear a lot. Late one night, it got too cold to walk over to the ferry, so we took a taxi from Aunt Meixin's campus back to the hotel. The driver was a mean-looking, grouchy, unshaven middle-aged man with the casual, accepting manner of working people everywhere. First, he complained bitterly that he only made 70 renminbee a month, which actually is a pretty good salary, better than the average factory worker's. All the way across the bridge, he cursed nonstop. Pedestrians who didn't move fast enough were "walking stiffs" and "sons of bitches," the drivers of other cars were the equivalent of motherf——s, and everyone else was a rotting turtle's egg. "How many little bastards do you have?" he asked us finally, in a relatively pleasant tone of voice. Then he wanted to know how much money we earned in the U.S. Don impressed himself by responding to all these vulgarities in the deepest local Hubei dialect he could muster.

We left Wuhan reluctantly because we would miss our new relatives and because we knew we'd never experience anything like it again during our visit. "China" is a different place for every visitor. Some enter the elegant world of tourist China, with its antiques and monuments, its guides and Western hotels. Others come into contact with government officials. They experience the excitement of sitting at the premier's table or dining with the mayor in a famous Beijing restaurant. And, of course, there is the China of universities and colleges where foreign experts live and teach. But the China of family and relatives exists only for the Overseas Chinese. The Shanghai Luo's had given us a sense of how important it is to have relatives. In Wuhan we began to realize the full implication of a familist world; for fourteen days we never left the company of a relative, we spent the whole time inventing and reinventing the connections between us, which they hoped, and we wanted, to extend into the future. It meant, as the writer Lu Xun had put it, that we disappeared behind "the invisible walls of the Chinese family." Tani finally relaxed for the first time, feeling completely comfortable, no longer an alien, but a member of a family. Don had discovered an old home.

But our months at the college had made Shanghai our point of reference, and what a difference between Shanghainese and the people of the interior. Shanghainese, even the farmers in the suburbs, are less encumbered by inherited ways of doing things, since their city grew up so quickly and was completely dominated by foreigners until 1949. Shanghainese are all dealers, from the inner-city proletariat to the commune farmers who grow vegetables to sell on the booming free markets. They are brash and slick. No one seems to value or accept tradition, particularly the sort of really retrograde ones alive in the hills of Hubei. Shanghai people are grasping, curious, and easy for us to come to terms with, because we share so many of their traits in common—love of machines, instinctive concern for fashion, a broad sense of humor, a kind of flair and sophistication. Shanghainese are awfully patronizing to other Chinese.

We couldn't disguise our relief when the Yangtze River boat (*East Is Red No. 41*) steamed into Shanghai's dockyard, and we saw the skyscrapers looming up in the background. We'd enjoyed finding our family in Wuhan, but we had also felt a little lost out there in the interior. Standing so crisply on the dock, their *zhongshan* suits clean and freshly pressed, Xiao Qian and Lao Zheng waved at us, motioning to Lao Gu who climbed out of the college sedan. We glanced from the welcoming party to the city skyline. Life in central China is very, very hard, very tough. We appreciate that. But we are city people at heart. Driving down the streets of the former French concession on our way to the college, Shanghai looked more like Paris than ever before. Shanghai ships and trains are more elegant, efficient, clean, and dependable. Shanghai has more cars, trucks, skyscrapers. We were on the road too long. We're glad to be in town and have work to do.

21

Teachers and Disciples

Shanghai, February 22, 1982

Since the trip we've been extraordinarily pushed for time. Most days we write and edit the textbook we've developed for the sophomore students. Twice a week we take our drafts across campus to the teaching building and meet with the English Speaking World teaching group headed by Lao Yang. The group's most junior member, Xiao Wang, is one of our favorite political instructors. He associates mostly with other worker-peasant-soldier graduates, all of them now either instructors, part-time interpreters like Xiao Qian, or librarians. Wang is an intense, analytically-minded man who reprimanded us once for showing too many slides about poverty in U.S. cities, and not enough about the lives of the white middle classes. Then, there is Professor "Thirty-thousand" Hu. It's not that we dislike "Thirty-thousand," but we do get awfully frazzled dealing with him in the seminar. The whole school calls him "Thirty- thousand" because of his extraordinary memory and the way he collects disconnected bits of factual information. Sitting with him during a criticism section, when what we really want to know is whether our latest chapter is teachable, he suddenly, rather erratically asks how large is the population of Seattle, or how many tons of tobacco are grown in Carolina. We keep telling him we don't know offhand and don't think that kind of information is too useful; but we can't seem to repress or offend him. In fact, we sometimes get the eerie feeling he is quizzing us; how can we teach him anything about the U.S. if we don't even know these simple facts. We enjoy these sessions, though. Particularly, when we can explain things like the American credit system, or the political economy of consumption.

Both of our most intriguing social events lately involved us thinking once again about our primary social position here as teachers. Mingzhang walked us from his house through the cold, wet downtown boulevards, recently, to the home of painting Master Fu, whom we'd met briefly several months before at a banquet, and who is doing a landscape for us on commission from Mingzhang. Many years ago Fu, as a young man, studied under the great twentieth-century painter Zhang Daqian. Zhang died recently in California, an internationally known, wealthy man. Now in his late sixties, Fu greeted us at the front door of his apartment. We recognized his distinctive appearance; a tall white-haired man with a long, oval face, eyes that glanced casually over us, and a studied, deliberate manner. He and his wife have a large room with a bay window, opening off onto a small balcony. Apparently the couple used to own the building, and their children and grandchildren still live downstairs. Fu's own paintings, some colored prints, and one reproduction of a Qi Baishi hung on the walls of the cluttered, tastefully decorated room. The book cases were crammed with volumes of reproductions. We removed our gloves, but kept the rest of our things on, since the bay window was open.

Fu seated us. The three middle-aged men, Don, Mingzhang, and another distant relative chatted comfortably with each other. Fu talked to Tani occasionally. More often he sat complacently and played with his grandson and granddaughter, who ran good-naturedly in and out of the room. A daughter introduced herself, and brought in some peanuts and more brandy. We gave Fu a calendar of color photographs of the U.S., each one with a rainbow in it. He flicked through it chuckling.

Then, someone called up from the street. Several minutes later a sturdy young man in his twenties entered the room quietly and was introduced all around not by name, but by status—Master Fu's student. As though alone in a classroom, the teacher took his student's painting and hung it on the viewing board. Then he stood in front of it, ignoring the student who remained sitting on a stool to his side: Overly dark here; brush work too muddy; balance wrong in this corner; branches large and out of proportion. After he had finished his criticism, Fu turned to us and asked what we thought.

The distant relative gave his opinion from the standpoint of an experienced art collector, and gently reiterated the painting's weaknesses. The student took the wealth of advice impassively, without embarrassment. When it was over, he excused himself and left the room; his painting remained on the board, where from time to time Fu turned to reconsider.

A bit later, another voice came through the window from the street. A second student introduced and then excused himself. In the space of an hour three more retiring young men had arrived. Then, in just the right amount of time, one of them came back into the room to clear away the table and set out four plates of cold hors d'oeuvres they had prepared for us. Later from the kitchen came a six-course meal, all prepared by one of the students who worked as a cook in a famous Shanghai restaurant. Much later, the very last student arrived with the eight-precious rice pudding he had cooked at home. Fu sat through the meal without lifting a finger to help. As the brandy flowed, he got a little more expansive, discoursing on the time he had spent studying Western painting when he was a young man. He has a dry, precise, phlegmatic conversational style, and it was amusing to hear him dismiss Western painting as adequate but limited. Oil painting, particularly, he argued, only represents what the eye can see superficially. He recommended Chinese ink wash, because it engaged the spirit of nature, forcing the painter into contemplation and away from mechanical perspective. Nature after all is very big and has many aspects; how can they all be represented from a single perspective? He knew very well how to execute Western-style perspectival drawing, he said, but as he got older it seemed to him unrealistic to force a frame around the single perspective, since "objectively" anyone can shift his or her eyes in the natural world and instantly get a different view of reality. All the time he talked in his alert, nonchalant, sophisticated way, his students kept coming into the room, removing the dishes, pouring brandy, and offering more tidbits. Fu would slip them tiny pieces of candy, without pausing in his sentence, just as he did with his grandchildren. When we finally had eaten everything up, the five students came into the room for a brief chat, then excused themselves and left.

Fu's dinner party impressed us so much because we knew how much it had relied on an entire protocol of relations between teachers and students. Fu knows what to expect from his students, and they know how to ask him for things. Everyone knows this protocol without thinking. Even the students of "Thirty-thousand" Hu seem to distinguish clearly between their teacher's method of instruction, generally agreed to be awful, and his importance as a teacher, which they do not question. According to one story going around, students became worried about "Thirty-thousand" several years ago when they noticed that he wore the same summer shorts year in and year out, and carried around the same broken umbrella. They surmised that the authorities were not paying him enough, and organized a delegation to meet with the authorities and discuss a raise for their teacher. As it turned out, Hu had a rather substantial salary. He just never spent any of it. The students we heard this story from did not object to the teacher's eccentricity. They all said that his students' concern had been quite appropriate.

We have watched many Chinese teachers with their students. Lao Yang, Fang Quan, and the older professors all have special students who help them at school and visit them at home. Don has a fairly stable following among his senior students: they send cakes, holiday wishes, inquire if he gets sick, though Don does little to encourage them.

We sensed the strength of this bond when Tani began tutoring her student Wang privately each week. He is the most brilliant student in the 1977 class and the most capable of covering much literature quickly. But she took the step because Wang had petitioned her. That is, he had come to the office with a token, three oranges in the dead of winter, to signify his wish to become her special student. Tani took him up on it. After clearing things with the authorities, Wang began arriving every Friday night at seven. We always invite him in and politely ask if he would like tea. He always refuses, and does not drink the tea we give him, unless one of us urges him to do so. In Don's presence he feels uncomfortable even sitting down. So Don withdraws into the bedroom, while Tani tutors Wang in the living room. When the time comes for him to leave, he thanks Tani profusely and tells her how much he profited from the night's instruction.

Wang is a short, muscular man in his late twenties, with very short cropped hair, dark skin, and controlled, experienced features. He seems so earnestly serious that when he does make a joke it always comes as a bit of a shock. What we know about him is filtered through his favorite American literature, so when we look at him we see a little bit of Faulkner, Hemingway, Joseph Heller, and Ken Kesey. Wang is also the most formal student Tani has. Given a choice between two novels to read, Wang always replies in a determined voice that the teacher should make the final decision. He does not like to be asked his opinion of a book. He says he'd much rather have the teacher's interpretation. This does not come out of any great curiosity about how we Americans read literature, since Wang doesn't seem particularly interested in learning about the U.S. He just wants the correct interpretation and prefers to keep his own ideas to himself.

There is no doubt at all that he has very strong personal views. One night, Wang and Tani were sitting in the parlor on the overstuffed sofa chairs talking about the citywide prize for the best senior essay he had just won for his paper on Joseph Heller's *Catch 22*. Somehow the conversation touched the role of rock music in the 1960s youth culture, and why rock and drugs had been such an unstated part of books like *Catch 22*. At first Wang couldn't accept the fact that the same people who read *Catch 22* were the ones he'd been taught about during the GPCR, who took drugs, listened to obscene music, and so on. Tani got a little irritated because Wang seemed more accepting of U.S. drug culture than of rock and roll, and she'd already failed to get her lecture students to understand the historical importance of American music. The students had said they found Louis Armstrong's trumpet music ugly. She could not shake Wang of his belief that rock music had filthy sexual power over people. Even when she told him that she and Don not only listen to rock and roll at home, but had even gone to rock concerts, she could see him inwardly refusing to believe her. The more stubborn he got, the more he irritated the teacher. Finally Tani lost her temper and told him he would never understand the fiction of the 1960s until he learned to appreciate rock music; meanwhile he could consider himself only barely literate. We know what students like Wang see in *Catch 22*. To them, it expresses their own feelings about the GPCR and the terrible drag of bureaucracy on their present lives. No matter what we say, Wang refuses to contextualize his novel in the morally suspect American youth culture.

Even after such a fundamental disagreement, Wang still persisted in fitting Tani into his need for a teacher. Lately, he started inviting us to his parents' home. We turned down the first few invitations. If we accept, it would mean a great deal of trouble for his mother and father, and at least half a month's salary. But Wang repeated the request so often, we finally felt it would be rude for us not to go. Anyway, we were curious.

We took the bus down to the Bund, where Wang met us and walked us across the river, past the old Cathay Mansion into a well-kept, though not wealthy, neighborhood. He unlocked the gate to his parents' home, letting us into a small inner courtyard and then through the front door to where an ascetic-looking man in his early sixties stood. The senior Mr. Wang seated us against the wall of the freshly painted, small room—Tani in the middle, Don on one side, and himself on the other. To our left on the family's sleeping loft hung a fresh portrait of Chairman Mao shaking hands with Hua Guofeng. After some brief conversation, Wang's sister and her three-year-old daughter came in from the kitchen to be introduced, and helped us to a small tiled table placed in the center of the room.

We did not meet Mrs. Wang until the end of the evening when we insisted on thanking her for cooking the meal. As we sat waiting for the courses to arrive, we felt somewhat awkward. The Wangs' deferential attitude toward Tani seemed inappropriate to both of us, since she and Wang are almost the same age.

Wang's young niece seemed subdued at first. For a while, she stayed some distance off, not daring to come too close to Tani. Gradually we noticed she was getting restless. Clutching her bright red plastic handbag to her waist, she suddenly ran to the table where she struck Tani and screamed that Tani was a *waiguo ren*, a foreigner. In a very rude voice, she asked why the foreigner wasn't wearing lipstick like all the other foreigners. Then she abruptly demanded to sit on Tani's lap. We knew the little girl had been quite sick, so Tani lifted her up to cuddle her for a moment. Before anyone could stop her she suddenly lost her temper and started screaming, "foreigner, foreigner, I'm going to beat you to death." She hit Tani. Then she ran to the corner where she pretended to cower in fear for a moment, before rushing back to accuse Don of being a foreigner. When Wang asked why, she said it was because Don spoke English. Wang laughed and said that he too could speak English, did that make him a foreigner also? "No, you are my uncle," she shouted. After a lot of negotiating, the little girl agreed she would go away while Tani ate dinner, if later she could come back and play.

We ate the banquet awkwardly. The carefully prepared food and wine gradually improved the atmosphere, and we forgot our bargain with the little girl. Then she came back. Taking off the purse she'd strapped around her waist, she pulled out her flash cards and began impressing us with how many Chinese characters she knew. She also produced an old GPCR comic book from her bag. Climbing up onto Tani's lap once more, the little girl began turning the pages, revealing frame after frame of muscular, heroic Chinese proletarians using their huge fists to squash tiny, mean-looking white people. Above practically every scene flew images of Chairman Mao. Peasants and workers raised his smiling face on unfurled banners. Chairman Mao sailed through the sky like a comet and rose on the red rays of a million suns. The little girl insisted that Tani count the number of Chairman Maos in the book. By now, the dinner had become an absolute disaster. Wang's little niece had unwittingly brought to the surface the family's ambivalence about the foreign teacher. Once Tani would have been considered a national enemy. Now, she was important because potentially she could teach their only son so much, and because Wang truly loves American literature.

We think we understand Wang's complicated feelings. When he was a teenager he had felt morally superior to all Americans because of his redness, but also because Americans really are so decadent. Now, he is a specialist in foreign literature and culture. Tani can teach him how to get even more out of the fiction and poetry he always enjoys so much. The problem comes when Wang projects his need for a Chinese-style teacher on a young American woman, without ever really relinquishing his impression that Americans are somehow morally unhealthy. Tani is his teacher, and, as he paraphrased a famous quote by Chairman Mao, will always be his teacher. But strategy governs his behavior too. Students expect teachers to give them a great deal in return for the concrete offerings, like the oranges, which initiate the teacher-student relationship. Wang gives Tani an allegiance she is not really culturally equipped to accept, in exchange for preference, special tutoring, support, and attention.

Actually a student can do a great deal for a teacher, if the teacher knows how to ask. Untalented teachers or ones who attract less capable students do not have the network of *guanxi* that for example allowed Master Fu to offer us such an elaborate meal. And proper use of the relationship can set off a momentum that benefits everyone very concretely. The more *guanxi* you have, the more powerful you become. A teacher who cannot attract good students really does have concrete reasons to resent those who do. Jealousy is an occupational hazard for teachers in China.

A student from last semester came to visit a week ago. The encounter was typical and explains how we might develop our own system of *guanxi*, if we could become acculturated enough to make the proper responses. The woman opened the conversation with some exaggerated flattery. Then she talked about her own family. She had sisters studying abroad, and offered to put us in touch with one of them who was in a position of some importance. Finally she came to the point of her visit. She needed some information about the American consulate general's latest policy regarding student visas; not for herself, but for a cousin, she said. In return, she offered to supply the service of yet another relative who works in the foreign currency exchange section of the People's Bank.

We do not mean to say that Chinese social relations can be reduced to exchange relations. Quite the opposite actually, since inside all these networks people depend on human beings to get things done. In the U.S. we expect the bureaucracies to carry out our wishes. Our Chinese students know that the only way to get things accomplished here is through other human beings. Also, the dinner at the Wangs opened up a universe of feelings beyond mere strategy and power. Social relations, feelings, strategy, and power all come together. People really feel affection for their patrons. Valerie fell off her bike several days ago. She didn't even skin her knee. But news about her accident spread within a matter of hours. The next day, a student who hadn't been particularly close to her arrived to inquire whether the teacher was badly hurt. The solicitous student took two hours and came all the way across town to make the call.

February 18th taught us a slightly different lesson. The relationship between teacher and student is a personal one, but how you rate in your work unit has official implications. Our work unit let us know how many cakes a young foreign expert should expect on her birthday. None. Or almost none. We certainly did not expect three for Tani. But we were a little upset when none came. We sat around fuming about racism and sexism, and so on, knowing that primarily it was a matter of age and status. Finally at about 8 P.M. the FAO came rushing in with a cake so warm out of the oven the frosting had started dripping down the sides. They had almost forgotten. The whole incident gave us a twinge, too. We know we find it difficult to accommodate the expectations of people like Wang. We can't really be what our students expect of us. But, on the other hand, the special attention we get just because we are foreign experts—birthday cakes, special cars, deferential treatment, the best medical service in Shanghai—seems to be eroding our better senses.

22

Civic Virtues Month

Shanghai, March 7, 1982

*T*he government has promised that there will never be another full-scale mobilization like the GPCR. But it has said nothing about minor political campaigns, which go on continually. Beijing recently designated March as national Civic Virtues Month.* Premier Zhao kicked off the new campaign with a televised statement that Chinese "should pay attention to hygiene, observe social order and good manners in order to turn China into a cleaner, more united and prosperous country." Zhao is assuming that if people are clean and mannerly the moral climate of the entire society will improve. The next day, an official newsphoto of Party Chairman Hu sweeping a walkway inside Beijing's Beihai Park appeared in all the newspapers.

At the local level, the authorities are mobilizing clean-ups and sending out sanitation teams to do propaganda work on the street. In Xujiahui yesterday, we saw a sanitation fair, consisting of large

---

*This turned out to be the forerunner of the short-lived, 1983 spiritual pollution movement.

groups of doctors and nurses all wearing flowing, white surgical gowns and gauze facemasks, standing in front of colorful poster displays, and speaking earnestly about germ theory, with many references to the charts behind them. Mingzhang, who is a radiologist, told us later that his team was lecturing specifically on the medical danger of spitting. (Convention justifies spitting. Chinese medical theory argues that anything harmful must be expelled from the body, so people who have colds spit frequently, and the ground is covered with sputum during the winter.) A new youth forest park is being built in Shanghai by the city Communist Youth League. Middle-school students have been given responsibility for regulating bus lines, and actually succeeded in stopping some of the shoving. Since Shanghai Teachers College is an enclave of potential leaders, there was quite a flurry of activity last Sunday as faculty, staff, and students cleaned up the campus. We saw teams of students lugging baskets of dead leaves and refuse papers over to the dump, planting saplings, and doing a little gardening. The kitchen staff at our dorm took everything out of the kitchen and pantry, scrubbed, dumped a lot of garbage and generally made a fantastic improvement.

This is the first time we have seen an organized campaign up close. "Civic Virtues Month" has been in its preparatory stage for months, though we hadn't initially understood that slogans like "five stresses and four beautifuls" were its first indications. No one bothered to explain that the directive ordering dress reform on campus had come down as part of the same campaign. After we came back from winter vacation, we just found that all of our female students had either cut or braided their hair, the male students were shaving regularly, and everyone's dress seemed even more conservative than before. Another day, all the Communist Youth League members on campus suddenly started wearing their identification badges, which they had not done last semester.

Yet we seemed to be the only persons on campus interested in this campaign. Students didn't even think it was important enough to draw our attention to, although they willingly answered our questions about it. Nobody has said that they think it is unnecessary, either; they just say vaguely, in a sort of uninterested tone of voice, that the campaign won't last and eventually everything will return to the status quo ante. Take tree planting, for example. When we read in the papers that thousands of saplings would be planted and saw some of our own students lugging little cypress trees around the campus, we got visions of vast green forests. But according to the students we questioned, tree planting is usually a failure. The trees are set in, but no one bothers to water them regularly, so only a third of them actually take root and grow. Good intentions end up wasting money and time. As usual, our students have a different perspective than we do. As we see it the college campus is already lush, well kept, even pastoral. They keep telling us that before the GPCR the campus was more beautiful, the banks of flowering plants endless, the artificial lake near the fine arts building almost like a Suzhou garden. The rebel students destroyed the lake exactly because it was so beautiful. Now, the college gardeners have almost rebuilt it, but the new version is nowhere as graceful and restful as the old lake. Nothing will ever be as beautiful it was before the GPCR. Planting more flowers won't help either, they tell us. As part of the ethics campaign and the new government plan to honor the efforts of intellectuals, campuses and research organizations have been issued quotas of flowering plants. A student told us wryly that the last time ornamental plants appeared someone had dug them up and stolen them. The moral is clear. It would be nice to have a prettier campus, but since the GPCR it's smarter not to bother.

This mild cynicism doesn't mean that people necessarily disagree with the idea of a "civics month." Everyone we know has complained at one time or another about the breakdown of civic morality. In general though, people give two reasons why a civics month won't work now. First, it is only a drop in the ocean. What happens when March is over and April comes around? Second, they argue, beautiful environment is a reflection of genuine civic virtues not the other way around. The GPCR's impact on morality was devastating. Right now people are much too selfish, too alienated, too disillusioned for any genuine collective morality to be instilled by the authorities. Anyway, the Party has not demonstrated its own sincerity. In other words, the very same people who argue that an ethics campaign won't solve social problems persistently refer to morality as their reason for skepticism. The most disaffected student still assumes that civic morality is the baseline of any society and that social progress in China will begin again only when people's moral feelings are revived. The most startling illustration of this attitude occurred when a very disaffected student said to us that the Chinese government was "bad." His very next statement, "a good government should regulate people's sexual behavior," voiced his assumption that sex is a problem of community ethics which "good" states oversee for their people. Most of our students would agree that a "good" government is both authoritarian and morally unimpeachable. Since the present leadership was contaminated by its involvement in the GPCR, they like to argue, why should it be obeyed? Chinese students are not American liberals. They do not assume that government is a contract, or that law is impersonal and transcendent.

Social morality plays a similar role here as legal or religious absolutes do in Western societies. We in the West speak of "lawlessness" or disrespect for the law, the Chinese talk in terms of moral absolutes. In the past, this human-centered morality, immanent in every concrete human relationship, had a numinous religious quality to it. Recently, at least before the GPCR, people still thought in terms of Communist ideals. But now the problem facing China, many people argue, is to re-establish a set of norms or moral standards for behavior. One way of doing this, as intellectuals understand the problem, is to graft Western-style law onto the Chinese "feudal" inheritance. Particularly in light of what many thoughtful people consider the fascism of the GPCR, law might form a barrier protecting the defenseless.

That is why we were interested in attending the highly publicized municipal court proceeding which took place recently. Many resident foreigners had been invited to the Shanghai People's Court to observe, and we saw one of the American consuls sitting in the audience with two Caucasians who looked like news reporters. Doubtless they considered what we saw to be a "show trial." To a degree they were right. It was in no way an Anglo-Saxon legal proceeding, but more closely related to a sort of morality play about law. The court consisted of one judge, two assessors and a clerk, two prosecutors, and a lawyer for the defense. The accused had committed repeated burglaries, breaking into 23 homes and stealing cash, banknotes, jewelry, cassette tapes, and embroidered quilt covers. He was arrested at the scene of his last crime. The police officer had not linked the man to any other thefts, until apparently overcome by remorse the arrested man suddenly began confessing to one after another crime and leading the police to each crime scene, explaining when and how he had committed the burglaries. So the defendant's guilt had been predetermined.

The "trial" consisted of victims' testimonies and the defendant's confession, followed by prolonged debates between prosecutors and defense attorney about the defendant's motives for committing the crimes. The defense argued that the young man, who was a model worker, had turned to crime in order to get enough money to pay for an expensive wedding. The prosecutors, judge, and later many of our campus acquaintances who read about the case extensively in the newspaper, all agreed that marriage pressure was the social causation for the crime. There was some suspicion his motives had been mixed, since he had used some of the stolen money for a pleasure trip to Hangzhou. But the defense attorney showed convincingly that the young man had put the overwhelming proportion of the stolen money into a savings account marked wedding expenses. The defendant himself made a speech saying that social pressures to have a big expensive wedding had led him to steal. He said he was truly sorry and felt he'd already reformed a little bit by doing good repair work in jail, such as fixing up broken windows and doors. The court adjourned for twenty minutes and returned with a sentence of three years labor reform.

The matter of guilt had been decided beforehand. The trial formalized the deposition and arguments. The accused made a public apology to the victims, and the judge meted out justice. The sentence seemed light to us for a person who had committed so many crimes. But the court determined its sentence on the basis of various social, ethical considerations which would never be admitted into an Anglo-Saxon proceeding. In the case we saw, social causation outweighed personal motive, and the promise of reform attenuated the crime. But for the sake of general social morality —not just the defendant, but society at large—the entire proceeding was sanctified by law. We were really quite amazed later to find that many friends on campus had followed the case very carefully and believed that the sentence and the protocol were correct, that "law" was the proper medium for resolving the contradiction and that the good of society and the good of the defendant should be reconciled.

The new emphasis on legality, people hope, may avert another GPCR disaster. But law has never been as important as ethics in Chinese society. And the present emphasis on law is still ethically motivated. The law, for instance, ensures the right of personal choice in marriage. Yet in practice marriage is still very much a question of community ethics. Last December, the China Youth Theater in Beijing produced a new play, *The Moon Begins to Shine*, about the conflict between freedom of personal choice and public morality. Bai Fengxi wrote the play and another woman directed an all-female cast. The story concerned a strong defender of women's legal rights who discovers that her older daughter wants to marry a man who is the mother's own age. What's even worse, the man had once been the mother's own beau, many years ago. To complicate matters, the protagonist's younger daughter announces that she wants to marry a factory worker, someone "intellectually" (read socially) beneath herself. The mother struggles with the dilemma presented by her daughters' eccentric choices. Finally she decides that the legally guaranteed principle of the freedom to choose must override her own personal reservations in both cases.

In a press interview, the playwright said that she had used the character of the mother to voice her own conviction that women should have freedom of choice in marriage. But the actress who played the role of the mother said in the same interview that she had found the role uncomfortable at first, because it didn't seem right for a daughter to fall in love with her own mother's old "boyfriend," and the mother's condoning it troubled her even more. But since she agreed with the constitutional principle set out in the marriage law and in the modern idea of parents learning to trust their children, the actress finally decided that the character of the mother must be correct.

The play aroused quite a bit of controversy in spite of its outlandish plot, because it illustrated the tension between individual rights and the larger, still more powerful conventional morality often enforced by conservative families. Even our daring Shanghai students tell us stories about parents who forbid love marriages. The other interesting aspect of this play was the obvious way it used a semi-literary vehicle to argue an issue essentially connected to the problem of establishing social, moral norms. This is a common contemporary means of inventing "literary" texts. And the official press of course takes a much more conservative position than our students do. Even so, literature written by younger, less Party-oriented writers frequently reiterates similar themes, though in a less obviously didactic fashion.

Last week *Wenhui pao* ran an article entitled "The Question of Love in Literature":

> Love is a reflection of multiple relations such as the spirit of the epoch, the social foundations and class status. It represents in a concentrated way people's moral sentiments and inner feelings, and therefore is an important subject of characterization. ... However, love is not necessarily an eternal subject for literary and artistic creation.
> Major problems [in the handling of the subject] include lack of realism ... vulgarity and poor taste ... monotony. ...
>
> Correct description of love in literary and artistic works should involve these points:
>
> 1. It should have a certain limit. It must meet the requirements of the characters and the main theme. Works should include more profound social meaning.
>
> 2. Characters, psychology, customs and habits of different nationalities should be considered. ... Chinese express love differently from Europeans. Kissing on the street may be common in Europe and America, for instance, but is rarely seen in China.
>
> 3. Communist moral sentiments should be reflected. Description of healthy, lofty love will guide the young to treat life properly and handle well the relations between love and revolution, ideals and morality. On the other hand, obscene descriptions will only propagate feudalistic and capitalistic ideology.

Among students, love represents an issue for ethical argument. They may reject Communist moralizing, but they are genuinely concerned with questions like: if you kiss someone do you lose your virginity; how is it possible to determine your "prospect's" moral character before social pressure to get engaged becomes too strong; is it immoral to have more than one serious boyfriend, and so on.

Everyone, not just students, has an opinion to express on the subject of marital ethics. The All-China Women's Federation just held a symposium on the question recently: Shang Youyu, vice-president of the newly established Chinese Academy of Social Science affirmed that love is the basis for marriage in socialist China. The president of the China Marriage and Family Research Institute took a moderate position halfway between the old taboos against divorce and the bourgeois flippancy of divorce on demand, arguing that divorce should be made available when marriage mediation fails. The secretary of the Communist Youth League warned young people to resist the urge to marry on the basis of mere physical appeal. And the vice-president of the All-China Federation of Trade Unions said young couples should love and respect each other.

This outpouring underscores the awkward position of the young people. It has been thirty years since the state issued its first national decree ensuring freedom of marriage. Yet the social anxiety surrounding love, the moral problems raised by individual free choice—why should children choose marriage partners for themselves when they don't have the right to choose anything else—still preoccupies both old and young people, as well as the authorities. Our favorite example of this unresolved family tension involves a case that made a huge stir among our students recently. The following story in *China Daily* was accompanied by a picture of a man and a woman staring gravely into the camera's lense:

> Wedding photographs are commonplace, but Liu Jungui and Tan Zhongying ended their marriage with a photographic session. The couple marked their divorce, after three happy years of marriage, by posing for pictures together in a photographic studio in Sichuan province. Liu, a peasant from Jiangbei county, returned to the land and Tan, a primary school teacher returned to her first husband.
>
> Tan's former husband, Wang Yiliu, had written to tell them he was no longer a "rightist," a label which had plagued him for more than twenty years. Tan had divorced Wang at his insistence, as Wang did not want his family to suffer because of his political status. Wang had ended up looking after the two children. The children still missed their mother, and Wang—now rehabilitated—wrote saying the children wondered when she'd come back.
>
> This time it was Liu who insisted on a divorce, insisting that he did not want to stand in the way of a family reunion. . . . On August 20, 1980, the couple went to the local administration

*The divorce portrait of Tan Zhongying and Liu Jungui.
(China Daily)*

office to apply for a divorce. . . . Tan and Wang were remarried
after years of separation. But they couldn't forget Liu. They worried about him until they learned that he has now married a
widow.

We had glanced at the case but hadn't given it much thought.
Our students insisted on raising it with us, discussing all the
ramifications thoroughly. Who was the most virtuous person, under
the circumstances? Should Tan have given up Liu, whom she might
have loved, to go back to Wang whom she had not seen in many
years? Did Tan actually marry Liu for love, or had she secretly
maintained her love for her "real" husband, Wang, all these years,
marrying Liu only for convenience? Which should be more heavily
weighed, one's obligation to family or one's personal feelings?

23

Feminism

Shanghai, March 22, 1982

*I*n early March, all the foreign women in the dorm received big red invitations to Shanghai's annual Women's Day celebration. There are quite a few of us now. Valerie, Anne, and Tani are full-time teachers. Nelson's British wife Holly does no teaching at all because she is in the late months of pregnancy; Jane, who is married to John, tutors part time. Jane's husband is a retired English professor with a long-time interest in socialism and the Chinese revolution, but amazingly unenlightened ideas about his own marriage. Jane says dissatisfaction led her to join an older women's group at home so she could improve her marriage by making it a little more equitable.

On the day of the event, about a quarter of an hour before Tani was scheduled to leave, Lao Zheng appeared rather suddenly at our apartment to ask whether Don would like to go, too. Neither Tani nor Don had any idea what lay behind Lao Zheng's studied casualness, and both of us figured it would be an interesting official celebration so we said yes, and walked downstairs to the car. There we encountered Jane, angrier than we had ever seen her before, and

John skulking around about a hundred feet off. Days ago, Jane explained to Tani, the FAO had come around to formally ask John if he'd like to attend the Women's Day celebration. Jane, who'd initially felt so relieved at receiving her own invitation, the first in her own name since arriving in Shanghai, just didn't feel like spoiling her afternoon. Without consulting John, Jane—for both of them she had thought—told the FAO that since John's name had not appeared on the invitation and he wasn't a woman, she would prefer to go by herself. Then, Jane said, the cadres just laughed at her. It was one thing to have to put up with such patronizing behavior from John, quite another from people she didn't really know. Jane lost her temper. As she talked to Tani, it became increasingly clear that this unfortunate incident was only the last in a long string of insulting slights. Whenever the FAO comes over, she said, they either patronize her, or just talk to John, ignoring her completely. She explained why she does not show up at the Thursday movies any more. Their translator-guide won't take the seat of honor between them, but insists on sitting at John's side, which means Jane can't hear the translation. Even her own students run over to John if he happens to appear in her classroom. Not only did this rudeness irritate her to distraction it was also bad for John, and for their marriage, since it reinforced the very habits in him she now found intolerable.

We sympathized with Jane. Her story also clarified the mystery of Lao Zheng's sudden invitation to Don. Since Tani is a full-time teacher, the college felt confident sending her to a Women's Day party because she would reflect well on them. But sending a "woman" like Jane who has no status in Shanghai literary circles except being John's wife meant that the school would do better to send John too. Having run into such an unexpected, explosive reaction from Jane, we suspect the FAO strategy shifted and Don had to be invited in order to show Jane that no harm had been intended. This was the first time Jane had said anything to us, and, although we were not ignorant of Chinese attitudes toward status, position and gender and should actually have been able to anticipate this problem, the car was waiting, so we all got in and went to the party.

As this was a Women's Day celebration, Fang Quan accompanied us as the highest ranking woman in our department, rather than the usual FAO men. We got to the Municipal Building and joined the reception line. Tani, Jane, and Fang Quan stood together talking casually, until we reached the front of the line. Then, abruptly, Fang Quan disappeared, to reappear right beside John. As Jane and Tani stood politely, arms outstretched to the greeting committee, Fang Quan pulled John forward to introduce him, and apparently still unaware of how rudely she had just snubbed Jane and Tani carefully ushered us all inside seating the men in the seats of honor at the table. Don was embarrassed, but there was little he could do without causing a scene, so he sat there uncomfortably. Fang Quan excused herself to find some important persons to introduce to John. At this point Tani knew she was completely dispensable (being the youngest, and the wife of the less important male guest), so she went off to talk with some friends from other campuses.

After the speech by the female "chairman" of the Shanghai Women's Association, we went downstairs to the theater for a performance. The choice of a *Yueju* opera was a nice touch, for *Yueju* is a regional-style opera performed exclusively by women. Except, gradually the audience began to catch onto the opera's infelicitous message. A vain, stupid, manipulative princess decides not to attend her father-in-law's birthday party; her reasoning being that as a princess she outranks her husband and his father, who is a lowly minister. Husband and wife have a huge fight. He smashes a palace lantern given to them by her father, the emperor. Then he mistreats her by throwing her on the floor. The princess runs to her dad, the emperor, who listens to her exaggerated account of what had transpired. She asks him to punish her husband. The emperor announces, in all his patriarchal wisdom, that since the young man has turned out to be such a terrible son-in-law, they might as well execute the ingrate and be done with him forever. This threat has its intended effect. The frightened princess suddenly realizes how much she still loves her husband. She begs for clemency. Later, in a male supremacist scheme, the husband and father work out a strategy to humiliate the princess in public. The son-in-law gets a promotion, making him the social equal of his wife. The princess does penance by swearing she will never disrespect her husband or her father-in-law again.

The female foreign experts came stumbling out of the theater in an unbelieving state. Not exactly an appropriate theme for the international Women's Day celebration, one Canadian woman said. Later Tani took Fang Quan aside and explained how foreign women responded to the opera. At first Fang didn't understand Tani's point. She defended what she believed to be the moral of the opera: since both husband and wife criticized themselves in the end, and both had tried to oppress each other, how could we say that one character was more sexist than another. Tani did some more explaining, and Fang said she would bring the foreigners' criticism to the attention of the authorities.

A few days later, a letter to the editor appeared in *China Daily*:

Women's Day was celebrated in Shanghai by the presentation of a traditional opera, *Beating the Princess*. Many foreign women were displeased about this choice of performance. . . . The quality was not at stake; it was well done and therefore transmitted very efficiently its sexist bias. . . .

Firstly, the woman in this script was seen as an oppressor, which in fact is the complete reversal of both the feudal reality represented and the current situation where men still have, at least, the better "half of the sky."

Secondly, the princess was depicted as spoiled and immature, ready to exaggerate and even lie to obtain revenge. This reinforces the negative myth that women are manipulative and dishonest.

Our Chinese hosts were incredulous when a few foreign women questioned the appropriateness of their choice. We were equally incredulous that they didn't seem to perceive the opera's sexism.

Paule McNicoll.

Paule McNicoll's letter spoke eloquently about the real differences between the way we look at the importance of gender in social relations, and the way most Chinese around us do, even the most politically progressive.

Social hierarchies other than the simple one of sex cut across and outweigh gender in Chinese thinking. Paule McNicoll, Tani, Jane, and Don all saw *Beating the Princess* as a story about sexual politics in which men subordinated women, and where tradition cast the leading female character in a derogatory light. The issue of political hierarchies seemed a subordinate plot to the obviously primary sexual struggle. Indeed, the opera we saw really did reflect the common perception here in China that in most cases women are not as valuable as men. But that was not its central Chinese message.

The Chinese audience saw a story primarily about a conflict over rank. In it, two hierarchies collided, giving rise to a situation where rules of propriety were not clear-cut. In the first, the natural law of officialdom and the throne determined that the princess outranked her own husband, and thus was not under any obligation to attend his father's birthday party. The second involved the age hierarchy familiar to all families regardless of rank, which determines that any woman will attend the birthday party of her father-in-law. The resolution of this impasse did indeed involve the humiliation of the princess. But theoretically, a similar story could have been told about a junior son, if, for example, the boy had scorned a poor, elderly woman who happened to be a friend of his own father, or had disrespected virtue or seniority. This is not to say that junior men hold exactly the same position as junior women. But in the story we saw, the conflict between rank in political culture and rank in family could not be properly adjudicated until the emperor raised his son-in-law to his daughter's rank. He could not lower her status; and he did not want to order her to obey someone less exalted than herself. The only resolution was to promote the husband, compelling the princess to obey the family hierarchy of her in-laws, and preventing her from being able to revenge herself later on her husband or his father.

A similar dynamic holds true in everyday life. Our male students generally assume that all men are more talented and valuable than most women, with the exception of women teachers, specialists, or high cadres. Women who have official authority get the same public deference male officials do, since power is acknowledged in overt ways. The person with the highest status is automatically the "biggest" (*da*) person, regardless of gender. Fang Quan introduced John to the Women's Day officials first, because of the four of us John has the highest status. In the 1930s and 1940s, John traveled in China and happened to meet Zhu De, Kang Keqing, and Ding Ling. Every time Fang Quan reintroduces John, she establishes these key facts of his pedigree. But as we were sitting around the table at the Women's Day party, a woman arrived, a bureaucrat so "big" she even outranked John. Automatically she replaced him at the apex of the exclusive little hierarchy around the table. There was no nod to her gender or to his, only to their relative social positions.

We want to stress this point. In China, patterns of deference are at work in all social relationships, not just sexual politics. Sons defer to fathers, daughters to mothers, children to all adults, students to teachers, junior cadres to senior cadres; everyone has superiors they must defer to and subordinates they accept deference from. This is not exactly a reciprocal relationship because the junior members are not rewarded for good behavior, and the senior does not automatically have to look out for the welfare of the junior; but the authority of the senior will prevail. We're not sure how we can emphasize this point strongly enough. In China, when you step into a room, meet someone, eat a meal, walk down the street, your position and status determine what you do and what people do to you.

So, to return to the problem Jane has been encountering, John's high rank does not automatically carry over to her, because inside the family wives are, in a practical sense, subordinate to their husbands. We asked a female student to explain why students treated Jane so "badly," and received this response: Most people derogate wives, particularly "housewives" who stay at home and have no outside employment. Unless the wife has her own position, most people will assume that she is less intelligent, less interesting, less powerful than her husband; realistically, since no two people are ever exactly equal, one must be below the other. This is "natural." Most people, herself included, learn from experience to ignore the wife and concentrate on the husband, no matter whether the couple is foreign or Chinese, she continued. Were Jane a genuine teacher like Tani, adjustments would have to be made, because then her position vis-à-vis her students would be professional rather than wifely, even though she would certainly never outrank John, because his status derives not just from his profession but also from his being a "friend of China," which puts him in a similar category as people like the grandniece of Sung Jiaoren, or the best friend of Mao's martyred first wife, Yang Kaihui.

Students, like everyone else, draw these distinctions of status positions in explicit, obvious ways. At the end of last semester, Tani's class gave her an enormous personal seal. She noticed that their own seals were all very small, so she asked why they had thought she deserved such a big one. Their answer was partly sarcastic. "The teacher," they told her with deadpan faces, "is bigger than the students." More seriously, they explained that a seal must reflect the rank of its owner. In feudal times, the emperor had a seal as big as a fist, for example. To use a more recent illustration, during the GPCR small Red Guard splinter groups in Shanghai had had gigantic seals made, hoping that readers of their posters would think that the directives were coming from a really important faction.

Status positions exist independently of the individual persons who happen to be holding them. They are language every Chinese has learned to speak; living up to expectation means knowing how to act appropriately in terms of designated positions. Chinese society tends to subordinate sexual politics by absorbing gender relations into the language of social hierarchy. So, accompanying the idea that juniors should defer to seniors, there exists the expectation that the daughter is subordinate to mother, son is subordinate to parent (in practice usually the father), wife to husband, everyone to grandfather and grandmother. Another example we can think of to illustrate how this works was something we saw once in a hotel. The old manager of the dining hall had come into the room for her meal. Her junior female staff all clustered around her asking about her health, comfort, massaging her feet. As each rose for other duties, relieved of responsibility for coddling the old woman their faces changed abruptly and they proceeded with their work. This is not necessarily hypocrisy, although obviously it can degenerate into that very easily. The employees considered their pseudo-kin relationship to their boss to be necessary and "natural."

The difference in how our two cultures channel and code sexual politics is probably the most troubling problem facing American visitors, whether or not the American in question considers herself or himself a "feminist." Since the nineteenth century, the West has privileged a fundamental sexual opposition between male and female. This antagonism colors Western society thoroughly. In China, traditional or "feudal" society contained the opposition of men and women inside the status hierarchy of high and low, but maybe even more insistently inside an ancient opposition between inner and outer. The twelfth-century Confucian theorist Zhu Xi defined gender in terms of the innerness of women and the outerness of men. This was not the same as the modern Western distinction between public and private, which draws a line between the "masculine" area of production and "feminine" sanctuary of domesticity. Innerness was not and still is not considered the exclusive province of Chinese women, as domesticity was until recently for Western women. The "interior" consisted of an individual's patriarchal descent group in opposition to people of other surnames, other *jia* or families, other lineage groups, other villages, and so on. China has always drawn itself as the inner, in relations to the rest of the world. But inside this China, other inner areas exist which eventually place wife and husband both inside the *jia* together. Put another way, no *place* exists where men and women face each other in fundamental opposition. As long as the family or *jia* remains, individual women and their husbands will stand together "inside," in opposition to everything outside. Whether or not they love each other or even barely tolerate their marriage, except in the case of sophisticated or Westernized people like our students, married men and women consider themselves to be a far more solid social unit than merely the union of two "individuals."

A potentially explosive situation arises when feminist foreign experts and the Women's Day Celebration Committee disagree on what is appropriate entertainment for a Women's Day celebration. Western feminists cannot understand why Chinese women fail to reject retrograde, anti-feminist elements in Chinese culture, when it seems so obviously to devalue them. But Chinese culture is what makes people "Chinese," and since culture impresses a specific perspective on sensibility, Chinese women cannot understand why foreign women criticize them. They find Western feminism completely inexplicable. Sometimes they resent it as a form of cultural imperialism. They do not see *The Beating of the Princess* in primarily sexual terms. Not only that, but at least in the short run, the GPCR demonstrated how impossible it is to ban traditional opera. People resented having to watch the same boring revolutionary opera over and over. Not only because they hated Jiang Qing's abuse of authority, but also because *The Red Detachment of Women* cannot substitute for the rich traditional opera culture. Sexual imagery cannot be changed by fiat. After the GPCR, traditional opera sprang back with its rulers and ministers, ingenues and heroes, colors, tunes, and mannerisms, because it's part of the Chinese cultural imagination.

There are enormous differences in the experience of American and Chinese women, which Western feminism cannot explicate or bridge. Fang Quan's duty in a public situation is to introduce the most important person first. Privately she belongs to the female culture where older and younger women aid each other. As we sat down to watch *The Beating of the Princess*, Tani found herself seated next to the female bureaucrat who outranked even John, a woman introduced as one of the most important officials in Shanghai's educational circle. Throughout the opera, she translated the opera's regional dialect into *putong hua*, the Common Language, whispering steadily into Tani's ear. This official enjoyed the story, sneering at the princess, encouraging the husband, identifying of course with the emperor. When the lights came back, she smiled and returned to the apex of that invisible pyramid of social positions, leaving Tani, appropriately, at the bottom.

Western and Chinese customs meet most closely in the informal world of personal relations. In public situations, our acquaintances are all very formal. They have assigned positions—colleague, student, cadre, guide—and no foreigner can expect them to do more. Once their obligations are discharged, they can choose to turn a different side to us. This is particularly true in the relations among women, and Tani deeply appreciates the warmth she finds in friendships with Chinese women. But that holds generally true in all sorts of relations outside the social hierarchies. Each week, we test out draft chapters of our *Contemporary USA* in a seminar of senior and junior faculty from the department. It has taken us several weeks to adapt to the seminar's style. Unlike the relaxed, informal group discussions we would expect from American colleagues testing out new curriculum, the seminar is formal and more than a bit stilted. Teachers don't expect their students to ask questions in class, so find it unnecessary to ask any when they are put in the position of "student." They are more comfortable when we talk and they take notes. After six weeks of this, despite our repeated appeals for feedback, Xiao Wang made a special appointment to consult Tani in our office. There he suggested a number of truly excellent improvements for our text, none of which he would have made with Don present or in a group setting. When Tani, who is his age and general status level in the department, asked him why he had not spoken up in seminar, he said it was because he did not want to embarrass us by voicing public criticisms. Actually, he was being doubly sensitive. He did not want to embarrass his older Chinese colleagues, and he did not want to take the chance of asking a question which Don might conceivably not be able to answer.

We love to hear stories about this more spontaneous level of experience, where people have to jockey for position, use strategies, fall in love, get married, and live from day to day. A woman we know told us a story about matchmaking. A male student approached her and asked her repeatedly whether she would act as a matchmaker for him in his negotiations with a female factory worker. Our friend finally agreed and a meeting was set up between the boy, the girl, and their respective representatives. This was somewhat unusual, since most often only one matchmaker presides. The two sides had never met, and our friend did not make clear why her party had initiated the contact. On the girl's side it was very simple; she wanted a college-educated husband. After the initial meeting, the go-betweens decided to call off the deal because the boy wanted a prettier wife.

This was a slightly more formal meeting than the one arranged by the friends of Xiao Qian and Xiao Shen, but the same principles operated. Our friend said she thought that formal go-betweens make the process of looking for a spouse less uncomfortable for many people, because second parties take over all the embarrassing negotiations if one side wants to withdraw but doesn't want to offend. Our friend also said she discovered that she was pretty good at matchmaking. The girl's representative subsequently came by to ask that a little pressure be applied to the boy, but our friend refused, saying that you cannot talk a marriage into existence.

We also know of a case where a mother arranged marriages for both of her daughters. The mother, worried because her younger daughter had become too friendly with a handsome but insubstantial boy, found a substitute. The second boy had old parents but a Party membership. Later, this second boy's mother died, and the daughter's friends said she shouldn't go through with the marriage, since she would certainly be burdened with caring for the prospective father-in-law. The daughter actually did object to the marriage initially, but on completely different grounds. She said she and the boy didn't have much to say to each other. But the mother insisted and prevailed. The couple now has a nice fat baby, a good future, and a solid marriage according to everyone, including the couple themselves. And, as it happened, the old father-in-law did not survive his wife very long.

When the authorities became involved in matchmaking the consequence can be quite bad. Other foreign experts have told us about cases where local Party secretaries forcibly brokered young unmarried female subordinates into unwanted marriages with coworkers, or forced attractive subordinates to marry their superiors. We have not heard about anything like that on our campus. But we did hear about a very embarrassing situation of a different kind. A top male student, "three good," all sorts of scholastic awards, just admitted to the Party, had sometime earlier become engaged to another student. When the man won a prestigious national scholarship to study abroad, he broke off the engagement without warning. Everyone was appalled. The Party branch secretary began an endless series of meetings to try and persuade him to change his mind. In breaking the engagement he had publicly compromised his fiancée and therefore ruined her reputation. The Party branch's integrity was on the line as well, since the man's action reflected adversely on the branch's ability to judge character. All of the relatives had a stake in the outcome, since they would also be implicated in any disaster or disgrace. But the man refused to budge. The secretary can try to have the scholarship rescinded, though that is unlikely. Too many people are already implicated in the decision to promote him, so all their reputations would suffer along with his. The person who told us the story thought it hilarious.

Not all women want to marry. Everyone, women and men, feel the tremendous pressure not only to get married but to find a really outstanding partner with high social status, good income, decent family, and good prospects for study abroad. And although everyone says that eventually, like it or not, they will have to marry, a growing number of women say they don't really want to. At one function Tani met two women in their early thirties. One was engaged, the other still resisting marriage. Both said that what they really wanted to do was to live together as spinsters. Quite spontaneously one of them asked Tani about lesbians in America. They assured Tani they had no interest in "becoming" lesbians. Far from it, they had no interest in sex at all. They were afraid though, that if they lived together much longer people would say they were lesbians and the gossip would ruin their reputations. One of the women said that she didn't want to marry because she had many scholarly interests and hobbies, and a family would take too much time away from her own pursuits. When Tani asked why they felt they had to marry, they both said social pressure. Another single woman we know just said that's what people expect you to do.

We hedge a little when people ask us to talk about marriage, love, sexual attitudes, perceptions of gender, and social expectations of husbands and wives in America. Attitudes and customs are so different here that we just can't bring ourselves to explain how relatively unexclusive we are in sexual matters, and how far outside the sphere of moral discourse marriage has become in our culture. Love, marriage, and sex are issues people here agonize over. During the GPCR, Western observers found so-called revolutionary love a little difficult to swallow whole. The criteria have changed, but people still pour enormous amounts of calculation into falling in love and enjoying the sensation once it does arrive. Recently, we heard some firsthand testimony about what educated women look for in love. The experience of falling in love is like being overwhelmed by a tidal wave, which sweeps over your old personality. An educated woman expects to forget her feelings of self-sufficiency. Since she usually has an attitude of superiority in relation to most people most of the time, when she's with her fiancé she looks forward to melting with happiness that someone so great, intelligent, powerful, and interesting as *him* takes an interest in her. Even young women who long for it, do recognize the danger of this kind of love. They all know of someone who let her defenses down and ended up with an unworthy partner. We ourselves know of a woman who initially felt this kind of love for her fiancé, but now that the marriage date is approaching she is terrified. She has discovered "moral flaws" in him, but things have gone too far for her to break the engagement. Marriages based on love encounter such problems quite often. People fall in love, get married, but after a year or so become disillusioned with each other. Since they have little in common, they turn to friends, kin, and colleagues as their real community. In this, the GPCR generation is not so different from their grandparents' generation. Both cohorts looked to Dumas's *Woman of the Camelias* for romantic inspiration. Our students have added D. H. Lawrence, but the pattern of expectation seems not to have changed dramatically.

The formal institution which deals with women's issues is the National Women's Federation. It operates under an official provision that prohibits "feminism" or special attention to women at the expense of "other social groups." Nonetheless, if you can scratch a young Chinese woman, even a very worldly one, you will not find an oppressed Western feminist. Sensitive, experienced, educated young women are not blind to sexual inequality. As one pointed out, she sees the problem as enormously complex and as one of the greatest burdens inherited from the old society. But when she thinks about sexual equality what springs into her mind is her grandmother, the distance separating her from her grandmother is unimaginable. Another student said that she thought women her age had "internal problems." She spent her childhood with her mother and grandmother. She learned certain attitudes from them which were incompatible with the more progressive ideas she learned about later in school. The GPCR thrust another set of expectations on her generation of Chinese women. Now, she has been at least three different women, and she isn't even an adult (i.e., forty) yet.

It has taken us some time to adjust to how thoroughly culture determines the relations between the sexes. In some regards Chinese women look very strong. The government bureaucrat, scientist, and teacher do exist, and they in turn act in an unofficial way as mentors promoting younger women. Women drive trucks and buses, they do labor, they work in heavy industrial factories as well as sex-segregated light industry. A new genre of fiction has emerged to discuss the social problems encountered by these new women. Educated women have trouble finding husbands. Men fear women who have high positions and they don't want their wives to make more money than they do. Our students' claim to the contrary, there is a growing number of women who avoid marriage or get divorced. Students always mention equal pay for equal work as the most important achievement of Chinese women. Some even echo the official claim that the Chinese family will never be the same again because women earn money now. But the signs of sexual inequality remain, transmitted in language, customs, proverbs, stereotypes, operas, manners, and protocols.

The difference between how we see them and how they see themselves is the key. Chinese women submerge the sexual dialectic into the fine gradations of hierarchical status and power. Individual women have the chance to side-step inequalities through examination, education, and Party hierarchy. Status and position can reinforce notions of female inferiority, since men still occupy most of the high positions. But this social hierarchy has also undercut simple sexual domination in reality and in cultural imagination.

One day Xiao Qian arrived at our dorm while we were figuring our expense accounts. We have a domestic money account that belongs to both of us, but the rest each of us controls separately. Tani was paying back some cash she'd borrowed from the common pot. Xiao Qian couldn't believe his eyes. He thought the whole idea of separate money so ludicrous he laughed all the way down the hall. He didn't find it at all funny though, when Tani told him she would not miss the professional conference she had been scheduled to attend in Berlin next August, and regrettably could not attend her father-in-law's eightieth birthday party.

24

Sexism

Shanghai, April 4, 1982

Some students had told us we should see *Dangdai Ren (Contemporaries)*, a new film by Huang Shuqin. So when it came to the campus we went. The five other foreign experts—Nelson and Holly, Anne, Valerie, and John and Jane—decided to go too, because their classes also recommended it. The story takes place at a tractor factory outside Guilin. Production overfulfills its quota, but it turns out shoddy goods. Neighboring communes keep returning the machines to maintenance for repair. The young production chief doesn't care, since on paper he's doing his job. Complicating things, this production chief wants to marry the factory manager's daughter, Wang Weidan. Cai Ming, the handsome, charismatic, musical (he does a soft-shoe routine in one scene) assistant factory manager, really wants to reform the entire plant, and the story's main plot line focuses on Cai Ming's attempts to rectify the situation. After a number of amusing, frustrating setbacks, he sends his fiancée, a fellow worker at the factory, off to Beijing to obtain new investment capital to update the plant. The last scenes show the old factory manager finally retiring after a moving self-criticism, as Cai Ming takes over.

Contemporaries had two important subplots. The first centered on Wang Weidan, the privileged, fashionable daughter of the factory manager. She has an unrequited passion for Cai Ming. Soft filters exaggerated the actress's good looks, and heavy make-up made her seductive and pouty. She wore unusually provocative costumes. In one scene, she emerges from a public bathhouse wearing short shorts and a sleeveless shirt to accost Cai Ming on a deserted street corner. The second subplot introduced a domestic tragicomedy. The factory's chief engineer and his wife, an assemblyline worker, have twin boys. This is a real blessing under the current birth control policy, but since both parents work, childcare becomes an irresolvable problem. Initially the engineer shoulders his share of the housework and childcare. However, his obligations mount every time Cai Ming makes a successful effort to modernize the plant, and the wife ends up being overwhelmed by the "lucky" burden. A serious conflict develops between socialist loyalty and sexual equality.

Huang Shuqin shot the film in vivid technicolor and heightened its pace with many short scenes and fast transitions. Most Chinese films favor a deadly slow version of the 1930s French *mise en scène*, which subordinates cinematographic technique to filmic narrativity. In *Contemporaries*, the images supported the narrative. Shots of automobiles, motor scooters, cement highways, airplanes, and a long sequence of Chinese passengers mingling with foreign tourists at the Guilin airport reconfirmed the theme of modernization. Huang used images to contrast the old and the new. In one sequence, a car containing visiting dignitaries slows to a crawl behind what appears to be a very slow-moving tractor. The camera pans around to the front of the tractor to reveal a water buffalo towing the tractor back to the factory. Another skillfully edited sequence shows factory officials at the top of a flight of stairs leading to the auditorium. As guests arrive, Huang cut to a closeup of feet running down the stairs to greet the visitor, then marching back up the stairs. Since the guests keep arriving, the feet keep running up and down the stairs. We also saw some obvious borrowings. Though not exactly a musical, Huang seemed to have been influenced by the light, facile pace and color scheme of films like *The Umbrellas of Cherbourg*. A thoroughly gratuitous scene showed the hero in a shower, naked to the waist several times; female characters began taking off their dresses before the camera moved away. During an airport arrival scene, the jet exhaust lifted the fiancée's already short skirt up around her thighs. All these cinematic clichés have become second nature to Western films. It startled us to see them for the first time in a Chinese film.

Generally, Chinese audiences don't make much noise. The night we saw *Contemporaries*, the audience went crazy, laughing, grunting, groaning, talking. The sequence which evoked the most knowing roars of laughter was a long slapstick routine where the requisition clerk finds himself caught between the competing demands of the production and maintenance departments. The competitors physically pull the clerk from side to side and he ends up drenched with sweat but still unable to satisfy either of them. Finally, he slips on a big wooden abacus and falls flat on his face.

When the film was over and the lights came on the five other foreign experts looked quite irritable. John and Jane, who usually find nothing but good in anything Chinese, shifted uneasily in their seats. "Why was Wang Weidan always lounging around, showing off her legs and bare arms, and screwing up her mouth provocatively?" Valerie asked. Jane and John said they thought the love scenes between Cai Ming and his fiancée had been too steamy. They all were repulsed by the Wang Weidan character. Her pursuit of Cai Ming seemed completely gratuitous. Jane said she couldn't see how Wang could claim she had emancipated herself just because she refused to marry the production chief. Valerie thought the so-called "emancipated" Wang Weidan promoted all the old clichés about female weakness by crying everytime she didn't like something. "This is what we complain about at home," Holly said. "It's certainly disheartening to see it here."

Holly said she thought that the most sexist scene in the movie was the exchange between Cai Ming and the wife of the chief engineer. The female assembly workers confront Cai Ming. They say they will go on a sympathy strike unless he does something about their friend's childcare problem. The twins' mother snorts at so-called women's liberation, saying it's liberated her right into slavery. Cai Ming resolves the problem not by giving his chief engineer some time off, but by sending the wife home to take care of the children. "For God's sake," said Holly who is pregnant, "why is the answer to the woman's question the same in a socialist country as in a capitalist one—send the women home?"

We felt just as vehemently but were curious as to why the regular audience responded so enthusiastically to the film. So we decided to check with our students and ask them what they had thought of it. One of the older men said he and his group of friends had enjoyed the movie because of its wit and humor. It was a nice little film that took a caustic look at mundane problems like bureaucracy, backdoorism, incompetent management, and domestic contradiction. "Chinese audiences live with these problems," he said. "They know Huang was aiming the camera at ordinary people." He suggested that maybe the foreign experts could not appreciate the film because we do not lead regular lives and have no way to measure how close to reality the film got. We let the student talk, waiting for him to mention the sexism. He never did.

We thought maybe he hadn't said anything because being male, he might not be sensitive to the issue. We turned to a female student, who repeated what the man had already said. We pushed her a little. We asked her what she thought about the Wang Weidan character. "Oh," she said, "there are so many girls like Wang around now. They're only interested in clothes and boyfriends. Their parents spoil them, so they think they should get everything they want." We asked her if she found Wang too sexy. "Not at all," she replied. "You must have seen her type around." We just didn't feel like admitting we hadn't. The woman apparently hadn't noticed the uncomfortable pause. "Where did you see the sex?" she asked. We marshalled the evidence: the shorts, the skimpy, tight sweater, the fiancée's thighs, the shower scene, the bathhouse scene, the kissing. The more we talked, the less convinced she looked. Finally, she just shrugged her shoulders, as though to say something had gone wrong with our eyes. Since she obviously hadn't noticed the sexual images, we wondered what she thought about the ploy to send the twins' mother home. She responded immediately, saying that all women these days want to spend the first three years of their baby's life at home on extended maternity leave, if possible.

By this time we were more interested in the gap of perception than in the film itself. We heard that Huang Shuqin was giving a talk on campus a couple of days later, so we decided to go and find out what the director had intended to do with the film. The auditorium was packed. Huang turned out to be a pleasant, solid-looking woman in her fifties with a commanding voice. Her talk focused mainly on how she'd created characters and how she'd chosen the actors. She said she had wanted Cai Ming to be extraordinary but not superhuman, and that's why she gave him the ability to maintain presence of mind when others became confused, yet included a scene of him getting drunk to make his character plausible. Her most trying moment had come when she decided on an ugly actor to play the role. That came as a big surprise to us, since the actor had seemed perfectly handsome to us.

Finally Huang got around to discussing female characters. She began by defending the actress who had played Cai Ming's fiancée. Those who had criticized her failed to understand that the fiancée was a secondary, passive character, whose only function was to highlight the active nature of Wang Weidan. Huang called Wang an "instinctual" woman, not too intelligent or educated, a good-natured woman whose love for Cai Ming was genuine. Her role in the plot had been intended to show how even ordinary people can deepen their own self-understanding. Cai Ming understood Wang

Weidan and helped her transfer her feelings for him to the collective unit. That was why she appeared in the last scene as his secretary. This was another surprise. We actually hadn't recognized the vague, well-dressed clerk hovering around Cai Ming in the last scene as Wang Weidan. Wang's instinctual nature, continued Huang, had positive elements because passionate impulses in women should not be condemned. But Wang had to learn how to turn selfish desire to more productive ends. Wang Weidan had also taken a big step in the struggle for a personal choice in marriage. She rejected the young production chief, even though he had already given her parents a color television set as a "feudal" bride price. Wang had genuinely emancipated herself and contributed to the modernization of the individual.

Huang's gloss was plausible, but did not convince us. Movies communicate messages through complex cultural codes, embodied in images. Huang's intention had turned out to be quite different from what we expected. But our original objection still existed. Those were sexual images we had seen. It did not matter that Huang never once referred to having sexualized her "instinctual" character or that the Chinese audience didn't see any sex in the film. From a long-range point of view, sexualized clichés borrowed from the West will eventually alter Chinese perception.

Huang had a great deal to say about the engineer's wife, but none of it had anything to do with the issue of sexual equality raised by Holly. According to Huang, the character illustrated the worst problem faced by young families—the childcare problem. Even when the young generation acts selflessly, the irresolvable problem of childcare interferes with their work and domestic happiness. Huang repeated the contention that the childcare problem affected both the husband and the wife. The only solution was "to probe around for a gap," to find a quasi-legal justification for letting the twins' mother go home on extended leave. Huang remained blandly unconcerned with the problem of sexual equality that her solution had raised at least from our Western standpoint. She said only that she had made a special effort to create realistic female characters. She admitted that she had gotten her inspiration from old Western films. In the 1930s and 1940s Hollywood turned out fabulous movies starring unrealistically beautiful women, she said, but after World War II neo-realism successfully reversed that tendency. The new directors in China could learn a lot about characters by studying European neo-realism. And that was as close as Huang got that night to a discussion of feminine images in *Contemporaries*.

Huang's discussion added to our understanding of *Contemporaries*. But we also noticed that some people in the audience were getting restless. Quite a number just got up and walked out. When we left we caught up with one of our students and asked him why. Some people left, he replied, because they wanted Huang to gossip more about the lives of the movie stars, and they thought the lecture was too serious and boring. He himself felt that Huang just didn't have anything to say. This student criticized the character of Cai Ming. No man who lived through the turmoil of the GPCR would ever have been so defiant and obvious. The GPCR made people very cautious. Real contemporaries scheme, maneuver, and strategize to avoid direct confrontations with problems. Cai Ming was a false, unbelievable character. In fact, the student went on, the whole movie was phony, silly and second-rate.

This student and a number of others then asked us why we were so interested in this particular film. We decided to give them a copy of what we had written. They apparently circulated this letter around, because we started getting all sorts of responses soon afterwards. The woman who had told us most mothers wanted extended maternity leaves walked straight up to Tani and told her bluntly that she had found the quality of our observations really disappointing. It showed her how foreign we still were, and that we still didn't understand how difficult balancing family and work is for Chinese women. When Tani became more aware and sensitive, she would drop her objections to the twins' mother wanting to go home. Several people said they were a little shocked at all the emphasis we have put on sexuality. They really didn't see it. Finally, a very well-informed man came around to say he'd considered our analysis peculiar when he first read it. Then he heard from a friend at another university that a similar story was circulating around his campus. A foreign expert there had taken her visiting parents to see *Contemporaries*, and all three of them had had the same reaction to the film as we did. This student wanted to say the entire round robin finally made him realize that even the perception of sex differed from culture to culture.

25

Mountain Climbing

Shanghai, April 27, 1982

*A*pril 17 we joined John and Jane, Lao Zheng, and our former student Xiao Zhong, now assigned as a junior member of the college FAO, and set out to climb Huangshan in southern Anhui. We had to get up around 3:30 A.M. in order to take the 5 A.M. train to Wuhu via Nanjing, and arrived there early in the afternoon. Wuhu lies along the Yangtze River, a little provincial town with a population of less than half a million. Still it forms one of the country's major rice-producing centers, and has broad new boulevards, many new buildings, and a lovely Mirror Lake with a pavilion for tea-drinking. The next day we drove by minibus from Wuhu to the foot of Huangshan, a six-hour trip into the countryside. Fields of green rice buds, yellow rape, and purple clover stretched out en route. Mostly the farmers use buffalo for ploughing, but we also saw a few tractors turning over the fields for the spring rice planting. We arrived at the foot of the mountain and spent the night in a comfortable inn.

We arose early the next morning and began the climb up the back of the mountain about 8 A.M., arriving at the Beihai peak just

Hotel at the top of Huangshan, where we spent the night. (China Publishing House)

before noon. The next day we would begin descending the front. We were not going to "mountain climb" California-style. The FAO and Lao Yang had instructed us to wear raincoats so that we could stand in the mist and rain and enjoy the scenery; and big, rubber-bottomed shoes so we wouldn't slip on the mountain staircases. We carried no backpacks, no survival kits, or Bowie knives. In the next few days, we would see Shanghai women climbing the mountain stairs in high-heeled shoes, honeymooners in their new suits, and workers wearing ordinary blue pants and jackets. No one made any concession to the rusticity of the site. That is precisely the point. No one seemed to acknowledge that we have come out of the city into "Nature." Rather innocently, we asked Xiao Zhong whether she thought of Huangshan as wilderness. Not at all, she replied. So we explained that when we go mountain climbing in the U.S. we like to imagine that we've escaped from civilization and gone into the wilderness. Actually we had asked Xiao Zhong an idle question because we knew Huangshan had been domesticated since at least the Tang dynasty. Staircases riddle the back and front of the mountain. We walked down the ones cut after Liberation. But abandoned stairs date all the way back to the seventh century. Every peak has a staircase, every cave has been found and named, at each turn in the path you step into a familiar vista, commemorated by former poets,

Tani and Don at Huangshan. (Zheng Xuexuan)

and dotted conveniently along the paths are temples, pavilions, and shops offering hot meals and cold drinks, or just a comfortable place to rest your legs.

Since Liberation, people climb Huangshan for two reasons. First, for the physical sport. Most of the journey up Xiao Zhong looked glum, because she had climbed this mountain before. Then, during the GPCR, the objective had been to climb the more difficult, precipitous front in one day; it took us two days coming down leisurely. After ten hours of climbing, she had spent four days in bed recovering. People also climb Huangshan just to look at it. Scaling the mountain means virtually entering a Chinese painting, or a "fairy land" as another friend put it. Walking becomes the means to enter into the world of traditional landscape. Just as *penjing* (an artificial scene of rock in a small flat bowl) represents a microcosmic reduction of this fairy land, Huangshan allows a macrocosmic dilation of a painting. Huangshan does not exactly provide the prototype of a painting, although painters and poets have been seeking inspirations here for centuries. More accurately Huangshan expresses one level of the macro-microcosmic space, the stacking quality which encourages the eye and imagination to see the natural site as a painting and painting as the imagined reality of the natural site. You must go to Huangshan to see how faithfully the landscape painting adheres to the presentation of nature as a series of contemplative vistas, and how the natural world has been tamed and cultivated to conform to a painterly human visuality. *Penjing*, Huangshan, painting are *all* expressions of the same aesthetic convention.

The pressure of time meant we could not wait for the weather. Some couples we know from the college spent a week at the peak, waiting hours for the mist to clear or appear, the clouds to gather, the sun to rise or set, so that they might take a photograph of the same view an artist could duplicate from memory in a painting. As we expected, every peak in the range has a name—Carp's Back Ridge, Lotus Mountain Ridge, individual rocks have names—Monkey Looking at the Mountain Scenery, for example; at one very famous location an ancient pine supposedly greets the guests, another sends them on their way. Hardly the equivalent of going to the Redwood National Park and looking at the tall trees. The pines which greet and send the guests have more in common with domesticated animals, pets.

Anyway, we spent the afternoon of the 19th enjoying the Beihai vistas. It rained the next morning as we began the first leg of our descent. We felt quite disappointed, because this leg is the most exquisite of all. Sleet, hail, and rain continued falling, and we saw virtually nothing but the rock paths in front of us. It wasn't a complete disappointment; one attractive feature of the rocks is that they are covered with lichen and moss, all shades and colors, even the phosphorescent blue familiar from paintings, so we at least had that to watch through the fog. We crossed streams, following granite steps down through the caves in boulders, up across gently rounded ridges which seemed to fall off nowhere, since we couldn't see more than a few feet ahead. In one small forest we stopped at a rude wooden shack for cups of coffee and tea, which inspired all kinds of jokes about travelers in the famous novel *Water Margin* who stop innocently at wine shops and get drugged, minced, and made into dumplings by the bandit proprietors.

But the weather kept getting worse. About three hours into the climb, Jane noticed that we were going up more than coming down. No one paid any attention to her. We continued our journey. The path got more beautiful and more wild. The steps seemed less kempt. Finally we began a straight ascent; the hand railings disappeared. We emerged onto a sloped, huge, egg-shaped stone crest, separated from a second rather more spiny crest, by a path about a foot wide. Up through the gap came blasts of fog and wind almost blowing us off balance. We went ahead anyway; Lao Zheng and Xiao Zhong, followed by John and Jane, Tani and Don. Then we heard panic. There was no more path in front of us, just a sheer precipitous, slippery drop. Predictably the wind increased in velocity. Safety lay on the other side of the gap. Each of us turned around and waited for a lull in the wind, when we could jump back across the gap to the rounder peak and climb down very slowly. Jane leaped, and then, safe, she panicked and began trembling.

Nearly an hour later, still in a windy storm, we found the turn we had missed, and descended safely to the midmountain hostel. In all we had been climbing up and down for six hours. We were thoroughly soaked, exhausted from the exertion and fright, and now felt suddenly numbed, famished, giddy. Lao Zheng, our now completely discredited guide, kept laughing in embarrassment, telling us we had accidentally climbed the infamous Lotus Peak in a windstorm, the highest, most dangerous mountain in the entire chain. When the weather cleared the next morning and we looked over at the bald, rocky Lotus Peak rising in the distance, we finally realized what real danger we had been in. Jane unfortunately never entirely recovered. She was too tired and frightened, too cold even to eat, so she could not fall asleep that night, and so embarrassed she wouldn't come out and sit around the pail of hot coal the hostel staff brought out to warm up its chilled, wet, frightened guests. The rest of us spent the evening bragging about our climb, telling jokes with a group of Hong Kong tourists, and laughing ourselves silly with relief.

We woke up to a clear, sunny dawn. Coming out of the hostel onto the front yard, we discovered literally a "sea of clouds" in full tide, right in front of us, punctured at spots by sharp peaks, all of it illuminated from behind by the rising sun. It was so fantastically beautiful we laughed, overjoyed. That morning, the descent really took us through a fairy land. We could see the steps stretching out before us, down into the mist at the bottom of the mountain. Each time we turned a corner a delicate, new perspective opened up before us: extraordinary, twisted pines pushing out of sheer rocks, orchids growing upside down from rock ceilings, boulders lodged together allowing only the narrowest path through the cleft, banks of violets in bloom in the shady areas, and, as we descended further, flame-colored, wild azaleas everywhere. When we were in Guilin during the winter vacation we had experienced that common shock at finding the limestone mountains exactly as painters had represented them. We had a stronger feeling of recognition when climbing Huangshan, because everything felt so small and because the mountain in the sunlight seemed so familiar, despite our momentary danger in the storm. The conventional cliché painting of orchid grass on rocks became a reality we could frame simply by the lazy movement of a shifting gaze. The tortured pine recalled a former vision. Inside the repetitive stacking of macro-microcosms we discovered a dense richness of possibilities for looking and representation, limited only by the randomness of chance. In the warm sunlight our final descent was poignant and we regretted that it was over so soon.

26

Graves and Bound Feet

Shanghai, May 10, 1982

We particularly wanted to see Qufu and Taishan. Qufu, Shandong province, is Confucius's birthplace and the site of the imperial monument to him. Confucius, whose surname was Kung, and 76 generations of Kung descendents are buried there. Nearby Taishan is one of China's five sacred mountains. Since we'd missed Omei Mountain in Sichuan last winter, we were particularly eager to climb Taishan. The first nine days of the trip took us through the Yangtze River basin, wandering leisurely through a series of old towns: Zhenjiang where the Yangtze meets the Grand Canal, to pretty sluggish Yangzhou across the river which had been Marco Polo's fief under the Yuan dynasty, and after a wild bus ride—somehow we'd forgotten about the first of May, the Labor Day celebration—to the provincial capital of Nanjing. We remained there for several days, visiting relatives and leisurely seeing the sights. Then we left by train for the north.

We arrived in Qufu the evening of May 4, anniversary of the 1919 anti-Confucian movement. The coincidence seemed particularly appropriate. We didn't know what to expect from Qufu, except what we'd read about the devastation left behind by Red Guard attacks. Still, Qufu held out the possibility we might learn something about what we keep calling Chinese "tradition," for lack of a better word. And maybe a little more about the logic of the GPCR attack on it.

An attendant led us through the darkness to our room in the Kung family mansion, part of which is now a tourist hotel. Our first impression was disappointing. The compound looked like an ugly, little cement storehouse with too many windows. But the next morning we realized how wrong we'd been. The one-storied buildings were brick, not concrete. The barracks were actually wings of a huge, sprawling complex, each room opening out into a courtyard formed by the backwalls of the previous wing. It certainly wasn't what we had expected, a venerable, precious old antique firmly secured in the past. In fact it didn't resemble a museum at all. Nothing had died. We walked over to the actors' dressing rooms which a member of the seventy-second generation had built at the end of the Qing dynasty. *Nagel's* was perfectly correct: the man had indeed destroyed the balance of the courtyard. It was wonderful evidence, both that the Kungs had never stopped living in this mansion, and that not all Kungs had infallibly good taste. Windows installed in some of the rooms in the early twentieth century had changed the building's original conception. So did the garden house we found at the back of the compound which would have been more appropriate somewhere in colonial India. For better or worse, the Kungs kept everything alive, and transformed their heritage with time.

We spent the whole morning in the residence. We were aware the buildings had been placed according to extremely fine geomantic reckonings, *fengshui*, but knowing nothing about geomancy we had no idea the significance the layout actually had. Practically, the residents benefited. During the day the rooms are cool, and at night they are warm. Everything in the entire complex is made of gray, fired brick. It's as though the builders had banished mud, leaving it to the common people outside the walls. Even the tiny gardens are lined with rock, hiding the soil from view. Stones pave the courtyards. Huge, chiseled rocks form stairsteps or, when up-ended, become rough benches. Weird stones set into two-foot high pedestals stand against the walls. In the area where our room was located, shades of gray, faded, white mortar and granite predominated. But in one area at the back of the residence we found a series of rooms fixed up as museum displays. The small rooms glowed. On the walls were large, polished marble slabs hung in mahogany frames, and yellowed calligraphy scrolls. Each of the rosewood chairs, big as thrones, had a brilliant red silk cover, richly embroidered in blue, gold, violet, and pink threads. The doors had been hung with a profusion of fuschia, orange, and yellow silks which accentuated the deeper, conservative tones of the walls and furniture. Although the silks were old and faded, we could still see the basic aesthetic: silk, polished wood, fired brick, and stone. Thus, we got a glimpse of the old world of privilege.

The Kungs lived in Qufu as Confucius's living issue, and as the caretakers of the Confucian cult. After lunch we walked from the Kung mansion around the corner to the Confucius temple. It stands in its own large, rectangular compound separated from the flattened mud outside by enormous red walls. We crossed a stone bridge and entered the compound though a gate in the red wall. Beyond us lay more and more gates, some set into walls, others just standing there in open space. Except for the gates, the first half of the temple ground is completely free of structures. Rows of ancient cypress trees fill the empty space, forming right angles against the protective outer wall. The earth at the foot of each tree rises slightly into a round, nodular bulge. We walked slowly, slightly beyond the trees, into the inner shrines—the twelfth-century Great Pavilion of the Constellation of Scholars (*Guiwen ge*), the thirteen bulking pavilions sheltering the imperial steles all mounted on giant rock turtles, and the Great Temple of Confucius (*Dacheng dian*).

As we penetrated farther we increasingly felt the power of the intelligence that had shaped the architectural space. Some of the temple structures are actually very tall. Yet the overall design masks their height. The illusion is created that the structures are pinned to the ground. The large, tense buildings and the lush marble terraces encircling them like bibs give the whole inner complex a padded quality, quite unlike the severe geometry of the cypress trees. The Great Temple of Confucius stands at the back of the rectangular field. Its marble columns, hollowed in the center and formed into writhing dragons, clouds, and flowers support an enormous two-storied structure. The oceanic sweep of the roof, the columns, and the huge inner beams contributed to our fantasy that maybe the building had not been built but inflated. It seemed almost to have been made originally of a soft malleable plastic which, once filled with air, had stiffened over the centuries into its present solid form. We knew *Dacheng dian* was monumentally tall, but we kept sinking into its deepness and width, like hard things into a pillow.

The temple yard and the administrative offices around the perimeter are filled with steles commemorating Confucius. Steles maintain their essential rock quality. That is, the building blocks which are used to make a cathedral or shrine are more than just themselves, since they become parts of an edifice. You can forget, in the case of a famous cathedral, that you are looking at something as fundamental as stones. We stood in the center of the memorial yard surrounded by tall granite steles. They were big, ponderous, heavy and will last forever. All of a sudden, it seemed very clear why the Red Guards had to attack the steles, the imperial turtles on which important steles are mounted, and even the old cypress trees.

A friendly attendant took us to a side courtyard where we could see what the temple had looked like before the restoration. Pieces of wrecked stele lay scattered in the long grass in front of an abandoned building. The scene conveyed the hilarious sadness of the GPCR. To buy gasoline in China one needs official coupons. The Red Guards did not have them, so they could not burn the temple down. All they could do was break the rocks. Now all of the broken steles are being put back together and hoisted onto their pedestals again. We could almost feel the frustration of the rebels. Later, when we went to see the shrine of the Duke of Zhou who was Confucius's own model ruler, we found a new stele standing by the gate, which said that on such and such a date the Gang of Four had destroyed precious historical objects here. Inside the little temple we saw a man on a ladder bent over the chest of a large clay image, carefully molding slip around the gown of the new Duke of Zhou. Another man standing nearby remarked that the destruction in Qufu by the Red Guards had been heartbreaking. They see wreckage when they see what remains of their monuments. We see an almost unendurable permanence.

Standing at the center of the Confucius cult solved little for us. The Qufu temple had once been the physical center of something very important. It's difficult to say exactly what Confucianism was. At one level, just the ideology of the ruling class, legitimated by the state. But its vitality made it much more. At a deeper level, all Chinese who worshiped ancestors, submitted to the obligation of filiality, subscribed to the view that the universe is held together by the Three Human Bonds linking monarch and subject, father and son, husband and wife—that is practically all Chinese—were Confucianists. None of the people we've met could by any stretch of imagination be called Confucianists. But we keep getting the impression that Red Guards who attacked Confucian temples all over the country had been stabbing themselves in the heart.

Our last stop was the Kung family burial ground. We left our taxi at the gate and walked into a huge, round, rambling cypress forest. On the ground lay hundreds of grave mounds and burial stones, scattered in what looked like random fashion. Anywhere we stood we could see leaning stones and strange lumps pushing out of the ground. Many older grave stones had fallen years ago, their inscriptions worn away by the weather. Some must have been shoved over by vandals. Others were more like tombs, with free-standing commemorative gates in front of them. Really important Kungs who married into the imperial families or won degrees in the examination system had miniature "spirit ways" lined with tiny elephants and camels leading to their tombs. But there were so many stones and the earth had buckled in such peculiar ways, the animals looked a little dazed. The sun shone through the haze and the shadows fell across the graves, increasing the ramshackleness of the strange forested graveyard.

We walked back to the entrance and turned right into a walled-off courtyard. Behind some empty buildings, inside a small rectangular space, are three hillocks. One of them is Confucius's grave. A wooden sign asks visitors not to climb the mounds, that is all. We hung around. The crowds jamming the temple had either decided graves weren't worthy of a visit or still felt the strength of powerful GPCR taboos. After a while, an old farmer came by. He stopped and asked us very defensively whether we thought Confucius had been a great, cultivated person. We said yes, of course. The man smiled and relaxed. He led us to a stone griffin standing on the path leading to the grave mound. This statue, he explained, used to be alive. In Confucius's own time, the griffin spoke every language of the world, and could travel 18,000 *li* (roughly 6,000 miles) a day. Confucius rode the griffin, and the two of them visited many foreign countries, like the United States, where the griffin translated for the sage. The storyteller did not say whether the griffin had died or would come back to life again some day.

We should have paid more attention to the griffin legend. We left for Taishan, once a living deity and so long a center of pilgrimage that even Confucius is reputed to have worshiped there. Emperors sacrificed to Taishan and gave it official rank. Along its stone staircases are temples to the Princess of the Colored Clouds, goddesses who healed the blind and the infertile, and various other Daoist deities. We reached the foot of the mountain on May 6 and began climbing the next morning. It didn't take us long to figure out that most of the people around us were not tourists but devotees. Among them were crowds of old peasant women dressed in black padded pants and shirts, their hair tied back in little buns, climbing the holy mountain on bound feet. Some of them had brought their daughters or granddaughters along. But most seemed to have come in sisterhoods of about a dozen women. All of them carried bundles and would climb very rapidly for about fifteen minutes, then sit down on the stone benches along the steps to rest and smoke. Some of them wanted to examine Tani up close. One woman was sitting alone when we turned a curve. She patted the place next to her on the bench invitingly and waved a cigarette. Tani and the old woman sat companionably together smoking in silence, but neither of us could understand her regional peasant dialect.

Bound feet on Taishan pilgrimage. (T. E. Barlow)

Without exception every rural woman on that mountain over the age of forty had bound feet. Tani has a memory from years ago when she started studying Chinese, of seeing a photograph of a lily foot for the first time: it made her nauseated. Gradually, her feelings have changed somewhat. The feet themselves have become more familiar, and so have taken on many different meanings. Once when she was a student in Taiwan, Tani was sitting on a street corner in the old city of Lugang, when a woman came out of a door carrying a bowl of water. Unaware she was being watched, the woman unwrapped her tiny feet, washed them very slowly, and then carefully wrapped them up again. Unbound, those little feet look very commonplace, like little fleshy elbows. The mundane actuality was a little frightening. Tani began to question her own previous feelings. The rage she had previously felt was not purely rage. It included a little shame at the grotesquery of the women who had had to accept the binding, who even now, like the Taishan pilgrim women, offer replicas of tiny shoes to the fertility goddesses. Also, perhaps most of all, the bound foot signifies what is strangest about Chinese custom. It is the sign of the Other, of the "Orient." At some level, we are all disgusted by alien customs, yet our own culturally peculiar forms of oppression must be equally alien and repulsive to other peoples. In the case of Chinese women, it's so easy to displace repulsion with pity and rage. Because what's far more puzzling than the feet themselves is that women whose feet are bound do not consider their feet to be the most important part of them. Peasant women with bound feet are not cripples. They are not pitiable. They do not perceive themselves as primarily victimized. Their feet hurt them and make it hard for them to climb the mountain. But their feet are "normal," in the sense that all oppressions are cultural and local in nature.

It took us seven and a half hours to reach the peak. The Red Guards either didn't think the women's deities worth the bother, or didn't have enough energy to climb all the way up. The numerous statues of the Princess of the Colored Clouds and her retinue were all intact. Entering the shrine compound, we saw pilgrims making food and money offerings. It startled us to see young men burning incense before the goddesses. In many of the shrines and temples we've visited elsewhere we'd seen young men kneeling awkwardly, self-conscious, and embarrassed. On Taishan, these young men prayed with the practice and concentration of the older folks. But it was already late afternoon and the fierce whistling wind and deep fog had come up. We checked into the mountaintop hostel.

At 4 A.M., just before dawn, the hostel attendants began pounding on the doors up and down the hall, awakening all the guests in time for the sunrise. We had assumed the object of witnessing dawn was to see the famous sea of clouds. But we discovered the dawn had religious significance. As the peak began to light up we saw about a thousand or so people hunched on the rocks. Some had spent the night in the hostel or in tents nearby, but quite a number had obviously remained out in the open. Unfortunately the cloud that morning was too dense. The sun rose, but we didn't see it. The pilgrims didn't seem to care. We followed them toward the Temple of the Jade Emperor, where groups of people were milling around trying to squeeze their way in. We pressed forward too, not so much because we wanted to, but because we couldn't help it. The crowd thrust us briefly past the open, uncovered rock, the peak's highest point, enshrined like a fetish. Then we were pulled along into a room where a gilded image sat, wearing a heavily beaded cap. People shouted and jostled as they scrambled past the Jade Emperor. Pulling each other along, the crowd exited and we were expelled. One glimpse was enough. It was a wild, sensuous shrine.

The wind continued to howl. The cold ripped through our padded jackets. We went back inside the hostel for a warm breakfast. Later, beginning our descent, we saw devotees hunched around the Princess shrine eating wheatcakes and corn bread stuffed with scallions. Many women had put twigs into their buns. Further down, we saw pilgrims burning incense and paper, carefully wrapping the ash into envelopes to carry home to their villages.

The folk devotees are fascinating, and something in us was moved by the intensity of their worship. But how does that square with the modern world, socialism, and the four modernizations? The impatience of Mao and his Red Guard seemed more understandable. Later, on the train back to Shanghai we talked about the "contradiction" with the provincial official who shared our compartment. He was an intense, rustic man in his thirties, very curious about the U.S. But the interest was not abstract. He wanted a point of comparison outside of China. His conversation reverted constantly to China and its problems, particularly the issue of popular belief.

We found ourselves in agreement with much of what he said. The effect of the GPCR was the revival of superstition and religion, he argued. Unless the Party actively combats cult worship it springs back to fill the gap left by a discredited Marxism. This failure pained him most. To illustrate his point, he told us he and his wife both work long hours, so they had hired a village woman to look after their child. At first she seemed quite satisfactory. But gradually they realized she was purposely subverting their child with bits and pieces of local religion, plus a little Catholicism she had picked up from somewhere. So they had to let her go. But the incident pointed to the more fundamental, disturbing problem. People turn to folk religion because the Party no longer has anything better to offer them. Marxism should not be offered as a belief, he said. It is a method of analysis, a practice. As a method, Marxism should change and adapt to material, social conditions. If it cannot do that it has no worth. Failures of ideology have already led to the collapse of discipline among village cadres. Local officials skip political meetings so they can go to temple or church. Village Party members are ignorant and know far too little about economics. Cadres use naked power and mask it with hypocritical rhetoric. They violate the law and alienate villages, so the Princess cult is thriving again. His implication was that the cults in themselves are not a threat to modernization. But they represent a backlash against the government and that does threaten progress, since the central government is the only entity capable of supporting modernization.

Every time this man said anything, he prefaced it with the comment that it represented his personal opinion and might not be "correct." After a while, we asked him how he could be so critical of the Party. He chuckled. Freedom to criticize was not the issue anymore, he said. He and his colleagues who hold similar ideas criticize until they exhaust themselves. But nothing happens. That was the problem. He still felt that one overriding fact justifies the existence of the Party, no matter what it does. A strong central government assures China's independence, and prevents China's recolonization by the industrial West, a genuine possibility should the center collapse.

We talked with him for several hours and came away with the admiration we've had so many times in China. The problems are so numerous; the past so unhappy. Yet, time after time, we met young men and women possessed with dedication and vision.

27

Aliens

Shanghai, May 27, 1982

*T*he two of us are what Xiao Hu calls "friendly foreigners." Imperceptibly we've found our balance. If we invite a guest over to the dorm for dinner now, we unself-consciously adopt appropriate behaviors and make the occasion into something our Chinese guests can enjoy without feeling uncomfortable. This came home to us when we got together with another cousin of Don's, who had visited us briefly in San Francisco a couple of years ago, and more recently came by to see us at S.T.C. When we first met him we spoke English, asked superficial questions about China, and offered him our best American hospitality. This time in Shanghai everything was reversed. We spoke Chinese, felt at ease inside the conventions of Chinese hospitality, and talked knowledgeably about our perception of the campus. Tani knew how to place the right parts of the fish on his plate, and Don filled his glass, urging him to drink. At the end of the meal we knew just how long to prolong the conversation and that we must walk him all the way from the foreign expert dorm to the college gate before finally saying goodbye.

It's a compromise. Being in a Chinese society seems often to elicit a kind of frank, jovial, brashly good humor in some Americans. Maybe Chinese value these stereotyped "American" characteristics in us. We don't think either of us has adopted that sort of persona, nor have we gone native. Differences will always be an issue for us, particularly for Tani. Once in Chongqing we were sitting eating dinner in a hotel restaurant, when a large Chinese family arrived. The daughter and her Caucasian husband were visiting from America with their small baby girl. The husband spoke Chinese like a native. He played with his daughter the way Chinese men do, using little endearments and clucking noises. But no matter how he adjusted his mannerisms or how many cups of tea and wine he poured for his older, Chinese in-laws, the invisible barriers remained. The relatives, who had clearly not had time to get used to him, leaned forward when talking to the wife, but imperceptibly away when responding to him. By the end of the meal, they had almost completely squeezed him out of the conversation.

There is a place for foreigners, or maybe it would be more accurate to say a range of foreignness tolerable in Shanghai. Aliens who refuse to modulate any of their habits remain beyond the pale. We know, for example, a story about a very patriotic British teacher who wore a Union Jack T-shirt and crash helmet and raced his bike, which he had decorated with red, white, and blue tape, up and down Huaihai Road. But the best example still remains our infamous predecessor Mr. Gross. A whole new round of Gross stories has surfaced recently. According to one, Gross never really loved the woman he married. Rather, before he had even the most rudimentary understanding of Chinese social convention, he had already started taking her out at night for walks. One evening they stayed in the park too long ("going to the park" is the euphemism for necking sessions), and the door guard accidentally locked them inside. After that Gross had to marry her because even he was "human" enough to realize that he had ruined her reputation. Another recent account has it that Gross is so stupid about social relations that he probably still has no idea that the woman he is married to recognized her passport out of China the minute she laid eyes on him. A third theory proposes China made Gross mentally ill, and that is why he married the first woman who was kind to him. There are even less plausible interpretations: The deranged Gross married the woman to keep her in bondage and humiliate her in some weird foreign way; he married her only to rescue her, after she told him the real story about her rightist family's suffering during the GPCR; his objective in coming to China was to find a wife so he could have a Chinese mother-in-law. People really did not understand Gross's foreignness. He in turn refused to act like a proper foreign expert.

He had quarrelsome, sloppy, lazy habits. He shot his mouth off whenever he felt like it, apparently almost purposely to scandalize the people around him. Once during a summer heat wave, students noticed that he was sweating profusely and thoughtfully brought him an electric fan. This infuriated Gross. "I came to China to get away from machines," he reportedly yelled at the students. They knew they had done something to upset him, but they could not conceive of a reason why anyone would want to get away from machines.

We think that Gross's innovations probably served some students' needs. In his composition class, he insisted that each essay be organized with an introduction, discussion, and conclusion. Any essay not following this Western format he literally threw directly into his large garbage can. We heard from one student that Gross was aggressive, but fair-minded. One day in class he asked students to talk about their most interesting experiences. One student began his speech very politely by saying he felt his talk would be inferior because his life had been rather dull. "If your life is so dull," Gross commented, "we don't want to hear about it at all." The student was publicly humiliated. Yet beneath this polite student's mild exterior was an ego as big as Gross's. Sometime later, when the occasion arose, he publicly returned the slight. Gross's feelings were very hurt; and he asked the student why he had been so rude all of a sudden. The student said that he'd only meant to return the insult. They talked it over and became close friends.

And despite all the misunderstanding Gross seems to have had some effect. Just recently three very good students approached us separately and told us special Gross stories. One said, "I must discharge an obligation to my teacher, Mr. Gross. He told me that to repay what he did for me, I should go around telling 'good stories about him, when he's gone.'" This loyal student told us how Gross had actually been an incredibly conscientious teacher. He required every student to keep a journal in English and criticized each journal meticulously. "We learned how to think straight from him, and how to write a decent essay," he said. Gross had a very good effect on some of his best students, but he also clearly alienated many, many others.

The more general legacy of Gross and others like him is not enlightenment but anxiety, a paralyzing sense of failure on the part of almost everyone involved. We realize this fully now, only because we are leaving, and the official summing up of our experience began several days ago at a special meeting hosted by the FAO and foreign languages department authorities. As per convention in these kinds of meetings, they asked us to give our "frank criticisms" of their department. We took the chance to talk a little about some of the

teaching problems foreign experts commonly encounter, particularly how the different expectations we and the Chinese have toward
learning affect classroom performance. We suggested that the
Chinese faculty be more explicit about what they want from us in
advance, and told them foreign teachers needed a little more
guidance. Presumptuously we described the sort of foreign experts
we thought the college should hire—young people with sufficient
knowledge about China, generalists rather than specialists in grammar (the Chinese favorite), or linguistics (the Western favorite). We
talked a little about book hoarding, insufficient library facilities,
the problem of the senior thesis, how to teach students to use the
card catalogue and the stacks. But mostly we discussed with them
our very strong feelings that the foreign experts' job should more
realistically be seen as a relatively humble one. The department
shouldn't expect too much from foreign experts or make too much
of us. A better plan might be to use us simply as foreign native
speakers in order to upgrade the language level of the department's
young, junior faculty. All of these suggestions represented our genuine feelings. And we got the sense that our Chinese colleagues who
were listening so politely had all had similar thoughts before.
Nothing we could tell them seemed particularly novel, although
they obviously recognized our good intentions.

Later Fang Quan came around. In light of our evaluations, she
said, she needed some advice about dealing with foreign experts
who have personal problems. But before she consulted with us, she
would have to tell us a Gross story. She had been responsible for
supervising Gross, she said, and when he first arrived he seemed
perfectly normal and enthusiastic about his job. For several
months, he dutifully prepared his lessons and met the classes on
time. But then things began happening. Talking with us during the
general evaluation session, she realized it had probably been a problem of cultural adjustment. But at that time, his eccentric behavior
in class had totally mystified her. Delegates of irate students began
arriving in her office, asking that she discipline Gross. Faculty
members displaced their anger onto her, since they felt it improper
to criticize the foreigner. For once, even the FAO did not know how
to handle the situation. Fang Quan had done nothing in spite of all
the pressures. Now she asked, "Should I have reprimanded him? I
didn't want to hurt his feelings, so I didn't say anything at the time."

We could not believe the amount of abuse the authorities
tolerated from Gross. We told her that the situation had nothing to
do with feelings. In the West contract outweighs social harmony. A
foreign expert should be expected to honor the contract in China, as
much as one did at home. Then we talked about firing an employee
for breach of contract. We felt that Fang Quan was interested in our

theory of contracts, but had no intention of ever firing anyone. What she seemed more intent on getting from us was some human explanation for why Gross had become, as she saw it, mentally ill. Gross, she said at one point, had actually begun to behave better at the beginning of his second year. Unfortunately, he fell in love shortly after that. Then he stopped doing class preparation all together. What should be done with foreign experts who have personal problems?

We had no answer. By now Fang Quan knows us fairly well. In soliciting our remarks, she wanted to see how we would approach a familiar problem from a slightly different angle. Gross had just been too strong a dose. The Gross problem may actually have brought Fang Quan and the students closer to the raw America than our own cautious, heavily mediated representations. And we suppose that if for that reason only, Gross's crashing around the department the way he did might have served some purpose. Yet with very few exceptions, he left behind almost universal bewilderment and disapproval.

Aliens like Gross who resisted all the attempts made to moderate his extremely peculiar behavior end up like the man we heard about (not Gross this time) who became so frustrated he threw his own mini-refrigerator out the dorm window. Foreigners who try to ignore the fine distinctions of race, background, and custom delude themselves. But if you neither resist, nor are overwhelmed by the pressure of Chinese culture, then it's possible to make a place for yourself here. We both have learned the difference between official patterns of behavior and personal relations where we are free to have friends and exchange feelings.

Realizing lately what has happened to us gave us a bit of a start. We think probably we've lost the defensiveness that often goes along with being an alien. We no longer see campus life as a challenge to our other, American personalities. It seems possible, in other words, for us to be foreigners of a certain kind: Xiao Hu's "friendly foreigners." Many of the other foreign experts we've met here, particularly those who have to live at the Jin Jiang Hotel instead of having dorms on campuses, really resent the terms of their duty in Shanghai. They don't know any Chinese people outside their students and the FAO cadres, and they have lots of complaints about the way they are treated. We had to think about the difference between our experience and the majority's experience. Partly we have escaped this resentment because our reception at S.T.C. has been so remarkably intelligent. The other reason lies in something we discovered about ourselves: We like Chinese social relations.

This sounds naive, and almost chauvinist on Don's part; actually it's more complicated than that, because we know of Overseas

Chinese who react against the Chinese just as vehemently as other foreigners. We recently received an American magazine article from Tani's mother, written by two former foreign experts, entitled "China Stinks." It catalogued all the ways life in China had proved intolerable to the couple, beginning with their perception that China is ugly, and listing the unfriendliness of the officials, the boredom, the hierarchies, the differential treatment, the controls, the inadequacies of their school, the *guanxi*, the efforts by students to exploit them, GPCR horror stories. Everything. Same problems; but different point of view. Underneath the article we detected a basic dislike of Chinese for being Chinese, and a kind of yearning that it would be so much easier for foreigners if Chinese people would just behave like Americans, like us.

One important reason why we have ended up liking Chinese rather than despising them is how we look at the differences between them and us. We do not explain one culture in terms of the other, a way of "understanding" that patches over key differences. We assume a Chinese feels as normal being Chinese as we do being Americans, and then try to figure what is distinctive about their version of "normalcy." A hierarchical, authoritarian society where everyone has a place is a society where everyone belongs. When we accepted the political, social, and academic positions designated to us by campus life, we started belonging here too. From our base we began extending out, developing a certain skill in personal encounters, and learning more about the depths of meaning that Chinese social relationships create. We now appreciate conventionalized behavior, like banqueting; ritualizing banishes the irrational in human beings, side-stepping it. The explicitness of *guanxi* does not seem gross to us, as it does to many of our foreign expert friends, because it makes social necessity more bearable. We even enjoy the arrogance and bravado of our students who can criticize their country's backwardness and not feel any need at all to *apologize* for being Chinese.

Several months ago, a slogan went up on campus, along the path from our dorm to the foreign language buildings. It said, "There is no such thing as a bystander." Yes, we still analyze our experiences and encounters, which is a way of detaching ourselves; but we see ourselves lately not so much as bystanders, but as temporary residents with specific, cumulative perspectives. Because we like the people around us doesn't mean that we accept them uncritically. We find the impulse to hide unpleasant things from our view quite unnecessary. The charade simply leads to judgments like those expressed in "China Stinks," that Chinese people are hypocrites and liars. We also still stumble sometimes, not knowing exactly what can be said publicly and what only privately. The conventional expectation that ugly situations should be beautified even when everyone involved knows better rubs very hard against the American habit of putting things out in the open.

28

Provincials

Beijing, June 20, 1982

We had a lot of trouble leaving S.T.C. Students kept coming around to say goodbye. We thought of last minute improvements on *Contemporary USA*, though it was much too late for revisions. Professor "Thirty-thousand" Hu, our colleague from the teaching seminar, graciously did the proofreading and Lao Yang delivered the completed manuscript to Comrade Wang for typing. During the days leading up to our departure, colleagues and FAO officers dropped in and out of the dorm, finishing last minute projects, requesting materials, making final clarifications in a translation. It was very easy to deny that we were leaving. The college community is so close and stable (too stable, too close, say many of the students), that we could easily confine our entire social lives exclusively to it. Each time we'd returned to Shanghai from a trip before, there had always been new gossip to catch up on. It was easy to half pretend we would be away for a while and then return to pick up from where we'd left off. Engagements, love affairs, job assignments, promotions, even a stroke last week.

The low standard of living means people invest more in each other. This is very painful to think about. Even Shanghai, the Paris of the P.R.C., has no twenty-four-hour television. There are no movie retrospectives, concerts in the park, or coffee houses or bars where people socialize. So human affairs acquire an extra quality. People express their sentiment very explicitly. A group of students gave us a winter scarf and a summer fan, saying these tokens would insure that all year round we would be reminded of them. At home we can have dozens of scarves, drawers full of fans. But as life gets more comfortable, it also loses intensity. We know that sensitivity cannot substitute for comfort, nor justify poverty and hardship. This hurts very much. Many people we know here have depth of feeling only suffering inflicts. But again, the depth doesn't justify the pain. And many suffer without learning anything.

The morning of May 28 we said our final goodbyes at the train station, where we had departed so many times before. But we would not be returning after this trip. Lao Yang and Xiao Qian sat in the compartment with Tani while Don and the FAO cadres stood clustered just outside in the corridor. We told them we hoped to return in five years or so, and see them all again. They departed. The train pulled out.

However, even if we do return in a few years, it won't be the same. When we come back, many of the friends we've made at the college will still be there, a reassuring fact of Chinese life. But the group that impressed us most deeply will be gone. There will never be another generation of students like the classes of 1977 and 1978. One day we were telling old Professor Luo how much we respected them, again. Luo finally decided to bring out his ace card: "You can admire them now," he said, "because in spite of all their social experience, they haven't been assigned jobs yet. Give them ten years, then judge." It was an important point, one which the students themselves anticipate. Many of them find themselves assigned not to schools, but to bureaucracies, where chances for corruption and "bureaucratism" are much greater. Each will have innumerable choices to make over the next ten years. And Professor Luo is right about us, too. We must adjust our own vision because we see China, to some extent, through our student's eyes. But Professor Luo's caution does not completely bridge the gap between our point of view and his. His job is to discipline and mold students. He looks forward to educating a fresh generation, untouched by the trauma and ambivalence of the GPCR, and better schooled in an academic sense. We have the more oblique perspective of friendly, sympathetic outsiders who, because we are Americans, tend to value nonconformity for itself.

On the train, we met a young FAO cadre en route to pick up a group of visiting foreign scholars. She started talking about the

Yanan revolutionary tradition and how she wished she could have lived during that era, before power meant the growth of bureaucracy and corruption. When she found that we agreed with her mild Maoist romanticism her mood changed. She seemed to feel that she could talk to us. She apologized defensively because she'd never been to college. Asking whether we thought her generation should be called "lost," we told her that we didn't agree with that evaluation. It implied that their experience had been wasted, and all of them had been ruined. We thought maybe the GPCR generation should be called the "modern" generation, rather than the lost generation. At least for the educated minority, and those like this FAO comrade who deal with outsiders, their GPCR experience will probably help them in coming to terms with the Western world. Not because they "know" what the U.S. is like, but rather because of certain personal qualities many of them have. These young people have pride and distance. They are proud because despite later disillusionment they grew up in security and were taught to value themselves for being Chinese. But the distance produced by the disillusionment is also important. Professor Luo may be right. But we see this generation as flexible, open to change. They love action and will always guard against blind faith.

So we entered the tourist world for awhile. Sightseeing in China is intriguing. You can rummage through centuries and never come out. We spent a week in Xian, seeing all the funerary remains, everything from the prehistoric archeological remains at Banpo, to the First Emperor of the Qin's grave mound, reveling in antiquarian delight. From Xian we took the train westward to Baoji, the railroad-junction town where the central trunk line branches southwest to Sichuan and northwest to Xinjiang. It's a small town not open to tourists as there is nothing anyone would want to see there, except as in our case we happened to have relatives. We'd received permission to visit Mingyao and his family. Don's sturdy, slow-moving, "northern"-looking cousin met us at the station and took us to the Baoji Railroad Hospital, the work unit where both he and his wife work. He checked us in at the railroad's spacious, bungalow-style guest house. Then we all walked across the street to their small two room apartment, one of many in the row houses, to meet Tianxia and their son Xunjie.

Mingyao, whom we had seen earlier in Shanghai, is a dental surgeon, and Tianxia is a gynecologist. They have worked at the Railroad Hospital for many years, and have been responsible, with their *danwei*, for innumerable improvements in community health. Once there was no hospital here, no modern doctors. The progress gives them pride. But they also work against frustrating circumstances. The local people have little interest in medical information beyond rudimentary hygiene, and even that is difficult to get across. Tianxia teaches birth control. Not many peasants are interested in controlling births, and when they are, she said, they turn to quacks and traditional cures that not only fail to prevent pregnancies but end up killing them. As they talked about their work, we saw the poem by the old Communist general, Yeh Jianying, written in a strong, hard calligraphic hand, hanging in scroll form up on the wall over the dining table:

> In attacking the city do not be afraid of its sturdiness.
> In study do not brood on its difficulties.
> Scientific knowledge has its limitations.
> Bitter struggle alone will enable us to storm the gate.

The poem made perfect sense in rustic, provincial Baoji. A person from Shanghai might express intensity of feeling by copying the poems of the Tang poet Du Fu or even maybe something composed recently by a new post-GPCR writer. But the Ye Jianying poem simply would not make sense; nobody in Shanghai's educated circles has to worry about rudimentary sanitation, or the open sewers still common in Baoji, or local quacks and witch doctors, or convincing people of the necessity for scientific reason. The next morning we went up the hill north of Baoji. From the top we could see the small junction town lying below us this side of the Wei River, to the east is Xian, to the west Xinjiang, and further to the southwest Sichuan. Baoji controls access to three provinces. Mingyao told us stories about some of the famous battles fought for this strategic terrain ever since the beginning of historic times. His railroad takes advantage of the terrain, for the same reasons as dynastic generals used to. Yeh's poem came to mind.

Mingyao, Tianxia, and Xunjie saw us off to Taiyuan, capital of Shanxi province. With a population of 2 million, the modernized city of Taiyuan still feels overwhelmingly rural, as though someone had set up a modern city on a sound stage and invited the local peasants over. The people move even more slowly than in Baoji, and Tani was the only foreign person at the modern skyscraper hotel. The whole place was filled with middle-level rural cadres "in conference." Conferencing is a phenomenon similar to "on outside assignment," Most people don't get vacations. But whoever can tries to attend local, regional, provincial, and national conferences, which always are held in faraway, scenic places. The habit has been getting some criticism lately in the papers. Inadvertently at first, but quite intentionally later on, Don asks delegates whether they are enjoying themselves. The reply is a huffy, "I'm here in conference, not to enjoy myself." Usually mid-level, urban, male cadres dominate conferences. But in Taiyuan this time the delegates included large numbers of shy, squat, middle-aged, rural female cadres. Many had never ridden in an elevator before. Sometimes they stood right near the button panel, just to make sure the automatic door would open. A few tried to press all the buttons and watch the door open at each floor. One clutched the wall in anxious panic, as the elevator shot up.

We did the sightseeing we had planned for Taiyuan and then tried to go on to Wutaishan in central Shanxi, a leading Buddhist pilgrimage site. One look at blonde Tani, and the provincial China Travel Service comrade gleefully turned us down. It was the first time on this trip that we really felt a strong nativism. After searching his mind for a sturdy enough excuse to deny us a permit, he came up with "modern facilities," meaning none of the guest houses on the mountain had flush toilets yet. We knew that Overseas Chinese and Japanese Buddhist tourists were all getting permission to go. Besides, we argued fruitlessly, we'd just been to Taishan, where there were no "modern facilities." In the end, it came down to race. The comrade gave Don permission to go alone if he wanted to, but the facilities were not adequate for "foreign" tourists like Tani. We could not budge the little bureaucrat, so we decided to go to the town of Wutai anyway, to see the wooden temples of Foguan si (built in 845), Nanchang si (built in 782) and the somewhat later, Yuan-dynasty Guangji si.

Immediately on arrival at the rail junction, we took off by jeep into the north China loess. The long, straight, paved road cut across yellow earth. On either side of the road ran unending rows of half-grown shade trees sheltering the asphalt from the blistering heat outside. At regular intervals, the road bisected other tree-lined roads. We started getting the eerie feeling of traveling down a soft, green tunnel that had been burrowed through the baking clay fields. Inside the tunnel with us were men and women walking slowly along the roadside, carrying huge loads of long, fresh scallions on their backs. Horse-drawn wooden carts, big green trucks, and little wooden wheelbarrows were all carrying the freshly harvested green scallions, filling the air with scent.

At a small junction we turned into an oasis. Suddenly everywhere we looked we saw water from artesian wells. Around the oasis settlement stood tall shade trees and fertile crop fields and private vegetable plots. In the middle of this was a pond large enough to accommodate a dozen women doing their laundry in the cool shade. We climbed up the hill behind the lake. Looking down into the small valley hidden behind the hill, we could see at each carefully terraced level a door opening out from inside the hill.

Small drying yards protruded slightly, and then dropped off down the gentle cliff to the next row of cave doors. Chickens pecked silently at invisible grain. The only colors besides gold, green, and brown were the patched quilts drying on the lines, and the painted, papered lattice windows of the loess cave homes. This must be Laotzu's dream of paradise, we thought.

Nanchang si sat serenely at the very top of the hill, a small, other-worldly structure with a flower garden around it. Tang dynasty architecture survives in relative abundance in Kyoto, and most Americans recognize it immediately as "Japanese" because the Japanese borrowed during the Tang, then formalized the style. Chinese taste moved further and further toward the baroque, exaggerated, highly decorative fashions we now associate with a "Chinese" aesthetic. So Guangji si, while exquisite, seemed quite familiar to us. What impressed us even more than the temple building were the larger than life-size Tang statues locked inside. Each one of the dozen or so figures was made of yellow loess clay, just like the houses, roads, and fields surrounding us. Marble and bronze sculpture is showy, in a sense, because the material used in their production is valuable. But mud sculptures take what exists in great abundance and form it around simple, straw-padded wooden frames. These are dried, burnished, and painted. The result was a roomful of richly colored, enormous, androgynous figures, each with its own peculiarities, none a standard size or shape. They seemed entirely magical, like very sophisticated fetishes.

We spent the night in a simple, white-washed hotel room attached to the huge Wutai municipal dormitory and cafeteria serving the local rural cadres. The service attendants brought us a farm dinner, every dish either freshly killed or just picked from the garden, and everything laced with black and red peppers and cilantro. With the dishes, the kitchen sent along bowls of fresh, flat noodles made of brown flour, platters of steamed wheat buns, fried pancakes and mounds of rice.

We set off for Datong from Wutai, to see the famous Yungang grottoes carved out of rock during the Northern Wei dynasty. And we recommend them highly. But more of interest happened in Datong than sightseeing. So far we haven't mentioned hotel or restaurant service. It has generally been adequate, and besides we hate to complain about minor annoyances. But our Datong experience illustrated a very key propensity in provincial life, particularly in tourist hotels. Most Chinese restaurants where Chinese eat have no "service" at all; wiped out, people say, by the GPCR. Unless you have good *guanxi*, you can expect comrades to be surly, slothful, grim, intolerant, and unhelpful. The China Travel Service catering to Western tourists has begun instructing tourist hotel staffs in the Western habit of service, with extremely fascinating consequences.

The Datong hotel's restaurant staff apparently had the impression that "service" meant being friendly and hospitable all the time. And they were. But the staff had not yet developed a sense of efficiency. The entire group of attendants continued to work along the older lines of jurisdiction instead, meaning that no one had been delegated responsibility over an entire table. One person set the chairs, another placed the condiments on the tables. If you order orange juice for breakfast, you need to wait for the beverage comrade to check in to work, because no one else has the authority or the keys. The problem extends to the different courses of a meal. Sometimes we were served the rice without the soup, or dishes of food and no rice, or just one dish, no rice, no soup. When we ordered anything slightly out of the ordinary, the waiters preferred not to bring the matter up with the cooks, the kitchen evidently being an alien territory. The problem worsened because none of the waiters could figure out a polite way of telling us we couldn't have what we ordered. So they just waited. After prolonged delays we finally figured that under such circumstances we had better order something else. Each attendant was unfailingly courteous. Sometimes when we asked for something, the attendant would say yes, then stand nearby loitering around. That, we learned gradually, was a good indication that whatever we wanted was beyond his or her reach. This scene, repeated three times a day began to make us think we'd strayed onto a set for the Marx brothers' *The Coconuts.* When the floor attendant "fixed" our leaking toilet by offering us a friendly stick of incense to mask the rather powerful odor filling the room, we knew it was time to go on to Beijing. But not before we wrote in the hotel recommendation book a plan for a service-oriented, nonjurisdictional training for the staff. Hopeless pedagogues.

There is another approach. One day a group from the French embassy arrived at the Datong hotel. Their first meal was no different from ours. About an hour before their next meal, an envoy arrived to rebuke the Chinese staff in French-accentuated *putong hua.* Haughtily, she forced the attendants to change the dirty table linen. Then she stood, imperiously, waiting until all the condiments and utensils had been laid out, the beer had been put into the refrigerator to chill, and the order written down in minutest detail. It worked, at least for the French. The rest of us noticed that our service level dipped precipitously. After the French left the next day, service returned to "normalcy."

29

Centrality and the Walls

San Francisco, August 5, 1982

We had been traveling for nearly a month in the interior by the time we got to Beijing. Living in hotels and traveling by jeep, car, and train had fatigued us. At some levels we hadn't really left the college. Once we settled down in Beijing airmail letters kept arriving from Shanghai telling us how students had done during the *fenpei*, the job assignment; when the FAO planned to put our large bags of farewell presents on the train; and other more trivial matters that just reminded us of what we were leaving. Beijing is almost unbearably hot during the summer. And the city didn't seem too hospitable, either. The FAO officer who met us at the station was in a big hurry to be rid of us and said we had no alternative but to stay at the Friendship Hotel, which is inconveniently located in the northwestern part of the capital. When we arrived there, the autocrat in charge of foreign experts turned out to be the rudest, most supercilious sort of petty bureaucrat we'd ever met. He insisted that we pay the standard, exorbitant tourist rate rather than the discount we were used to, on the grounds that we're only volunteers and not genuine foreign experts. So we stayed one night, then rushed off to make some new *guanxi* for ourselves, and ended up in a very comfortable, medium-priced hotel below the Qianmen gate, just a decent walk to Tiananmen Square. We stayed at the Beiwei Hotel for the next five weeks.

Mostly we felt the heavy lassitude brought on by the heat and a peculiar feeling of suspension, as though we were not in one place or the other. So we drifted around the city, following other tourists. Eight and a half million people live in Beijing. Thousands more come in everyday on conference, business, and sightseeing. Japanese tour buses with air conditioners so big you can hear them humming from a distance glide around the city. Chinese tourists mill bug-eyed through monuments. Also it seemed to us that in Beijing, the fashionable, privileged children of high cadres stood out in a way we hadn't noticed in Shanghai. Beijing people really are more polite, smoother, more in tune with the latest government pronouncements, as people always say. But shopping is poor, and compared to Shanghainese, Beijingers are larger, heavier, more ponderous, and reserved. Most of the year they eat animal fat and pickled vegetables together with dumplings, noodles, fried bread, and gruel. So they really do move more slowly than southerners and have to take long naps after all the carbohydrates. We walked and observed. But, mostly, we succumbed to an incredible lethargy. We felt increasingly detached. No one felt genuine. The only people who seemed as displaced as we were the poet Ai Qing and his wife Gao Ying, who were living at the same hotel while their old house, confiscated during the GPCR, was renovated for them.

The monarchs and geomancers laid out Beijing on a north-south axis. The city walls have been dismantled and modern buildings tower over old neighborhoods. But the primary north-south, east-west grids still dominate the city. Cosmology is stamped into the city plan. Dead center of the city lies the Imperial Palace, and directly in front of it the huge open Tiananmen Square. Changan Avenue cuts east-west across the city between the palace and the square. We climbed Coal Hill in the shimmering heat one day to get the overview, the palace directly in front, and beyond it the square stretching out with the large, bulky People's Heroes Monument and the Mao Mausoleum, and then farther off in the distance, the old Qianmen.

We both find the ornate architectural style of the Imperial Palace distancing and forbidding. It doesn't move us directly in the same way that the simple, elegant, mud and wood complex at Nanchang si did, but we kept being drawn back to its architectonic arrangement of space. The "forbidden city" was the meeting point of Heaven, Earth, and Humanity. The person representing Humanity

Don and Tani in front of the Lama Temple, Beijing. (Anon.)

was the Son of Heaven. This basic triad formed the immovable structure of premodern Chinese thinking. And just like all palaces or mansions, the Imperial Palace lies on a north-south axis, and is composed of walled rectangles lying within walled rectangles. To enter the palace grounds, you walk in through the massive front gate and down a ceremonial entry way which leads through marble staircases and bridges, huge, empty stone-paved courtyards, to a succession of three imperial audience halls, and finally, beyond that to the three inner halls. To the left and right beyond the empty courtyards are the household quarters for wives and eunuchs, the emperor being the only potent male in the entire inner palace. However, unlike all the other mansions and palaces we've ever seen, this one was not human size. The enormous open courtyards, the overly stark, yellow buildings, the ruby-colored walls, and the harsh, low-hanging blue sky all dwarfed human individuals and monumentalized the emperor.

Actually Xian is much closer to the geographic center of China than Beijing. The Imperial Palace, the cosmological center of the "central kingdom," tilts to the northeast and Inner Mongolia and Manchuria, the area where the Manchus who founded the Qing dynasty came from originally. Beijing is the "real" center of China because for 600 years the Ming and Qing emperors resided there. In the same manner of speaking, the Temple of Heaven where the emperor went twice a year to perform ritual sacrifice "is" the center of the entire world. But it doesn't even stand dead-center of Beijing. The eccentricity of both the capital and the Temple of Heaven illustrates a basic point. The Chinese sense of order is not

Aerial photo of Imperial Palace showing the Wumen Gate leading to a succession of imperial halls, all along the north-south axis. (Beijing Slides Studio)

mathematical in the quantitative sense. It is human. Premodern thought placed the emperor at the center, just as it spread a human grid over physical geography. The richer and more powerful a man became the more closely he could approximate centeredness. He could, for example, provide himself and his family with more and more walls, rectangular courtyards, and inner residences. And the higher he climbed in the official hierarchy, the closer he got to the real center of power, Beijing.

A world with a concrete center has a concrete periphery. Something has to separate these places from each other. That is the cosmic function of the Beijing walls and microcosmically, of all the walls of China. In north China especially, walls have been important since prehistoric times. They were useful for defense, breaking the force of the wind, and to demarcate the inside from the outside. Individual families built walls around their houses to keep the harsh northern wind from blowing their fortune away. But all premodern Chinese cities of any worth had walls—walls surrounding city blocks, walls separating quarters of the city, and walls defining the family compound from the outside. Nothing can outdo the significance of the Great Wall of China as a stark physical evidence of this cosmological ordering of things.

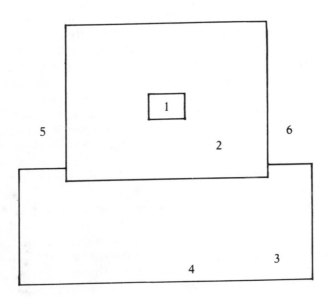

1. Imperial City
2. Inner walled city
3. Outer walled city

4. Temple of Heaven
5. Temple of the Moon
6. Temple of the Sun

Old Beijing

The spatialized Chinese material world is reflected in a spatialized cultural world. The whole idea that places and time can be carved into pieces to mark out areas of human existence is ever present in the living language. Place names rely heavily on spatial, on directional terminologies. Beijing is literally the northern capital, Qianmen the front gate, Shanghai above the sea, and so on *ad infinitum*. China has many binary spatial oppositions—up and down, front and back, left and right, big and small, distant and near. Each opposition combines to indicate a collectivity. Therefore, "big and small" indicates the concept of size; "up and down" the concept of height; etc. Frequently, verbs are constructed by attaching a spatially charged character to an action. The verb for "I can't eat it" literally translates as "I can't eat it down."

We have mentioned before the hierarchical nature of Chinese family relations. In a sense these too are spatialized. In actual living experience, the family consists of three, or at most four generational blocks of relatives, the great-grandparents, grandparents, parents, and children. This stacking of generations as if they were concrete components is stabilized by the use of very sophisticated, clearly delineated kinship terms rather than actual personal names, so that each person is constantly aware of to which generation one belongs within the kinship hierarchy. Eventually each older generation will die off; but the kin names will remain stable, open to occupation by members of the next generation. As people age, in effect, they displace the previous generational block and take on the responsibility of nurturing another lower generation.

Lest we get too academic, everyday Chinese habit provides ample evidence of the workings of the spatial ordering of social relation. All day long, but especially in the morning and at dusk, grandmas and grandpas stroll through Beijing streets wheeling their grandchildren in enormous pushcarts. These have nothing in common with Western baby carriages. Chinese baby carts are oblong, bamboo jitneys, more like cribs on wheels. They are spacious enough for a child to stand up in and walk three or four steps. Two or even three babies can sleep in it, and with only one occupant, it's big enough for the groceries as well. Often we saw children as old as three or four still confined inside these things. The pushcart initiates children into human social life by containing them at an early age and restricting their mobility until they get to be four or five years old. We saw children screaming with rage, pounding the sides of the cart in frustration at not being able to get out. The adults just laugh. The attitude children have developed toward the cart once they are liberated from it struck us as well. Three-year-olds sometimes push their buggies as far away as possible, and then run screaming after them, in a half pretend panic. Generally children haven't much opportunity to play this repulsion-attraction game, since adults rarely let them out, and even when parents do take them out to teach them how to walk, the cart is never far away. This infant training reminds Don of the courtyard, where his family rented rooms from a local landlord in the village of Xizhou, Yunan, during the Second World War. Only the wealthy people could afford a courtyard surrounded by buildings and the walled gate, inside of which children, chickens, dogs, and piglets, all spent their days. The courtyard formed the perfectly safe enclosure, walled off from the outside world.

We asked a Beijing pediatrician friend about children, and happened to mention that Americans think Chinese babies are particularly adorable. She surprised us by saying that most people she knows like "foreign" babies better, because Caucasian babies have white skin, taller noses, and tend to be livelier than Chinese babies. She had one good point. Chinese babies are much more sedate. Adults discourage acts of self-will. Children express aggression primarily by throwing public tantrums as soon as they figure out how embarrassing that can be to their parents. We have yet to see an urban parent punishing a child in public. In fact, children's misbehavior usually upsets all the adults around, not just the parents. Recently on a bus, we were sitting near a boy of about five or six who was making a gigantic nuisance of himself by trying to wrest a jar of goldfish away from a passenger. No one, including the woman trying to hold on to her goldfish, did anything except to tell him mildly not to be naughty. They did not act as an American parent might, just reach out and grab or smack him. As always with this sort of vignette, we're not completely sure whether this boy's parents hesitated because we were watching and nobody wants to make a scene in front of a foreigner and her cadre. But children do behave remarkably well, so well, in fact that Don thinks it's a form of psychic strangulation. The one great exception is when they travel together in large groups. We learned fast to get out of the way when we saw lots of kids coming toward us and no adult around.

Language contains the baby's behavior as well. People treat children as though they were little adults, and expect them to behave accordingly. Not just mothers, but everyone around infants impresses on the baby the need to be an intelligent, intelligible human being by talking to it constantly. Adults always talk to children, in and out of the pushcarts. Caretakers direct a constant stream of endearments, questions, jokes, laughter, instructions, and teasing at children. And our pediatrician friend said educated parents right now are consciously increasing the amount of talking, in order to accelerate language facility. But we have noticed that even what look like workers' children ordinarily learn nouns at a very early age, because adults are always asking them "what is this," "who's that," before they can even sit up. No one uses baby talk, either. The questions adults ask are simple, but grammatically indistinguishable from adult conversations. In general, Chinese children seem to develop language skill at an earlier age than American kids. It's also clear that adults stimulate language precisely for the purpose of molding and restraining children, preventing them from acting like "children."

One area where Chinese parents don't restrain and American parents do is infantile sex play. On a walk one evening we stumbled across a two-year-old absentmindedly masturbating against his little toy. The mother sat behind him. All she did when she noticed us looking was to make a hand gesture, brushing her pointed finger against her cheek, to signify loss of face to the child. She didn't try to stop him. The common custom of dressing children in open-slit pants, more customary in places other than Beijing actually, means genitalia are exposed until three or four. In Beijing we often saw children playing sexual games with each other. The taboo against women exposing their breasts seems only partially observed.

Children commonly see elderly and peasant women open their upper garments, fanning themselves in the midday heat, or nursing infants on the street. Still, this is clearly a leftover. Younger, urban women wear tight bras to contain and mask their breasts. And several intellectuals have told Tani that public nursing is a repulsive peasant habit.

In many parts of China, though again not as commonly in Beijing, children are toilet trained by putting them in open-slit pants. The parent periodically lifts the baby into a squatting position, simultaneously opening the slit and making a whistling noise. The baby learns to urinate in response. As children begin walking they remain in open-slit pants and learn to relieve themselves. This custom takes a great deal more time and patience than diapers, at least initially. The parent has to remember to take the infant out every hour or so. No daycare center could possibly train each child this way; another reason why families prefer grandmas. As all of this implies, bodily waste is acceptable, as long as it doesn't come into the house. Children in rural areas learn early to save their own excrement for fertilizing the private plot.

By the time children are seven or eight they seem to take enormous pleasure in being adult. After dinner, all over the Beijing neighborhoods, we saw parents and children walking gravely hand-in-hand, talking. Children discuss things very seriously with their parents, particularly their fathers. They seem extraordinarily secure and confident with all the attentions they receive. We also noticed an interesting displacement going on now with girls and their mothers. Little girls are becoming fashion surrogates. Some young adults on Beijing streets are wearing seductive dresses, lipstick, high heels, earrings, and even the old "Suzie Wong" *qipao* with side slits. Far more often we see little girls dressed up in all these previously forbidden things, except the high heels. Mostly these heavily made-up girls of five or seven, wearing enormous glass earrings, long strings of plastic beads, a gaudy party dress, and hair ribbons appear in parks on Sunday sedately walking alongside their drab, undecorated mothers.

In Shanghai we had lived inside the campus walls, enclosed by our *danwei*. During our stay in Beijing, though physically in the center of the city, we became outsiders, mere tourists and onlookers. Even the street scenes failed to interest us as the weeks went by. We began buying the *International Herald Tribune* every day, and read *Time* and *Newsweek*. We spent more and more time in tourist dining rooms and even ran into an old schoolmate of Tani's from Davis, California. We started letting go. We lost interest in traveling outside the city. When we walked it was as though suspended in time. Looking at the walls and gates we realized for the first time what they really meant. They are there to shelter and contain, but also to cast out. Chinese culture draws its own lines between inner and outer. That's one fundamental reason for the depth of difference separating them from us. Innerness, what lies inside the rectangular walled spaces, accepts guests on its own terms. We saw the gates. But we couldn't quite bring ourselves to leave through them yet.

Postscript

Tani left China through Hong Kong and spent four hours walking in and out of downtown Victoria's luxury shops in frustration. Don came directly home to the same extreme disorientation. At first nothing seemed familiar. Close friends gave us a welcome home party and we watched helplessly as the conversation slipped past us. We tried talking to people about our experience in China, but somehow could not convey much to friends who had not shared our experience. Unconsciously we ended up withdrawing to think over what had happened to us.

We had loaned ourselves to China, to its ambiance and general way of seeing things and to some extent China changed us. A different "we" came back to a slightly unfamiliar United States. We re-experienced our society through the fresh eyes of newly arrived immigrants. Of course, we don't have the eternally displaced feeling they have, and we know a great deal about both countries. We know the extravagant wealth of the United States enrages us. We did not talk about poverty in our letters because, being so much a part of Chinese existence, no one belabors the obvious (particularly to a foreigner), except to mutter the cliché that China is a poor country. We can protest the uniformity of Chinese culture, the pressure of family, the bureaucracy of the work unit, the oppression of sex roles, and so on. But the America we live in is a frustratingly surreal world which offers no stable perspective and no common standpoint. Now, we evaluate our own alienated bourgeois liberties against the burdens and pleasures of Chinese social life, its obligations, responsibilities, and intimacies. Most troubling of all, we discovered what an extraordinary sense of security hierarchical, heavily formalized, patriarchal, authoritarian China gives to people living there. This discovery surprised us. Visiting scholars from China told us the same thing; they too, but at a more profound level, accept the personal liberties American society has to offer individuals, but miss knowing they belong somewhere.

Place, time, location, and the given terms of our own personality make-up determined what and how we encountered "China." For example, Shanghai does not really resemble any other Chinese city. One look at its modern, Westernized skyline and fashionable population makes that very clear. Chinese mostly live in the countryside. But living in Shanghai, working there, and traveling to the interior, taught us how to distinguish northerners from southerners, Shanghainese from *Hubei lao*, the Han from the minorities, the city from the countryside. Chinese people from different regions look differently, dress differently, talk and behave differently.

We went to China at a very specific time, 1981–82. The Cultural Revolution had been over for several years, but had left a very deep wound. The euphoria following the downfall of the Gang of Four and the New Realism of 1979–81 had also become things of the immediate past. We found people trying to adjust to the policy of the four modernizations. The five stresses and four beautifuls campaign had begun, but not yet the socialist spiritual culture campaign which unfolded shortly after we left. Our account differs from those of Delia Jenner and Edoarda Masi, who wrote memoirs about working in China as foreign experts at earlier points in time. The people we met and talked to in 1981–82 had different preoccupations and concerns than those before or since; different even from feelings they themselves had had at other times. During our stay, nobody had anything good to say about the GPCR, which all agreed had been a total disaster, a personality cult, a political conspiracy without ideological significance. It's not that people lied to us. Yet what we heard came inevitably through the rage, pain, and suffering of our urban, educated informants. So, many of our questions remain unanswered.

Location also matters. In our case, we had the luck to be placed in a remarkably well-organized work unit. Not all work situations compare favorably to Shanghai Teachers College. We learned about one FAO cadre in Kunming who used to work as an English-language interrogator during the Korean War and treated his foreign colleagues thirty years later more or less the same way he'd handled American prisoners of war. As a consequence of much negotiating and planning with the Shanghai Teachers College FAO, we participated in the workings of a well-run Chinese bureaucracy, despite the inevitable few mishaps and misunderstandings.

Finally, our interest as historians defined our approach. We have been trained to look at things in long-range terms, and place them in what we believe to be proper context. In this regard, we differ from journalists like Thomas Bernstein and Fox Butterfield who by profession must seek the new. Instead of the sensational, the new, the political, we have tried to look at the human, cultural, and historical. The trip deepened and altered the ways we have been taught to look at China. Yet, taking the long look doesn't mean we have become conservatives.

We spent the first few weeks after our arrival in China trying to figure out what in the things we encountered could be considered Chinese and what Communist. But we soon had to abandon that false dichotomy. The two are inextricably part of the current Chinese reality. What is "Chinese-ness?" Can it be extracted from a specific place or time in China, isolated as a norm? "Communism" is everywhere, even if nowhere completely realized. What is Communist—the Central Committee of the Party or the local branch secretariat, the cadre, the bureaucrat, or the disillusioned GPCR generation still dreaming in terms of the Lin Biao morality burned into its imagination 15 years ago?

We had read about the importance of personal, social connection in Chinese culture, its emphasis on specific kin and group relations, its preoccupation with ethics. It took the experience of actually living and working in China to realize that these things form a social psychology we ended up calling Chinese communality. Inside this context, we began to understand phenomena like ethics campaigns (even unsuccessful ones), the pleasures and pitfalls of *guanxi*, and why Chinese in turn find it so difficult to really grasp what Western individualism is all about. We comprehended the difference before only in an academic sense. Living and working in China made it a social-psychological reality and a part of daily life.

We want to stress the incomparability of our two worlds. China has lived a different history from the West. In the last century, it has experienced a transformation immeasurably different from the West's capitalist development. China's present demographic and economic legacies as well as its social and political organizations are not like the West's. Even assuming that the current four modernizations policy succeeds, the underlying social and cultural patterns will not be transformed that quickly. Chinese culture will modify, and be in turn modified by the modernization to come. The consequence, a "modern" China, will differ from modernity in other countries. Everyone has an intellectual and psychological need to compare. Mistakes occur when we try to fit the course of Chinese history into a Western schema of development. China is not the West, and the Western pattern does not have universal applicability. It is so inviting to take one aspect or theme out of the Chinese context and identify it with something seemingly analogous in the West, be that "love," "feminism," "freedom," "democracy,"' or what have you. We have reported many examples of how our Chinese students misread Western phenomena in precisely this way. Westerners do the same with China. The insight we have gotten from our experience is this: Universality does not exist. Once the comfortable illusion of universality is gone, the different dynamics of Chinese and Western societies present a tremendous intellectual challenge to understanding. Emotionally that realization has complicated our own passage from one world to the other, as we live out the formations of human needs and desire in China and the U.S.

Index

Advertising, 108, 111

Baoji, 231
Beijing, 235ff

Chengdu, 160
children, 100, 102, 103, 116, 127ff,
    146ff, 240ff
Chongqing, 163
communality, Chinese, 7, 13, 26ff,
    39–40, 46, 49–#50, 60ff, 99ff,
    127–28, 130ff, 184ff, 192–93
commune, 61ff
Confucianism, 133–34, 195, 212
cross-cutural perception, 45, 58,
    72–73, 93–95, 108, 133,
    134–35, 142, 144–45, 177,
    189ff, 201ff, 226, 233–34, 240,
    245ff (See also the Other)
cultural dichotomies, 74–75,
    80–81ff, 83, 90, 126–27,
    183–84, 195

Danwei (work unit), 1, 26, 27,
    29–30, 65, 103–04, 158–59
Datong, 233–34
Dazu grottoes, 163ff

Eating as social occasion, 8ff,
    64–65, 101ff, 115, 117ff, 167,
    169–70, 174ff, 177ff, 221
enclosed space, 33, 51, 90, 159,
    212ff, 236ff

Family (See kinship)
film, 16, 17, 20, 35, 89ff, 110, 201ff

foreigners, attitudes to (See Gross;
    the Other)

Garden, 32ff, 54 (See also landscape
    and mountain)
gaze, 25ff, 99ff
gender (See love and marriage; sex;
    and women)
generational conflict, 44, 66–67,
    74–75, 115, 130, 148–49,
    151–52, 185ff, 229
Great Cultural Proletarian Revolu-
    tion (GPCR), ix–xii; attitudes
    to, ix, 15ff, 78ff, 83, 170, 219,
    229–30
Gross, Mr., 26, 42ff, 87ff, 222ff
guanxi (social connection), 29,
    104ff, 138, 179, 235
Guilin, 159ff

Hangzhou, 54ff
health care, 75–76ff
Huangshan, 207ff

Ideographic language, 21ff, 80, 108
intellectual elitism, 43, 83–84

kinship, 5, 47–48, 93, 101ff, 240ff
    (See also Lowe family)
knowledge, attitudes to, 43, 45–46,
    74, 81ff, 84, 139–40, 152, 155,
    173–74, 176ff

Labor intensiveness, 16–17, 31
landscape and mountain, 159–60,
    182–83, 207ff, 216ff (See also
    garden)

literature, attitudes to, 12, 44ff, 73,
    142, 154ff
love and marriage, 42, 43, 65ff,
    149ff, 185ff, 197ff (*See also*
    sex; women)
Lowe family, 5, 24–25, 101ff, 112ff,
    144–45, 166ff, 230–31 (also
    spelled as Luo, in ping-ying
    Romanization)

May Fourth Movement, 93
moralism, 43, 47ff, 65, 85, 97, 123ff,
    140, 152ff, 162–63, 181ff

Narrativity, Chinese, 36, 90, 92,
    110, 111ff, 160, 162, 164

Other, the, ix, xiv, 13–14, 51, 57,
    85ff, 98, 139, 140ff, 143ff,
    176ff, 221ff (*See also* Gross)

Painting, 91ff, 174–75
patriotism, 54, 97, 114
perspective (*See* enclosed space;
    film; garden; landscape and
    mountain; narrativity, pain-
    ting; photography; television;
    and theater)
photography, 106ff
political observance, 35ff, 52ff, 55ff
propaganda campaign, 20ff, 53–54,
    120, 123ff, 181ff

Qufu, 212ff

Sex, 12, 71ff, 90, 109, 129, 131ff,
    198–99, 200, 201ff, 241 (*See
    also* love and marriage;
    women)
Shanghai in comparison with the
    rest of China, 31ff, 69, 159,
    163, 172, 228
Suzhou, 31ff

Taishan, 216ff
Taiyuan, 231–32
television, 110–11
theater, 18–19, 35–36, 93, 111,
    134, 190ff
travels inside China, 29ff, 54ff,
    158ff, 166ff, 207ff, 212ff, 228ff

Women, 48, 63–64, 74–75, 78, 90ff
    101, 102, 119, 146–47, 185ff,
    189ff, 201ff, 216ff (*See* love
    and marriage; sex)
Wuhan, 166ff
Wutai, 232–33

Xian, 230, 237
xiangxiang (to think in similarities),
    159–60

Youth, 128

About the Authors

Tani Barlow is Assistant Professor of History at the University of Missouri-Columbia, specializing in Chinese history. She has published articles on the contemporary Chinese woman writer, Ding Ling, and is now revising a manuscript on gender relations in twentieth-century China.

Donald M. Lowe was born in China and lived there during his childhood. He teaches critical social thought at San Francisco State University, has published *The Function of "China" in Marx, Lenin, and Mao* (1966) and *History of Bourgeois Perception* (1982), and is now writing "Desire in Late Capitalist USA."

In 1981–82, Barlow and Lowe were foreign experts at Shanghai Teachers College. While there, they wrote *Contemporary USA: An English Reader for Chinese Students.*

This book is an account of their experiences in China, and an analysis of the differences separating Chinese and American social realities.